THE
SCHOOL
-TO-
WORK
REVOLUTION

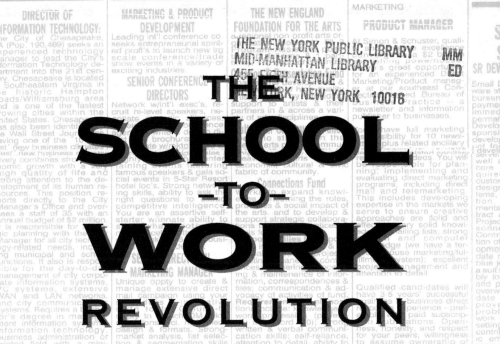

THE SCHOOL -TO- WORK REVOLUTION

HOW EMPLOYERS AND EDUCATORS ARE JOINING FORCES TO PREPARE TOMORROW'S SKILLED WORKFORCE

LYNN OLSON

ADDISON-WESLEY
Reading, Massachusetts

Many of the designations used by manufacturers and sellers to distinguish their products are claimed as trademarks. Where those designations appear in this book, and Addison-Wesley was aware of a trademark claim, the designations have been printed in initial capital letters.

Library of Congress Cataloging-in-Publication Data
Olson, Lynn (Lynn Amy)
   The school-to-work revolution : how employers and educators
joining forces to prepare tomorrow's skilled workforce / Lynn Olson.
      p.   cm.
   Includes bibliographical references and index.
   ISBN 0-201-14940-0
   1. School-to-work transition—United States. 2. Career education—
United States. 3. Education, Cooperative—United States.
4. Industry and education—United States.   I. Title.
LC1037.5.057 1997
370.11'3—dc21   97-25348
                                                       CIP

Copyright © 1997 by Lynn Olson

Addison-Wesley is an imprint of Addison Wesley Longman, Inc.

Jacket design: Peter Blaiwas
Text design: Greg Johnson, Art Directions
Set in 12 point Goudy Oldstyle by Vicki L. Hochstedler

1 2 3 4 5 6 7 8 9-MA-0100999897
First printing, July 1997

Find us on the World Wide Web at
http://www.aw.com/gb

Contents

Preface

In 1993, as a reporter for the newspaper *Education Week*, I began traveling around the country to visit a new generation of programs that link work and learning in high schools. I admit that I began this odyssey as a skeptic. Like many Americans who graduated from college and work in white-collar professions, I had a very traditional image of career-related education in my head. I grew up in an affluent suburb, took my full share of college-preparatory and advanced-placement courses, and graduated from a good college. The only vocational class I ever took was a dull course in home economics in junior high school, where we girls learned to sew and to cook while the boys grappled with large pieces of wood down the hall. The experience left me with the impression that career-related education was uninspiring and inconsequential.

This book is not about those kinds of programs. It focuses on efforts to create a much more substantive connection between education and work so that young people can be better prepared for the rapidly changing world that awaits them. Today's economy has little room for those who cannot read, write, compute, frame and solve problems, use technology, manage resources, work in teams, and continue to learn on the job. Well-paying jobs for unskilled labor are disappearing at an alarming rate.

The traditional shop class is wholly inadequate to prepare young people for this new world. So, too, is the traditional academic class, with its emphasis on learning that is disconnected from the learning's application. As a recent national commission noted, "The skills that students need are not just more of what the schools have always taught, such as basic skills in mathematics, but also skills that the schools have rarely taught—the ability to work with complex knowledge and to make decisions under conditions of conflicting or inadequate evidence."

The challenges posed for schools are enormous. But quietly, in places around the country like Tulsa, Oklahoma; Austin, Texas; Portland, Oregon; and Cambridge, Massachusetts, a new kind of education is emerging. In these communities, educators and employers are joining forces to make the system of education work by making academics more rigorous and by tying schools more closely to the realities and the demands of the modern workplace.

This revolution is already happening, although it is often overlooked in the weekly tirades against the public schools. It is, admittedly, uneven in its implementation. But it represents a grassroots response to a growing problem: how to prepare young people for a knowledge-based economy that will be radically different from the one we knew as children.

The story begins in the mid-1980s, when national reports highlighted the gap between changes in the workplace and in education. These reports documented the steep decline in earnings among young people with only a high school diploma and their difficulty in finding steady, well-paying jobs. The reports cautioned that for the nation to remain competitive, more young men and women would have to achieve at levels once expected only of the few. In a world where what you know and can do increasingly determines what you earn, what young people learn and how well they learn it have enormous consequences, both for individuals and for society.

One response to these problems has been new efforts to link work and school in a more meaningful way. Originally, the focus was on young people who may not complete a bachelor's degree. But the discussion has since broadened into one about how best to prepare all young people for work and for adulthood. Even college students, after all, eventually go to work.

The goal is not to create a few hothouse programs but a "school-to-work" or "school-to-career" system capable of serving large numbers of young people. This system would differ in substantial ways from its predecessors: It would integrate academic and career-oriented studies, rather than keeping them separate. It would stress an upgraded academic content for all students. It would emphasize learning in the context of work—not just work experience. And it would tie these activities back to activities in the classroom. Equally important, it would erect ladders to both higher education and employment, not to just one or the other. It also would require collaboration and oversight by both schools and businesses.

Such efforts are creating a growing conversation among educators and employers about the role *both* must play in preparing the next generation.

I think this conversation is enormously important. But as a journalist who is interested in the human side of things, what has most impressed me is the students. As I visited fledgling school-to-work initiatives around the country and talked with teenagers, I heard an almost constant refrain: Now I understand why I have to learn this. What I do at work matters because somebody else is relying on me. Suddenly, there are lots of adults talking to me about my future.

The comments were the same, whether I was talking with a straight-A student who hoped to become a surgeon or a C-average student who just wanted to get out of school and find a job. Many young people whom I interviewed had enrolled in tougher academic courses and were developing a stronger sense of their career options because of their involvement in school-to-work efforts that gave them exposure to real workplaces.

I changed from a skeptic to an interested observer. Then, in April 1995, the Alfred P. Sloan Foundation of New York approached me with the idea of writing a book on the topic. Hirsh Cohen, the vice president of the foundation, wanted a fair-minded account by a journalist who had spent some time looking at school-to-work systems up close. The goal was to write a publication for parents, businesspeople, educators, and students that would explain what these ideas were about and whether they were worth pursuing. Cohen stressed that I should emphasize what worked and what didn't. This book would not have been possible without the foundation's support.

I have spent the better part of a year on the road, traveling to sites from Oregon to South Carolina, from Michigan to Texas. Everywhere I went, people have been unfailingly gracious and thoughtful and generous with their time.

I am also grateful to the German Marshall Fund of the United States and to the Center for Learning and Competitiveness at the University of Maryland in College Park for enabling me to travel to Denmark, Germany, and Scotland in October 1995 with a group of fellow journalists. My editors at *Education Week* generously allowed me a year's absence to research and write this book.

In writing a book for a general audience, I have relied heavily on the research of experts in the field. I am particularly grateful for the work of the Center for Learning and Competitiveness; the National Center on the Educational Quality of the Workforce at the University of Pennsylvania; the Institute on Education and the Economy at Columbia University; Jobs for the Future in Boston; the National Center for Research in Vocational Education, based in Berkeley, California; Mathematica Policy Research, Inc., in Princeton, New Jersey; and the Manpower Demonstration Research Corporation in New York. I have tried to summarize and reflect what their studies on school-to-work have produced without misrepresenting their findings.

I also want to thank Tom Bailey, Sandra Byrne, Stephen and Mary Agnes Hamilton, Anne Heald, Peter Joyce, Hilary Pennington, Marsha Silverberg, Adria Steinberg, David Stern, and my husband, Steve Olson, for reviewing earlier drafts of this manuscript. This book would never have been published without the encouragement of my agent, Rafe Sagalyn, or the assistance of my editor, Henning Gutmann. Vicki Hochstedler ably steered the book through the production process. Kate Scott did a superb job copy editing.

This book seeks to present a realistic appraisal of where efforts to link work and schooling stand and what we can expect of them. It chronicles a quiet revolution in education and tries to differentiate real accomplishments from hot air. School-to-work has the potential to reengage in their education at least a portion of young people, many of whom are not being well served now. But to do so effectively, it must be done right and cannot be done poorly. This book will try to point out the difference. The result, I hope, is something on which we all can build.

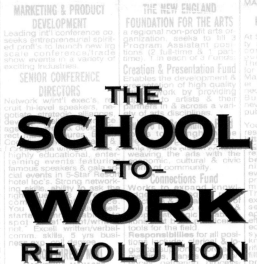

THE SCHOOL -TO- WORK REVOLUTION

CHAPTER 1

The Need for a New Alliance

*F*rom childhood until old age, two activities dominate the lives of most Americans: education and work. Yet educators and employers, despite their obvious interdependence, communicate poorly—or not at all. The gulf between them handicaps business, wastes the talents and energies of millions of young people, and threatens our future prosperity as a nation.

The signs of this disjuncture are everywhere.

Employers do not trust schools to teach students what they need to know. When asked whether our nation's public schools do a good job preparing students for the world of work, only 4 percent of business leaders in a 1995 survey said yes, compared with 44 percent of high school teachers and 68 percent of school superintendents. Because businesspeople have so little faith in schools, they tend not to use high school transcripts or other measures of school performance to make hiring decisions. Nor do they reward young people who take harder courses or earn higher grades. Companies with good jobs, career ladders, and fringe benefits don't even like to hire young people. Instead, they let most 20-somethings cycle through dead-end jobs, schooling, and periods of unemployment before plucking the lucky ones from the pack.

Educators, meanwhile, often view business with more than a little suspicion, distrust, and envy. They resent being blamed for economic problems beyond their control. They have deep misgivings about allowing business values to permeate the schools. And they question the motivation and commitment of corporate leaders who chastise public schools on the one hand, while fighting for tax breaks and private-school vouchers on the other.

The disconnect between educators and employers has contributed to a severe motivation problem in schools. Students see no connection between what they are learning—or how well they learn it—and their future career goals. So they have little incentive to work hard in school. "Across the country, whether surrounded by suburban affluence or urban poverty, students' commitment to school is at an all-time low," observes the psychologist Laurence Steinberg on the basis of surveys of more than 20,000 students. The majority of high school students describe their education as "boring." Too many think it is important to graduate but not to do well.

Meanwhile, parents worry that after 13 years of public schooling, and an often substantial investment in higher education, their offspring will be unable to secure or keep a job. Parents know that the economy is shifting but they are unsure what to do about it.

Today, the connection between work and learning is more important than ever. The skills required for well-paid employment are rising. Repetitive jobs on the assembly line are being replaced with new jobs that require workers who can think mathematically, read well, solve problems, and use computers. Such workers must be able to communicate orally and in writing, work in groups, and monitor their own performance. Constant change means that most jobs now require continued learning even after formal education ends. An increasingly fluid labor market requires individuals to keep learning so they can move from one job to the next. Many of tomorrow's jobs have not even been created yet.

Modern economies place a premium on higher skills, with drastic consequences for the youngest and least educated.

"Education is becoming the fault line that is dividing the winners from the losers in this economy to a far greater extent than ever before," asserts former U.S. labor secretary Robert Reich. "Just look at the difference in earnings of people with college degrees and people with high school degrees. If you had a college degree in 1979, you were earning around forty percent more than someone with a high school degree. Now, if you have a college degree, you are earning over eighty percent more than somebody with a high school degree."

Technology further winnows out the unskilled from the skilled. For low-skilled or unskilled workers, Reich notes, technology is taking away jobs. For those who know how to use it, technology adds value to what they do.

A good example can be found in any auto repair shop. It used to be that many teens could pop the hood of the family automobile, replace a starter or a few spark plugs, and drive away. "Today's vehicles have more computing power than the Apollo spaceship that went to the moon," says Stephen Ash, the chairman of automotive technology at Sinclair Community College in Ohio. The typical car today has eight onboard computers: to operate the radio, the climate-control system, the ride control and the suspension systems, the antilock brakes, the fuel-delivery system, the emissions-control system, and the automatic transmission. A new car may contain as many as 115 small electrical motors and have three miles of wiring. Today, if you want your car fixed, you bring it to a technician who analyzes the problem using complicated manuals, diagrams, and computerized diagnostic equipment. More than likely, your car will be repaired by a team of specialized technicians working together.

In this new economy, smart businesses rely on an educated workforce to thrive. And young people need to be educated in new ways to be employable.

The New Synthesis

The problem is not that our schools perform less well than in the past. In some respects, they are doing even better. More students graduate from high school than at any point in our history. And basic literacy levels are higher for a more diverse group of young people.

The problem is that changes in the economy require schools to reach much higher. Schools must ensure that most young people acquire the skills and knowledge once reserved for a few. They must emphasize a whole new set of skills—such as computer expertise and the ability to work in groups—that were never on their agenda. "School" may not even be the best place to teach some skills, such as how to learn in the context of work or how to use the latest high-tech equipment.

One solution is to reach beyond the boundaries of the school by creating a new relationship between schools and employers. Around the country, the first tentative steps have been taken toward this new alliance. It is called "school-to-work" or "school-to-career."

"School-to-work" assumes that one purpose of schooling—though not its only purpose—is broad preparation for work. School-to-work systems generally link learning at school and at work to help young people see the connections between the two. The best integrate high-level academic and technical knowledge and teach at least some content in context. They provide young people with career exploration and counseling so they can make more informed decisions about their academic and occupational goals. School-to-work systems build bridges among high schools, higher education, and the workplace to prepare young people for both careers and college. And they put young people in touch with adult role models who can help ease the shift into adulthood.

If properly structured, school-to-work has the potential to give students challenging academic instruction and a foundation for higher education and lifelong learning. It can help prepare workers who can meet the demands of a high-wage, high-skill economy. Many of these efforts are new, but they are starting to show results:

- In Boston, inner-city high school students are working in banks, hospitals, and environmental organizations prior to enrolling in college or taking a job.

- In Pennsylvania, Procter & Gamble is using the work site to teach high school students about teamwork, manufacturing processes, and quality control.

- In Oregon, thousands of students are shadowing employees to explore different career options, and businesspeople regularly visit the classroom to share their expertise.

- In Delaware, employers are helping assess student projects that combine academic research with its real-world applications.

- In California, students in "career academies" are gaining a broad exposure to occupations while preparing for both work and higher education.

The approaches differ, yet all share common features. They use exposure to the world of work to motivate young people to learn more rigorous academics. They give young people a better sense of how to take advantage of career opportunities. They foster the work ethics and social skills that employers say they want. And they teach young people how to learn in the context of work, as they will continue to do all their lives.

School-to-work systems also are changing the perspectives of employers. Businesspeople are discovering that young people can be productive workers, not just cheap, low-skilled laborers. Employers who train teenagers in the workplace generally are pleased with their students, find them productive, and believe that both sides benefit. Many say they would take part in such efforts again and would recommend them to their peers.

"Business absolutely needs an educated workforce to survive," says Mimi Bushman, who heads the education task force for the Oregon Business Council in Portland. "Everyone would say that. And what the schools are producing right now isn't adequate. It is not blaming the schools. Actually, the schools are probably doing a better job than twenty years ago. It's that they're not doing what we need in the next century. The world is changing so rapidly. The workplace is changing. Schools need to keep up."

School-to-Work in Action

The best way to get a sense of the potential for school-to-work is to see it in action.

As a high school sophomore, Erika Pyne of Kalamazoo, Michigan, was a fairly typical high school student. "I had absolutely no idea of what I was going to do with my life, and that really frustrated me," she recalls. Enrolled in a high school program that emphasized science and mathematics, she did not see any connection between her courses and what she might do with her life. "I was sinking," she says.

Then, in her junior year in high school, she enrolled in a school-to-work program run by the Education for Employment Consortium in Kalamazoo. For the next two years she spent part of each school day taking classes at Bronson Methodist Hospital, learning about such topics as anatomy and medical terminology. She also spent time shadowing health-care professionals and getting hands-on work experience. As a senior in high school, Erika interned afternoons on the family-care unit at Borgess Medical Center, where she helped out in the delivery room. "It was great," she says. "I just loved it. I mean, I was seventeen or eighteen and helping out in deliveries. I'd seen fifteen of them by the end of the year, half of which were cesareans. And I had all these wonderful experiences that most people my age couldn't talk about. I fell in love with health care."

Today, Erika is a patient-care assistant at Bronson Methodist Hospital and a junior at Western Michigan University, where she is enrolled in the nursing program. The $7.86 an hour that she earns helps pay for her education, and unlike many of her fellow students at the university, Erika has a clear sense of her career direction. Eventually, she would like to be a physician's assistant so that she has more authority and flexibility than a nurse.

Her employer also benefits. Robert Doud, the director of public affairs for the Bronson Health Care Group, says the hospital has employed several dozen graduates like Erika in entry-level positions. "It's very economical for us," says Doud. "We know these graduates are competent when we hire them. We know that their learning curve on the job is less than anybody else that we might bring in. We already know a little bit about their attendance history and their work ethics. So by the time they hit our front door, they are really ready to run."

Erika's experience reflects the most intensive end of the school-to-work continuum. Such apprenticeships (called "externships" in Kalamazoo) often are modeled closely on the education-and-training-system in Germany, where 70 percent of young people participate in apprenticeships that combine learning in school and on the job. Students in apprenticeships typically spend significant amounts of time learning at work sites, have classes related to their work experiences, and graduate with separate credentials attesting to their accomplishments. Many apprenticeship programs include at least one year of postsecondary education.

As would be expected in a country as large and diverse as the United States, there are many variations on school-to-work nationwide.

❀ *Cooperative learning* is one of the oldest forms of work-based learning, dating back to the early 1900s. It usually consists of part-time jobs offered as one component of vocational education in high schools. At the postsecondary level, engineering students often participate in coop programs. Coordination with school-based learning is often weak, however, and students usually do not receive credentials that are recognized by other employers.

❀ *Technical preparation* ("tech-prep") *programs* are four-year programs that combine the last two years of high school with two years in a community college earning a technical degree. They may or may not include work-based learning. At Sinclair Community College in Ohio and Tri-County Technical College in South Carolina, tech-prep programs ready students for careers in industrial engineering, automotive technologies, and health care, among others.

❀ *Career academies* are usually schools within a school or separate small schools that are organized around a broad career theme such as health-care, arts and communications, or finance. By offering settings where students and teachers stay together for several years, career academies try to break down the anonymity of large, comprehensive high schools. The career theme helps to focus academic course-taking. Students in career academies may participate in job shadows, have adult mentors, and engage in internships or work experiences over the summers. But there often is not a strong link between these work experiences and their classes. First established in Philadelphia about 1970, there are now more than 300 career academies scattered across the United States, with a heavy concentration in California.

❧ *Career majors* are similar to career academies, except that all students within a high school are encouraged to explore various careers such as health services or industrial engineering. Students then select a broad career area that interests them to help organize their academic courseload, not to lock them into a particular occupation. They also may take one or more sequential classes in their career area. Career majors provide a context in which students can learn and apply their academic skills and shape their future goals. At David Douglas High School in Portland, Oregon, juniors and seniors can take classes in seven broad areas— social and human services, health sciences, business and management, industrial and engineering systems, natural resources, arts and communications, or hospitality, tourism, and recreation—in addition to their core academic subjects.

❧ *School-based enterprises* and *service learning projects* allow students to identify and address community needs. At the Rindge School of Technical Arts in Cambridge, Massachusetts, a student-produced news program broadcasts once a week on a local cable channel; a student-run electronics service installs and maintains computer and telephone equipment in the building; and a community leadership and services corps encourages young people to design their own solutions to community problems.

❧ *Job shadowing* and *internships* give students a taste of different career options outside the school setting. These can range from a few hours spent at the work site to an entire summer devoted to exploring a career and learning skills. At Advanced Micro Devices in Austin, Texas, high school juniors and seniors work for the company during the summer to apply academic lessons learned at school.

The Origins of School-to-Work

Twenty years ago, the need to connect school and work was less urgent. Young people could finish high school with a minimal education and few skills and expect to enter the same factory where their parents worked. They could anticipate earning a decent, middle-class wage there for most of their working lives. But stable, well-paying jobs that do not require advanced training are going the way of the typewriter.

Charlie Coppola, a project engineer at the Procter & Gamble facility in Mehoopany, Pennsylvania, can attest to the transformation. Charlie graduated from high school and went into the service for four years before joining the company in 1970. The day he started at the plant, they hired 50 people. "In reality, it seemed like if you had a little work experience and you were breathing, you got hired," he recollects.

When Charlie began working at the factory, computers were hardly in evidence. Even the big paper machines that churn out paper towels, diapers, and other products were turned on manually, by throwing a series of switches on the plant floor. "There was no such thing as a hand-held calculator when I came to work," he laughs.

Today, P&G is more productive with fewer workers. The plant has shrunk from a high of about 3,100 employees in 1992 to about 2,500 today. An entire P&G assembly line can be operated by a team of five men and women whose job is to troubleshoot problems and oversee quality from a control booth on the factory floor. The team decides how to organize its work and how to improve productivity. P&G has its own training facility to continuously upgrade workers' skills.

"Anybody who starts in this place today had better know how to use computers," cautions Coppola. "These kids are coming into a much more structured Procter & Gamble. It's much harder for them now than it was for me. There's so much more to learn." A high school education won't necessarily get you through the factory door.

The seismic changes going on in the economy are among a number of forces that have added impetus to the school-to-work movement. Beginning in the 1980s, several national reports chronicled the declining wages and rising unemployment among workers with only a high school degree. In 1985, Dale Parnell's book, *The Neglected Majority*, accused public schools of ignoring the needs of the middle 50 percent of students, who were graduating unprepared for either work or college. In 1988, a report by a commission of the W. T. Grant Foundation, *The Forgotten Half: Non-College Youth in America*, focused on the need to provide a pathway from school to careers for young people who did not embark immediately upon undergraduate education. In 1990, *America's Choice: High Skills or Low Wages!* warned that America would lower its standard of living unless it invested in the skills of its front-line workforce and the productivity of its companies, so that they could compete in a high-wage, high-skill economy. By the early 1990s, no fewer than 20 reports had been published that bemoaned problems in preparing young people for careers and adulthood.

Meanwhile, U.S. companies began to express frustration with traditional school-business partnerships that failed to produce results. New forms of work organization in high-performance companies were underlining the need for a more highly skilled workforce and a new system of education and training. Increasingly, businesses began to call for a return on their investment in public education.

In looking for models, Americans were drawn repeatedly to the education-and-training systems in Europe. Countries such as Austria, Denmark, Germany, Switzerland, and Sweden had a high percentage of "average" kids who were well prepared for careers and college. These countries seemed to move young people into stable employment much faster than was typical in the United States.

Americans who traveled abroad noted that, despite differences in history and culture, education-and-training systems in these nations shared several features in common:

❖ *All students are expected to meet a high academic standard by about age 16, whether they are bound for work or for college.* In these countries, young students share a common curriculum at least through primary school and often through lower-secondary school.

❖ *There are clear incentives to work hard and excel in school because students must take exams that determine whether they will enter postsecondary education or have access to the best technical training.* Employers make hiring decisions on the basis of performance in school.

❖ *Students in Europe learn about careers beginning in middle school so that they can make informed choices.* In each of these countries, adolescents may spend up to two weeks a year in the workplace learning about different careers. Beginning in early adolescence, students and their parents also meet with advisers to discuss career and educational options.

❖ *Compared with the United States, students in these countries are not allowed to float through high school.* Focused pathways prepare young people for university, careers, or both. These pathways typically begin in late adolescence and include a year or two of postsecondary education and training.

❖ *Employers, employees, and educators collaborate to set national standards for the skills and experiences that students must have to enter different occupations.* Young people who meet the standards earn nationally recognized credentials that employers value. Education is not considered the sole responsibility of the schools.

Employers and educators work in concert.

❧ *Students have access to adults at school and at the work site who can guide them toward adulthood.*

"I think the single most important lesson from the European experience for the United States is to get education right the first time," says Anne Heald, the executive director of the Center for Learning and Competitiveness at the University of Maryland. "We have a low-expectations system. There is a set of incentives or signals working through the European systems that performance counts. So students bring more of themselves to school."

No one is suggesting that we adopt these systems in total. The European systems are far too rigid for our country. We would not want to push young people to select an occupation at age 14, as they do in Austria. We would not want our middle school students channeled into secondary schools on the basis of their achievement, as they are in Germany. Heavily subsidized government services and centralized labor markets run counter to our history and politics.

Moreover, the European systems are under great stress. High unemployment, inflated wages, generous benefits, and rigid labor rules hamstring their economies. Germany, in particular, has lost much of its luster. Its rate of long-term unemployment now is much higher than in the United States. The U.S. economy, in contrast, is relatively robust.

But we can apply some of the principles here that undergird the European systems, as we shall see later in this book. Moreover, the fact that many European countries are now revising their education-and-training systems in the same direction as incipient school-to-work efforts in this country affirms the logic of these changes.

Even as Americans were looking abroad for models, two parallel bodies of research in this country were bolstering the need for reform. Studies of large, comprehensive high schools suggested they are inhospitable places for both students and teachers. Too many students are going through the motions without any significant engagement in learning. Their education lacks focus and challenge. Too many teachers and students are engaged in a "conspiracy of the least" that demands little of anyone.

Two thirds of high school students responding to a national survey in 1996 admitted that they could do better in school if they tried. About half said school failed to challenge them to do their best.

Many teenagers in large high schools barely interact with adults. John Tobin, the director of vocational training for the Siemens Corporation, remembers how when he was the principal of a high school in New York City, he shadowed an average American student for an entire week. "Her name was Joelle, and she was a cheerleader. I shadowed her all through her academic days, and after school, too. Now, she had seven different subjects every day with different teachers, but there was very little interaction. A teacher might say, 'Oh, Joelle did her homework; I don't have to talk to her about that,' or another might say, 'I don't have to call on her in class because I know she knows the answer,' and so on. Joelle did have interaction with the head of the cheerleaders, but overall I found she only interacted with three adults in the course of a week."

A separate body of cognitive research highlighted the disjuncture between how people use knowledge at work and at school. At work, people increasingly are in situations that demand collaboration. They use tools such as calculators and spreadsheets to do their jobs. And they are constantly asked to do something with what they know. In school, students often sit isolated at their desks, work with pencils and paper, and memorize facts free of any immediate context or use. Whether bound for work or college, this research suggests, many students are too passive. They would likely benefit from having some of their instruction focus less on abstract concepts and more on how academics apply beyond the walls of the classroom.

By the late 1980s, these separate strands had generated a strong core of interest in new approaches to the transition from school to careers. A handful of states and communities began to experiment with creating a uniquely American school-to-work system. Industries with critical labor shortages launched youth apprenticeships as a way to recruit skilled employees. In 1990, Jobs for the Future, a nonprofit organization based in Boston, embarked on the National Youth Apprenticeship Initiative. With the support of such national foundations as the Pew Charitable Trusts, the DeWitt Wallace–Reader's Digest Fund, and the Ford, Lilly, and Charles Stewart Mott foundations, it hoped to demonstrate a high-end model for school-to-work in the United States. The U.S. Department of Labor also provided demonstration grants for a handful of school-to-work programs. In 1992 the administration extended the program and focused it more specifically on youth apprenticeships. That same year the Council of Chief State School Officers, which represents state superintendents of education, provided support to five states to develop school-to-work initiatives.

These early efforts drew support from across the political spectrum. In the 1992 presidential campaign, Republican candidate George Bush and Democratic candidate Bill Clinton both outlined initiatives to strengthen the school-to-work transition. The former Republican governor John R. McKernan, Jr., of Maine has been an outspoken advocate of school-to-work, as has Republican Governor Tommy G. Thompson of Wisconsin.

In 1994, Congress passed the School-to-Work Opportunities Act with overwhelming bipartisan support and the strong endorsement of national business and education groups. The National Association of Manufacturers, the National Alliance of Business, the U.S. Chamber of Commerce, the Committee for Economic Development, the National Coalition for Advanced Manufacturing, and the National Employer Leadership Council all threw their weight behind the law.

The act provided limited seed money for nearly every state to help carry out school-to-work plans, with most of that money going to local communities. By the fall of 1996, 37 states and about 100 communities had received implementation grants from the federal government. Federal funding through fiscal 1996 totaled $695 million. For every $2 in federal investment, another $1 in public and private monies was spent.

That same year, the first 11 states to compile data reported 210 school-to-work partnerships, encompassing about 1,800 schools and 135,000 businesses. These employers provided more than 39,000 work-based learning sites and nearly 53,000 slots for students.

Just a decade ago, no one had ever heard of school-to-work or school-to-career. Today it is a growing and evolving endeavor that has captured the attention of government officials, businesspeople, schools, and parents.

School-to-Work for Any Student

But whom is school-to-work for? Initially, the focus was on the "non-college-bound"—students who do not intend to continue their education after high school or who drop out before graduation. But as school-to-work has developed, its potential benefits for any student have become more apparent.

Certainly, the non-college-bound have an especially severe transition from education to employment. Job stability and real earnings have plummeted for those whose education stops at high school or before. Their prospects for earning a middle-class income that could support a family are dwindling rapidly. Between the ages of 18 and 27, the average high school graduate who does not enroll in postsecondary education holds nearly six different jobs—almost invariably low-paying ones—and experiences between four and five spells of joblessness.

In 1994 the unemployment rate for recent high school graduates not enrolled in college was 36 percent. For high school dropouts, it was 57 percent. The real earnings of high school dropouts have plummeted as much as 26 percent in the past 15 years. Today they are qualified for only the most menial employment.

The problems of finding good jobs are magnified for minority, disadvantaged, and inner-city youth, who are more isolated from the mainstream economy. The unemployment rate for black high school graduates in 1994 was nearly double that of white high school graduates.

When young people who have not gone to college find a job that pays enough to live on, they tend to keep it. The notion that this constitutes a real "career choice" is laughable. Some economists argue that this rocky transition to the world of work is a reasonable way to match up people's skills and interests with those of the labor market. Yet the experience of other countries suggests that this process can occur with far less financial and emotional trauma than occurs in this country.

Young people who see no productive role for themselves in the community contribute substantially to the nation's high juvenile-crime and teenage-pregnancy rates, as Lisbeth B. Schorr points out in her book *Within Our Reach: Breaking the Cycle of Disadvantage*. High school dropouts, she writes, are three and a half times as likely as high school graduates to be arrested and six times as likely to be unwed parents.

"Our common stake in preventing these damaging outcomes of adolescence is immense," cautions Schorr. "We all pay to support the unproductive and incarcerate the violent. We are all eco-nomically weakened by lost productivity. We all live with fear of crime in our homes and on our streets. We are all diminished when large numbers of parents are incapable of nurturing their depen-dent young, and when pervasive alienation erodes the national sense of community."

But school-to-work is not an opportunity just for the non-college-bound. Studies suggest that the *vast majority of students—*including those headed for college—also are having problems identifying career options and making the transition to college and careers. They too are bored and disillusioned with their education.

Take the case of Christina, who attends eleventh grade at a suburban high school in Fairfax County, Virginia. She's a solid A student who plans to go to college and whose courses include advanced-placement history, honors English and chemistry, and algebra 2. Yet she says of her education, "It's not like I'm thinking a lot here. You get all kinds of facts, and then you take the test, and then they all leave you. They don't mean anything. I get good grades by just going through the steps and doing the homework and turning it in. I feel like I come away from the year with just grades and nothing more."

What Christina finds exciting is her internship with a non-profit organization in Washington, D.C., after school. There she does research, answers the phones, and helps survey community-based groups about their volunteer needs. "At my internship, I feel like they treat me as someone who has a lot of ideas, and who's not just a kid," Christina says. "At school, you feel like your teach-ers are just talking at you. When I'm at my internship, I feel like they respect my work, and they respect what I do. And I get ex-cited about what I'm working on."

Today most high school students have wildly unrealistic expectations about their future. They expect to have high-paid,

high-status jobs. About one out of three expects to have a professional career. Ten percent think they will be doctors. Another 10
percent anticipate jobs in the sports or entertainment industry.

The majority of students do not even have a particular career
in mind. They vacillate between options as diverse as architecture
and dog training, surgery and singing. Their ambivalence about
career choices is coupled with scanty knowledge about what such
jobs actually entail or what their educational requirements are.
When researchers in a massive nationwide study of adolescents
asked students for precise information about the careers they
hoped to enter—such as the average income, the education
required, or the prospects for job openings—few could provide it.

We need to stop differentiating students as college-bound or
non-college-bound. Today most students think they are headed
for college. In a recent survey of high school seniors, 95 percent
said they planned to continue their education beyond high school
and 84 percent expected to earn at least a four-year degree. The
percentage of young people nationwide who are enrolled in college the fall after they graduate from high school now exceeds 60
percent.

Many of the rest will enroll in some sort of postsecondary
education and training eventually, especially when they see the
jobs available to those with just a high school diploma. We cannot predict who will go to college and who will not. In the future,
most people will cycle back and forth between work and learning
throughout their adult lives.

But the dirty little secret of college (as I discuss in chapter 6)
is that many students who enroll in two-year and four-year colleges never get a college degree. Poorly prepared for college-level
work and without a clear sense of their career prospects, they strug-
gle with the rigors and expense of college. Though college students pay as much as $25,000 a year or more, many arrive on

campus without adequate direction or academic preparation. Parents and others who foot the bills are increasingly anxious about whether colleges are giving students the skills they need to succeed.

Furthermore, even the cherished college diploma no longer guarantees success. A 1992 Labor Department study found one in six college graduates doing work that did not generally require a college degree. Meanwhile, well-paying, high-technology jobs that students could enter with a two-year degree from a community or technical college are going unfilled.

Many accomplished high school students see nothing unusual about school-to-work activities, and for good reason: Their own education often incorporates similar experiences. Maybe they did an internship after school or in the summer at a local business. In their science magnet high school, they might have conducted research in a real laboratory working under the guidance of a real scientist. They might have entered competitions sponsored by local companies to provide innovative solutions to real-world problems.

Work-based learning is how schools, colleges, and universities teach many high-achieving students. Doctors complete residencies and internships; lawyers clerk for judges and work in law firms over the summer; architects and engineers complete practicums. You would never go to a brain surgeon who had only read about surgical procedures in a book or trust a pilot who had never sat behind the wheel of a plane. If work-based experiences are valuable for our best students, they can be equally valuable for any student.

Colleges recognize this. According to *U.S. News & World Report*, they are increasingly providing experiential learning for their students. They recognize the value of practical, hands-on education. And they know that experience in the workplace can give their students a leg up after they graduate.

New Assumptions

At age 16, most young people legally can leave school. At age 18, they are ready to vote and assume adult citizenship. It is a time of intense exploration: Who am I? What do I want from life? What are my goals?

In my travels around the country I have met with hundreds of high school students. It remains one of my favorite ages. High school students are remarkably perceptive and fresh in their views. They have far more energy than most adults. Given a chance to assume responsibility, many do. They can be committed, creative, and very funny.

Yet we systematically deny these individuals the opportunity to engage in meaningful ways with the adult world. One striking comment heard repeatedly from students in school-to-work programs is that they are treated like adults in these programs and therefore act like adults. In regular high schools, they say, they are treated like nine-year-olds—and often act accordingly.

This is a book about the tremendous potential—and corresponding perils—of school-to-work. In it I will look at what happens when employers and educators begin to communicate across the chasm that now separates them. Effective school-to-work systems are not just a new and improved version of vocational education. And they are not just for the non-college-bound. Rather, they embody some very different assumptions about education and work for the twenty-first century.

Head and Hands

In the workplace and in our schools, we traditionally have distinguished those who can work with their heads from those who can work with their hands. But in the modern workplace, we need people with high-level academic *and* technical knowledge. Good school-to-career systems prepare students who can solve problems or produce something with their knowledge.

High Expectations for All

Public schools in the United States have excelled at separating students into different educational tracks. Typically, this has meant an abstract, symbolic education for some and a watered-down, dead-end curriculum for those headed toward work. In today's society, every student must be held to high academic and occupational standards.

The Basics Plus

It is generally agreed that all students need to master such basic academic skills as arithmetic, civics, and the appropriate use of the English language. But educators, business leaders, and colleges are identifying an additional set of skills that young people need to make it in the real world. "In addition to basic skills, all individuals must be able to think their way through the workday, analyzing problems, proposing solutions, communicating, working collaboratively, and managing resources such as time and materials," stated the nation's governors and corporate executives at the 1996 National Education Summit. "Providing all citizens with the opportunity to develop these skills will give the people of our country a competitive edge." These skills need much greater emphasis in schools, and work-based learning is ideally suited to acquiring them. School-to-work can equip young people with skills and knowledge that they would have a hard time acquiring in other ways.

The Power of Work

For hundreds of years, young people learned by working alongside their parents. Some became apprentices who worked beside a master craftsman to become competent in their field. But today students need more formal education to learn the academic skills that increasingly are required on the job. School-to-work systems are striving to create a new form of apprenticeship that combines formal learning in school and at work. That does not mean that every student will spend the last two years of high school in the workplace. Nor is it an argument for narrow vocational training that forces students into career tracks before they are ready. But every student should have the opportunity to explore career options while still in high school. All students should spend part of their time using case studies and real-world problems to learn and apply academic content. Young people should have a chance to engage in productive, responsible activities that make a difference for their communities and reinforce basic work values. And students should have the option of participating in more structured work-based learning if they choose.

The Benefits to Business

Many businesses have viewed their involvement with the schools as a civic responsibility or a nice public relations gesture. But to sustain school-to-work systems, businesses must recognize and take into account their self-interest and the collective self-interest of their industries. Some businesses have used school-to-work as a screening and recruitment device to "grow their own" workforce. Industries such as printing and metalworking have reached out to schools to fill labor shortages. Others have used school-to-work programs to increase diversity in the workplace. Businesses are not a monolithic group, and their reasons for participating in school-to-work will vary. But school-to-work systems will not survive if businesses view their involvement solely as a form of charity.

The K–16 Continuum

Actually, the phrase "school-to-work" is something of a misnomer, since high-wage, high-skill jobs increasingly require some postsecondary education and training. Many school-to-work initiatives more accurately could be called school-to-college-to-work. Typically, they include at least one year of postsecondary education. Some programs also are encouraging students to enter four-year colleges who might not have done so in the past. The challenge is to ensure that high school students not only are motivated but are *prepared* for postsecondary education. We need to improve the rates at which students who begin college actually earn a degree and make it easier for young people who do not pursue undergraduate education immediately to find challenging, well-paying work. In short, we must prepare young people for *both* work and college, since they will alternate back and forth between them as they engage in lifetime learning.

Where We Stand

School-to-work poses real risks, and I will not minimize them in this book. If school-to-work systems funnel students into narrow job categories based on immediate labor-market needs, they will have failed. If they are grafted onto existing vocational education—representing a change in name only—we will be worse off than when we started. If state and local officials permit anything to pass itself off as a school-to-work initiative, regardless of its academic or occupational rigor, the entire effort will be discredited. If school-to-career systems weaken academic preparation or close off college options, they should not be supported. And if school-to-work remains stalled as a handful of hothouse demonstration projects, it will suffer the fate of many good ideas: lost in the onslaught of change.

In 1996 the Clinton administration estimated that at least 500,000 students were engaged in intensive school-to-work experiences based on data from 11 states. But we still do not have anything approaching a school-to-work system that is capable of serving large numbers of American youths. Nor do we know anything about the quality or rigor of these experiences.

There are more than 5 million juniors and seniors in public high schools nationwide. Many of them have not been touched by the school-to-work movement. One of the biggest unanswered questions is whether enough employers will step forward to allow many more students to participate.

We know from the research to date that students who participate in school-to-work activities generally are motivated and engaged by what they are doing and have a better sense of their career options. Small-scale studies and anecdotes from individual programs suggest that, in some cases, high percentages of young people in these programs are pursuing higher education. Some studies have documented lower dropout rates, improved attendance, greater academic course-taking, and better academic performance.

But, in general, these early initiatives have had either no effect or only modest effects on students' grades and high school attendance. There is little evidence of economic outcomes. And the current round of programs is so new that there are no longitudinal studies on students' postsecondary education, employment, mobility, and earnings during the first few years after high school graduation. At present, we are left relying largely upon argument and anecdote.

Of course, preparing students for employment is just one goal of education. Schools also need to nurture good citizens and people who can understand and appreciate the world around them. But these three goals are not incompatible. On the contrary, they can be mutually reinforcing. If school-to-work systems can engage students in education, students can be expected to achieve more academically and intellectually. This is the promise at the heart of the school-to-work philosophy.

Ironically, the strong bipartisan spirit that once characterized school-to-work is now under attack. Following the Republican takeover of Congress in the 1994 elections, some conservative legislators began to question the federal involvement in education and training. Conservative groups such as the Eagle Forum derided school-to-work as a conspiracy by big business and big government to shape children's futures, charging that it will further vocationalize education and dilute academics. The most extreme critics compare school-to-work to the managed economies of the Soviet Union and construct paranoid scenarios of federalist plots.

Others question corporate motives and wonder how much we want businesses involved in the schools. They note the continued existence of large numbers of low-paying, low-skill jobs. And they worry that young people will be overeducated, not undereducated.

It is also true that many young people already work too much. One of the features that distinguishes the United States from other countries is the extent to which teenagers work. The majority of high school students work today in a shadow economy of fast-food jobs and retail chains, as do the majority of college students. Students who work during high school obtain higher earnings in the first few years after leaving school, largely because employers value work experience. But most of the jobs young people work at devote almost no time to education and training. They bear no relation to young people's schooling. And they are not connected with young people's long-term career goals. Some studies suggest that young people who work too much have poorer academic performance.

There is always a chance that school-to-work will be done badly. Structured improperly, school-to-work could further dumb-down education and channel students into low-expectation tracks. Business could be allowed to play too dominant a role in dictating school programs. And if we really want a high-wage, high-skill economy, we have to support policies that encourage the creation of high-wage, high-performance industries. We have to change both the demand side and the supply side of the equation.

But it is equally clear that the world around us is changing. If young people are not better educated and better prepared for this new world, the consequences will be severe for them personally and for the nation.

Today we teach students academic subjects out of context and then are perturbed when they ask, "Why do I have to learn this?" We hire young people without glancing at their high school transcripts and then wonder why they do not work harder in school. We sequester teenagers in high schools that are too big for them and then express dismay when they succumb to an adolescent peer culture. We tell young people to attend college to "get a good job" but then offer little in the way of career guidance. We convince students that we are preparing them for the "real world" but make their education as removed from the adult society as possible.

School-to-work offers the potential to address some of these issues. It cannot solve the problems of U.S. education or business. Education and the economy are both extraordinarily complicated—too complicated for a single solution.

But work and learning are becoming inseparable. We need to move beyond the distrust of both educators and employers and begin to engage in productive conversations. This is a book about the people who have begun those discussions—and about what those conversations mean for the future of the country.

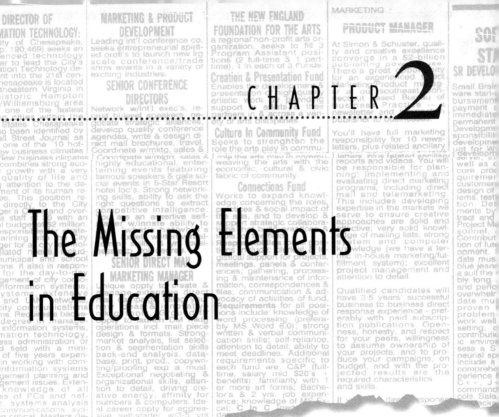

CHAPTER 2

The Missing Elements in Education

$\mathcal{I}$n a small conference room in Cambridge, Massachusetts, nine high school students sit around a table discussing the book *Working* by Studs Terkel. One after another they describe which of Terkel's 1972 portraits of working life in America appeals to them and why. "I chose the laborer because I can relate to him," says Christopher Scott-Martin, whose fair skin and blue eyes reflect his Irish heritage. "My whole life is a blue-collar life. . . . I can only work with my hands. I can't work with my mind."

At age 16, Chris has decided that he can't think. Why? A big reason is because American schools have told him so. Throughout the twentieth century, this country has built an educational system based on the premise that many students cannot think deeply and therefore cannot engage in serious intellectual work. Though

Americans embraced the very democratic notion of mass public education, we did not embrace the idea of the same public education for everyone. Instead, we created an academic education for the "head-smart" youngster and a vocational education for the "hands smart." This chasm has widened and deepened ever since. Even our expectations and standards of coursework for many college-bound students remain shockingly low. It is the reason many of us no longer trust the value of a high school diploma.

In their 1985 book *The Shopping Mall High School: Winners and Losers in the Educational Marketplace*, Arthur G. Powell, Eleanor Farrar, and David K. Cohen refer to the great mass of students as the "unspecial." These are the students who drift through classes without working too hard or being pushed too much. Their high school programs lack focus. Their teachers barely know them. Whether they choose to engage in serious intellectual work or not is up to them. For most, mediocrity, passivity, and anti-intellectualism prevail.

The greatest single challenge to American high schools is how to engage these tuned-out, turned-off students so that they can achieve more. So far, the approach we have taken is to crack the whip by raising standards and creating new tests and graduation requirements. That is part of the solution. But if students actively dislike school, higher standards and better assessments are not going to change their minds. And higher standards will do little to alter the self-image of a student like Chris.

As we shall see in chapter 6, the school reforms of the 1980s emphasized more testing and more academic coursework for American teenagers—and these reforms have had an important effect. But they have failed to address the deeper crisis of boredom and disengagement in U.S. high schools. Why should students take tough classes and study hard when they see no connection between education and their future? How can students get excited about learning when they spend much of their time glued passively in their seats?

New Building Blocks

Convincing young people that learning is worth the effort requires a different kind of instruction and organization of the schools. This chapter describes some of the new building blocks on which American high school education should be based:

❀ We need to stop categorizing students as academic and vocational, college-bound and non-college-bound. In the modern workplace, we need people with high-level academic and technical knowledge.

❀ We need higher standards and a solid academic core for all students. Everyone must be equipped to work and learn throughout their lives, as learning becomes a more prominent feature of all jobs.

❀ We need more active and engaging instruction. Students should have opportunities to extend and use their knowledge, not just regurgitate facts.

❀ We need to help young people explore careers so they can set realistic goals for the future and establish plans to achieve them.

❀ Underlying these four assumptions, we need to connect learning at work and in communities with activities in the classroom so that young people see how knowledge is applied.

I have visited many school-to-work efforts over the past several years, and I can honestly say that few achieve all of these objectives. Some have injected low-level academics into low-level vocational classes. Others have put students in the workplace with little or no connection back to the classroom. A few simply have slapped new names on old practices.

Still, the pieces of a compelling picture are there, even if they are scattered. And the picture slowly is coming into focus.

Hands and Minds

Few places better illustrate both the chasm between academic and technical education and a way to bridge it than the Rindge School of Technical Arts in Cambridge, Massachusetts.

For over a century, Rindge epitomized the divide between academic and occupational studies. It opened its doors in 1888 as the Rindge Manual Training School. Its chief benefactor, the industrialist Frederick Rindge, specified in his bequest that the school should serve "boys of average talents and strong physique." It was the first public vocational high school in Massachusetts and the second in the entire United States. An inscription carved in granite over the front door reads: "Work is one of our greatest blessings. Everyone should have an honest occupation." In the 1970s the school merged with the nearby college-preparatory high school to become the Cambridge Rindge and Latin High School, although Rindge still retained a somewhat separate identity within the larger school.

The Cambridge public schools operate under a system of controlled choice. All teenagers attend Cambridge Rindge and Latin, the only public high school in the district, with just under 2,000 students. Located a five-minute walk from Harvard Square, the gray stonework facade retains much of its former grandeur. Within the high school, students can choose to enroll in one of six semiautonomous houses, each with its own identity and focus; one of them is Rindge. But as the vocational option, Rindge was the least popular place to go. By the early 1990s, Rindge's enrollment had plummeted to about 235 adolescents, and its working-class students were those whom no one else wanted to teach.

This is what Larry Rosenstock encountered at the Rindge School of Technical Arts when he became its executive director in 1990. A former carpentry teacher, Rosenstock is always on the move, his wiry frame animated and words tumbling from his mouth.

Before coming to Rindge, Rosenstock spent two years working to change federal vocational-education laws as an attorney with the Harvard Center for Law and Education. He took the job at Rindge, he recalls, because "I wanted to see if we could do it."

Rosenstock's approach has been to make hands and minds work in harmony rather than in opposition. Sitting near the original director's rolltop desk, carved out of dark oak and filled with secret cubbyholes, he quips: "If anyone had told me at fifteen or sixteen that I was going to be spending my adult life in a high school, I would have ended it right there." Yet he has found a way to make Rindge not only bearable for its students but engaging: He has opened it up to the world.

The work-site seminar in which Chris participates, one of three courses he is taking as a senior, is a good example of Rindge's efforts to marry academic and technical studies. The seminar does not take place at the high school but at the Harvard Facilities Department, located just across the Charles River from Harvard University. The nondescript, one-story structure bears little resemblance to the statelier ivy-clad buildings across the way but without its services, Harvard would soon cease to function. From here, University Operations Services maintains the institution's buildings and transportation systems, its computers, and other technology. Two other university divisions, Harvard Real Estate and Harvard Dining Services, also participate in the Harvard internship program, which involved about a dozen students from all of Cambridge Rindge and Latin High School in 1995–96.

The students spend several mornings a week at work sites associated with their divisions. Chris, for example, wants to be a chef and works for the dining services preparing meals. Other students work at computers in the real estate division or accompany building supervisors on their rounds.

The twice-weekly seminar is where they all come together. Its purpose is not to teach specific job skills but to explore the meaning of work in society and in students' lives. Students also study Harvard as a large corporation. The teenagers receive both English and social studies credit for their participation. On this particular morning, teacher Maria Ferri coaxes the students to make comparisons between their work experiences and those described in Terkel's book. She prods them to differentiate between workers who are unhappy in their jobs and exert little control over their environment and those who consciously strive to make their lives better. When Chris complains that the laborer wasn't treated with respect by society even though "he's the person who's getting everything done in this world," Ferri asks, "Do you feel, at times, that you don't get respect for the work you do?"

Other weeks' seminars cover such questions as "What is work?" "What is success?" "Who am I as a worker and as a citizen?" Students interview their supervisors about their career history, interview people whom they consider successes, and contrast their student internship with previous jobs or volunteer experiences. The Cambridge Historical Society provides them with a walking tour of Cambridge's old factories and buildings, which they use to reconstruct the history of working life in the city. They draw upon the resources of the university to study the history of Harvard, the formation of labor unions and their role, and the differences between profit and nonprofit organizations. All students keep work-site logs and journals, which become the basis for classroom discussions. They produce a newsletter about their internships. They also complete an independent project at the work site that culminates in a research paper, a product of some kind, and an oral presentation before an audience of employers and educators.

"Work has authenticity and relevance, which leads, from my experience, to engagement," says Rosenstock. "So we need to preserve that part of vocational education but greatly diminish narrow training for specific jobs. There's very little role for that, in my opinion, at the secondary level."

The same basic concept of merging academic and technical studies extends throughout Rindge's programs. All ninth-graders take a class known as "CityWorks" taught by a team of academic and vocational teachers. Using the city of Cambridge as their laboratory, students make maps, take photographs, draw architectural blueprints, build models, and write up oral histories, as they learn about the city and its resources. At the end of the year they complete a community-development project, such as creating scale models and drawings for refurbishing a neighborhood park.

In an internship program on teaching, students spend two mornings a week working as teacher's aides in elementary school classrooms throughout Cambridge. The other three mornings they participate in an education seminar at Lesley College, which is co-taught by a Lesley professor and a teacher from Rindge. In 1994–95 the seminar focused on issues of justice and fairness in the classroom and used as some of its texts *Coming of Age in Mississippi,* by Anne Moody, and *The Autobiography of Malcolm X,* written with Alex Haley. One goal of the program is to encourage more students of color and from low-income backgrounds to pursue careers in education.

Even the architecture of the school speaks to the changes underway. Students helped tear down the walls of the traditional shop classes and construct large, open spaces that resemble art studios. In 1995–96 they were replacing Rindge's traditional woodworking shop with a technology lab, where students can build projects that allow them to apply knowledge from mathematics and science. The day I visited, a group of teenagers was huddled in the middle of the half-finished space. They were constructing a waterwheel and testing the maximum load that it could lift. This would lead into a study of kinetic and potential energy. In 1995–96 Rindge planned to offer two introduction-to-technology courses as well as a course in physics and engineering. These new classes were designed to emphasize the more analytical skills needed in today's job market.

Rindge also creates student-run enterprises that are tied directly in to its academic program. A student-produced news program broadcasts once a week on a local cable channel. A student-run electronics service installs and maintains computer and telephone equipment in the building. The student-operated "image center" designs and produces logos for school and community groups. In the auto shop, students are retrofitting trucks from Harvard and the Massachusetts Institute of Technology to run on electric power. Other students have joined a Community Leadership and Services Corps that combines classroom studies with efforts to address community needs.

Such programs can make a big difference for the students they serve. When Alfreda Cromwell, a vivacious and energetic senior, enrolled in Rindge, she was a streetwise, turned-off student. "I didn't like school," she recalls. "I didn't plan to go to college and all that good stuff. I hung out on the corners. Basically, I was more into my friends than school."

After her brother convinced her to try Rindge, she enrolled in CityWorks, where she learned about the community where she had lived most of her life. She began staying late to finish her projects. Sometimes she had to be pushed out the door. She got straight A's. In her junior year, she began an internship at the Harvard Real Estate offices. Five mornings a week she worked on campus, mastering the intricacies of various software programs. After learning one computer application, she discovered that it was easy to learn more. For her class project, she developed a brochure that introduces other students to the Internet, e-mail, and the university's bulletin board. She also produced a videotape of her training session. To her surprise, Alfreda found herself thinking about work at home and planning for the next day. She learned how to dress, how to prevent personal problems from spilling over into the workplace, and how to communicate. "I wasn't this big, bad person before," she recollects. "But I definitely wasn't into school and I definitely didn't want to go to college."

When I last spoke to Alfreda, she was in the midst of arranging her college interviews.

Chris also enjoyed his internship at Harvard Dining Services, which he described as a "great program" (though his teacher thought he was spending too much time on basic food preparation). He told me, "I'm not big into the academics, and I never did good in school with the books and the teachers and the papers and the pencils. I hated that stuff. I'd just sit there and fall asleep, or I wouldn't go to class, and my grades were affected." In contrast, he described the internship as "hands-on training. . . . I still have to use my mind and everything, but it's actually something that I enjoy using it for."

Chris envisions two future scenarios for himself immediately after high school. He plans to apply to four culinary arts colleges in New England. His family cannot pay for his education, but he can name several scholarships that might be available to him and that would help put him through college along with paid work in his chosen profession. If he cannot get into college, he has the immediate skills to begin working for a restaurant or a catering business. Harvard Dining Services already has hired him to work in the main kitchen on Saturdays for $10.75 an hour—not bad starting pay for a teenager. "It's excellent," enthuses Chris, "and a lot more opportunities, I hope, are going to arise from this program."

Rosenstock and a dedicated team of teachers and volunteers are slowly turning Rindge around. Everyone from the children of Harvard professors to the children of the working class are applying for its internship programs. The attendance rate at Rindge is higher—and the percentage of courses that students fail is lower—than at the other houses within the high school, including the more traditional college-preparatory program. Nearly all (99 percent) of the students who start internships complete them. Of those who complete internships, 85 percent go on to postsecondary education, compared with 74 percent for the high school as a whole.

A Dichotomy Rooted in the Past

Yet for all its success, Rindge has not shattered its image as a vocational school in the minds of many Cambridge parents. Its overall enrollment outside of the internship programs has remained flat. It is still the place where other people's children go. It takes a long time to overcome history.

The dichotomy that Rosenstock encountered at Rindge between vocational and academic education is deeply rooted in the evolution of U.S. public schools. When Rindge opened in 1888, public high schools enrolled under 9 percent of the high-school-age population, and a much smaller fraction actually graduated. The high school curriculum anticipated that of the universities: Latin, Greek, ancient history, and natural philosophy.

Between the turn of the century and the eve of World War II, a revolution occurred in American education. From a total high school enrollment of about a half million in 1900, enrollments swelled to over 6.5 million pupils by 1940. Attendance rates went from under 9 percent of the high-school-age population to over 60 percent.

The University of Michigan historian David K. Cohen ascribes this phenomenal growth to several sources. In a society that valued upward mobility, formal education became a gateway to economic and social success. Changes in industry and in the economy foreclosed many unskilled and semiskilled jobs to those under age 16. The passage of child-labor laws, the demise of apprenticeships, and the expansion of compulsory schooling also conspired to push more adolescents out of the labor market and into the classroom. Meanwhile, the emerging industrial factories needed workers who were at least literate and able to follow directions. Faced with a wave of immigrants who did not speak English and were unfamiliar with American customs, employers looked to the schools to socialize them. Teenagers went to school, Cohen observes, less because they wanted to learn than because there were few other options.

The question that occupied educational reformers for the first half of the century was, what kind of education would suit this much larger and more diverse population? On one side of the argument was the Committee of Ten, chaired by President Charles W. Eliot of Harvard. In its 1893 report, the group argued that all students should master an equally rigorous curriculum. "Every subject which is taught at all in secondary school should be taught in the same way and to the same extent to every pupil," the committee stressed, "no matter what the probable destination of the pupil may be, or at what point his education is to cease." The committee recommended at least four years of English, four years of a foreign language, and three years each of mathematics, science, and history.

Opposing the committee's recommendations were men who favored a much more practical, utilitarian curriculum for students not bound for college. In 1906, a report by the Massachusetts Commission on Industrial and Technical Education argued that the schools were "too exclusively literary" for the great body of children and youths. The report documented the large number of students who left school at age 12 or 14 for dead-end jobs because school held no interest for them. What these youngsters needed, the commission concluded, was "school training of a practical character" that would prepare them for jobs in industry.

These reformers were joined by powerful forces in the business community who wanted the schools to help train a skilled labor pool. The National Association of Manufacturers was particularly taken with the German system of technical and trade schools, which it believed contributed to that nation's growing commercial success. In a report published in 1912, it differentiated among three kinds of learners: the "abstract-minded and imaginative children," the "great intermediate class," and the "concrete, or hand-minded children." For the benefit of the latter group, it advocated the creation of separate trade schools in the United States.

As the debate between academics for all or vocationalism for some swirled throughout Massachusetts and the United States in the early twentieth century, the Columbia University philosophy professor John Dewey developed a perspective on education that remains compelling today. His views were more nuanced, and in the end more valuable, than those of either of the opposing camps.

Dewey advocated rewriting the curriculum to reflect the "urgent realities of contemporary life." He thought the study of occupations would help students make sense of the rapidly changing industrialized world. He believed that by engaging young children in projects and in manual activities that more closely reflected their daily lives, they could be drawn into a study of the traditional academic disciplines.

But Dewey adamantly opposed a dual system of education, with one curriculum for the college-bound and another for everyone else. He feared that a narrow vocationalism in the service of industry would serve to strengthen class divisions in American society.

"The problem of the educator," Dewey wrote in *Democracy and Education*, "is to engage pupils in [vocational] activities in such ways that while manual skill and technical efficiency are gained and immediate satisfaction found in the work together with preparation for later usefulness, these things shall be subordinated to *education*—that is, to intellectual results and the forming of a socialized disposition."

Dewey's insights were for naught. In the great debate about the purposes of public schooling, the vocationalists won decisively. In 1917, Congress passed the Smith-Hughes Act, which provided the first federal funds to states for the promotion of vocational education. The act encouraged the growing separation between academic and vocational instruction in American high schools by establishing a separate funding stream for the latter, geared toward skills training for specific industries.

By the 1930s, high schools had begun to resemble the "shopping-mall" schools that Arthur Powell and his colleagues would describe 50 years later—offering a little something for everyone. There were commercial, industrial, and home-economics studies to prepare young people for the labor market. Schools added new academic courses like "general math" and "general science" to educate the non-college-bound and those with no specific occupational plans. Such changes met the demands of mass-production factories for workers with a modicum of skills; a basic command of reading, writing, and arithmetic; and the ability to follow orders. Well-intentioned educators tried to mirror the efficiencies of modern industry by sorting children into distinct curriculum paths on the basis of their presumed abilities and their future role in society.

Over time, high schools developed three relatively distinct curricula: "college-preparatory," "general studies," and "vocational." Today, these tracks have become more muddled, with some college-preparatory students failing to take high-level mathematics and science courses that some vocational graduates take. But the differences in students' learning opportunities between the higher- and lower-level courses remain pronounced. Students in the more-advanced classes are more likely to receive better instruction and spend more time on learning. They have more homework and are held to higher standards than those in the low-level classes.

These distinctions stem from assumptions that are no longer valid. They presume that most students lack the interest or ability to attend college and that few jobs will require an education beyond a high school diploma. Only in the past two decades have educators and policymakers begun to reexamine these assumptions seriously. Indeed, the notion that all students should engage in serious academic work and learn it deeply is a relatively recent phenomenon.

The Failure of Vocationalism—and a Way Out

I have been in a large number of high schools to visit vocational programs. Many of these programs are located in the basement or in a separate wing of the school building. It is a fitting reminder of the isolation and second-class status of these efforts.

Throughout the twentieth century, criticisms of vocational programs have been remarkably consistent: Vocational education focuses too much on narrow job training. It is out of step with changes in industry. It prepares young people for occupations without regard to labor-market demands. It lacks intellectual content and academic rigor. It is too isolated from the rest of the curriculum. Vocational students take fewer academic classes, and fewer advanced courses, than do other students. And the more vocational classes students take, the worse they perform on national assessments of achievement.

Perhaps the lack of academic substance could be overlooked if students who took vocational courses did better in the job market. But many don't. Vocational students who secure a job in their field of study tend to earn higher salaries than other high school graduates. But fewer than half of vocational graduates find employment in the occupation for which they trained. The rest ride an educational track to nowhere.

One study of the high school class of 1982 examined the 1985 pretax earnings of those who went to work right after graduating. It found that students whose high school transcripts indicated they were enrolled in vocational programs fared significantly worse in the labor market, earning almost $1,000 less than the annual average. In contrast, students who proceeded directly into the workplace after completing an academic high school curriculum earned about $1,065 more than the average.

"The most serious problem is that vocational education in the high school has carved out as its domain those entry-level occupations that are relatively low-paid and low status—secretary, hairdresser, farmer, auto mechanic, electrician, carpenter—with few prospects for advancement and demanding relatively low academic skill levels," says University of California, Berkeley, education professor W. Norton Grubb. "From that fact, students with higher aspirations have shunned vocational education, converting it into a 'dumping ground' for those considered unable to (or perhaps just unwilling to) perform adequately in academic classes."

Since the early 1980s this pattern has become even more pronounced. As states and localities have increased the number of academic courses required for graduation, participation in vocational education has plummeted and students' vocational course taking has become even less coherent. A 1994 report to Congress from the U.S. Department of Education found a growing concentration of low-achieving and disabled youths in vocational classes. It cautioned that this trend could "slowly increase the isolation and stigmatization of these programs and students."

Of course, there are exceptions. Some vocational classes with strong connections to employers prepare students for high-demand, well-paid fields. Many of the teachers who work in these programs are dedicated professionals who want to do everything they can for their students. But the overall pattern is disturbing.

The general studies curriculum—in which about 40 percent of high school seniors are enrolled, compared with 48 percent in the college-preparatory track and 12 percent in vocational programs—is not much better. Critics have described general studies courses as preparing young people for neither work nor college. Classes like "basic English 12," "exploration in math I," and "general science" seem designed to fill time rather than to prepare students for a productive future.

In response to such criticisms, many school districts have scaled back vocational programs or have tried to align them more closely with labor-market needs. They have eliminated the general track and replaced low-level academic courses with ones that teach college-preparatory content in new ways. Some of these changes are more cosmetic than substantive. But they illustrate the second key task facing public schools: how to increase the academic content and standards for *all* students.

High Expectations for All

In modern economies, no students can afford to end their education when they are handed a high school or college diploma. Many of the students entering high school today will still be working in the year 2050. No job will go unchanged in that time. Many of today's jobs will have disappeared, and many new ones will have been created. To keep up with the dizzying pace of change, work and learning will have to occur throughout our lives. To prepare for a lifetime of learning, all students need to meet higher standards and master a solid academic core.

One place where those goals are being embraced is in the thriving economy surrounding Wilmington, Delaware. Like the Rindge School of Technical Arts, the New Castle County Vocational-Technical School District, which serves about 17 percent of the public high school students in the county, was on the rocks in 1990. Students from the county could opt to attend the county's three vocational-technical schools—and they weren't coming. The superintendent had just been fired for personnel improprieties. The governor had replaced half of the appointed school board. The school system's approximately 3,000 students routinely scored at or near the bottom on statewide tests. And its course offerings included an array of low-level options like "General Math 1 and 2," "Business Math," and "Consumer Math" that essentially allowed students to bypass academically demanding subject matter.

"It was a really bleak period for a lot of us," recalls superintendent Dennis Loftus, a big, beefy man with a salesman's handshake who was brought in to repair the damage. The school board gave the former assistant superintendent broad leeway to make changes as long as he staunched the flow of negative publicity. The school district's new motto was "Rising Above the Rest to Become the Very Best."

Loftus began by resurrecting the school district's moribund business advisory committees, which helped determine the content of vocational programs. He formed a high-profile task force, chaired by a former DuPont Company executive, to examine the problems at Howard High School, the school district's most urban and neglected facility.

Most important, Loftus launched a campaign to raise academic standards and expectations. Many low-level academic courses were eliminated. A one-semester technical writing course was added for all twelfth-graders. Programs of study spelled out both the academic subjects and the technical sequence that students must take to graduate, so that there would be less drifting through the curriculum. The district created three different levels of "career program certificates"—bronze, silver, and gold—to recognize students who had excelled in both their technical and academic course work. Students have to complete an additional year of mathematics and science beyond the state's minimum requirements to qualify for the silver or gold awards.

Working with the business community and the school board, the district set benchmarks in such areas as student attendance, discipline, academic skills, vocational skills, the percentage of students who made it to graduation, and their activities after they graduated. Some of the benchmarks stemmed from surveys of the school system's customers: parents, teachers, employers, and students. Other measures, such as the attendance goals, were based on the performance of the best-performing schools in the county or on feedback from employers. Business leaders had complained, for example, about the poor mathematics, reading, writing, and communications skills among graduates coming out of the schools.

The district published annual reports on each school describing how the school compared with the benchmarks. Where schools did well, they were asked to share their strategies. Where they did poorly, they were asked what steps they would take to improve. But within this framework, each of the three high schools in the district was allowed to steer its own course.

Some of the most noticeable changes have occurred at the Paul M. Hodgson Vocational-Technical High School, which is located in a growing suburb 20 miles outside Wilmington. Hodgson is a member of the Coalition of Essential Schools, a national group dedicated to reforming high schools. The coalition stresses teaching fewer subjects in more depth, restructuring high schools so that teachers can know students better, and graduating students on the basis of what they know and can do rather than the time spent in class.

At Hodgson, these themes converge in the form of a senior project. Since 1990, each senior has had to complete a year-long, career-related project that culminates in a research paper, a product, and an oral presentation before an audience. Projects can range from a scale model of an earthquake-resistant house to a brochure explaining the pros and cons of different health-insurance plans. The projects go beyond what students typically do in shop. One carpentry student I talked with was building a 13-foot by 4-foot flat-bottomed boat that he hoped to rig for sailing.

The senior project requires high school students to engage in the same basic tasks as Ph.D. candidates: to research, write, and orally defend their ideas. Demand for these skills has percolated throughout the curriculum. Because students must have both an English and a vocational teacher advise them on their project, teachers have to communicate across disciplines. And the principal, Stephen Godowsky, has championed the resulting collaborative efforts. For example, two eleventh-grade teachers developed a class called "the American Experience," which combines the study of history and literature. It makes extensive use of mock trials, simulations, and role-playing to reconstruct historical events. A team of ninth-grade teachers works with the same group of students to teach English, science, and social studies.

As teachers try to prepare their students for the rigors of senior year, they have added more research components, oral presentations, and projects to their academic and shop courses. "Some of the benefits that come out of senior project are those we never even imagined," says the carpentry teacher Dave Lutz, "benefits like time management, meeting deadlines, consultation with others, and research skills."

The projects also have raised teachers' expectations of students. Susan Holloway, a nurse-technician instructor, says, "My expectations of students have gotten much more demanding, and they have met them. The papers are more in-depth. The products and the care plans they produce are more in-depth. The expectations for the presentations have really increased. And the kids are meeting them. The more you ask of them, the more they're doing."

Since the initiative began, vocational students are spending more time on homework and classwork, their writing and oral communications skills have increased, and their grades have gone up. Today, Hodgson students score higher on the Delaware State Writing Assessment than do students from most nonvocational public high schools in the state.

At the Howard High School of Technology in downtown Wilmington, an outside task force spearheaded a drive to renovate the building and make the school a technology hub for the district. The school has tried to use technology and writing across subjects to improve students' academic performance. And it has developed plans to get students into the workplace earlier and more often, so they can see the benefits of what they are learning.

On one of the days I visited, students in the library were designing electrical circuits on computers and working on algebra problems. A geometry class was using computers to construct isosceles triangles and prove that two of their angles were equal. In a ninth-grade classroom, algebra students were balancing a yardstick on the edge of a desk, loading it with pennies, and then graphing on hand-held calculators how the balance point changed.

At Delcastle Technical High School in suburban Wilmington, the largest of the three schools, teachers switched to a block schedule in 1995–96. Instead of taking 45-minute classes in seven subjects each semester, students now take four subjects in 90-minute classes. The longer class periods permit more in-depth, active learning. Students prepare homework for four courses instead of seven, and teachers work with fewer students each semester, so that they know them well. The school also added a 45-minute period of sustained silent reading in the ninth grade and an additional period of reading and language arts in the tenth grade.

Surveys and test data indicate that the district is headed in the right direction. Customer satisfaction, as measured by parent and employer surveys, has improved. About 26 percent of the region's public school eighth-graders now apply for admission to the technical high schools. In writing, the school system's students score among the top six high schools statewide. Individual students at the three schools also make more progress from grades 8 to 10 in writing and mathematics than many other students in the state.

Academic course taking also is up. In 1994–95, more than half of the school system's graduates completed three years each of mathematics and science, although that was true of a smaller portion of Howard graduates.

All three of the New Castle schools are part of the High Schools That Work consortium, which was created in 1990 by the Southern Regional Education Board (SREB), a membership organization of 15 southeastern and Middle Atlantic states. In the 1980s, SREB published a series of reports that stressed the need for a common academic core for all high school students, particularly those in the general and vocational tracks. The goal of High Schools That Work is to prepare "career-bound" students who perform more like "college-preparatory" students.

"Students who reach these goals," the consortium states, "can read and interpret fairly complex materials, solve multistep mathematics problems using algebra and geometry concepts, and understand physical science concepts." To accomplish this, schools that join the consortium pledge to replace the general track with a solid academic core: at least four years or the equivalent of college-preparatory English; three years each in mathematics and science, of which two must be at the college-preparatory level; and a focused, well-planned vocational major.

In 1993, the consortium published a report on its seven most improved high schools. In just three years, these seven schools had managed to close the gap between their career-bound students and the consortium's goals by 65 percent in reading, 36 percent in mathematics, and 70 percent in science. Moreover, students who had taken the full sequence of mathematics, science, and English courses generally exceeded the consortium's targets.

There simply is no replacement for a rigorous, carefully planned sequence of academic course work. When Clifford Adelman of the U.S. Department of Education analyzed data from a longitudinal study of the high school class of 1972, he found that students who had strong academic backgrounds in high school were more likely to complete postsecondary education of *any kind*—academic or occupational. "I propose, very simply, that what you study is what you learn and that what you learn comprises a large part of what you bring to the workplace," he concluded.

Similarly, in a study of high school students in Indiana, the researchers Gary Orfield and Faith G. Paul found that students who have carefully-thought-out plans for high school generally enroll in courses that keep their career and college opportunities open. By comparison, the other 40 percent of students, who lack clearly defined plans, enroll in few academic courses and reduce their future options in work and in school. "The purpose of a plan is not to force students to make career decisions early in their experiences," the authors concluded, "but rather to ensure that they make no academic decisions that might close doors to opportunities that they later wish were open."

Indeed, some studies suggest that college graduates earn more because they have higher basic skills at the end of high school and not because of anything they learn in college. College is simply an easy way for employers to identify workers with strong basic skills. This argument suggests that if high schools could increase the basic skills of all young people and find a better way to attest to their competency, then a college degree would become less essential to get a good job.

But the most improved High Schools That Work sites have not just changed the amount and content of course work. They also have altered how content is taught to make it more active and engaging. Students in the seven most-improved schools reported that their vocational classes were more challenging and placed a greater emphasis on academic skills and content. They believed their mathematics, science, and English teachers related their academic studies more to real-world situations. Compared with students in schools that had just joined the consortium, more of these students reported making oral presentations, being asked to state and defend their opinions or compare ideas, write research papers, and read books outside of class. In mathematics, they were more likely to complete at least two major projects a year, participate in a mathematics lab at least once a month, use computers, work in small groups, and use mathematics to solve work-related problems. Similarly, in science, a higher percentage reported reading books and articles, writing reports, and making classroom presentations, and more students at these schools used equipment such as stethoscopes, electricity meters, and barometers in science labs.

In sum, students were rising to the higher expectations and standards that had been set for them.

Learning by Doing

Schools like those in New Castle County are trying to bridge the traditional divide between academic and vocational education. This divide stemmed in part from the premise that some children were "abstract minded" and others "hand minded." But recent research suggests that while there is a place for abstract learning, there are many occasions when it helps to have both the head and the hand engaged. Students benefit when they can see the practical application of knowledge and ideas, apply their skills to real-life problems, and communicate their thinking to others. As young people share and refine their thoughts, they can create communities of learners that mirror the quality circles and collaborative teamwork now so prominent in the workplace.

In contrast, most of today's high school students spend at least one quarter of their time in relatively autonomous, passive activities—such as listening to a lecture. Less than 4.5 percent of their time is spent in classroom discussions. This kind of passive high school experience helps explain why so many young people are so bored.

Paul Barton, a researcher with the Educational Testing Service, also argues that young people often have trouble applying what they learn in school outside the classroom. This may help explain why educators contend that their graduates can read, write, and compute, while employers contend that they cannot. Barton contends that "illiteracy" is not a problem among high school graduates but that a high proportion are "low-level literates, unable to do tasks commonly required in day-to-day living." Although they can read a newspaper article, for example, they cannot decipher the kinds of technical documents typically used in the workplace.

When properly structured, school-to-work initiatives can increase the opportunities for young people to connect learning in school and out of school so that they can continue learning on the job. They can help bridge the divide between "school learning" and real life. When I was at Howard High School of Technology in Delaware, I visited a group of students who were completing an internship at Riverside Hospital, a residential-care facility. The internship was part of a more traditional vocational program that prepared students to become certified nurse assistants, although many students had higher career aspirations.

Roxanne Lloyd, who hoped to become a maternity nurse, said, "Basically, what we learn in school we come out here and do. If you take medicine, you have to be really good in math." Christine Klingler, who was interested in sports medicine, discovered that "you have to keep notes as a nurse. You have to keep track of patients for the doctor." Although the program had not made many connections between the experiences of students in the hospital and their academic classes back in the high school, Christine had approached her English teacher for help with some of her report writing for the internship.

One study of 16 school-to-work programs by the Manpower Demonstration Research Corporation asked students to compare their experiences in school-to-work programs with their regular high school course work. Students said the school-to-work classes were better and more interesting. Students in more than half the programs characterized their course work as more demanding than their regular high school courses. Students also said they liked the hands-on activities and felt these would help them in the world outside school.

This is the kind of engagement that properly structured school-to-work experiences can provide. The results, however, should be interpreted with caution. Another study of students in 33 middle and high schools around the country found that students described their vocational classes as less challenging and less important to their future goals than their academic classes.

Career Exploration and Planning

School-to-work also can strengthen the fourth building block I listed at the beginning of this chapter: career exploration and guidance in high schools so that young people can plan for the future. Many high school students know very little about the wide range of career opportunities available to them. The majority think they are going to become professionals, such as doctors, lawyers, or architects. Yet many have not taken the high school courses that would permit them to succeed in college or after.

High schools generally do not engage in career exploration or counseling with students. In the early 1990s, Gary Orfield, a professor in the Graduate School of Education at Harvard University, and Faith G. Paul, the president of the Public Policy Research Consortium in Chicago, conducted one of the most extensive studies of postsecondary education and career planning in high schools. The Indiana Youth Opportunity Study surveyed more than 5,000 Hoosier students in grades 8, 10, and 12, their parents, and their counselors. It revealed that slightly more than half of the young people surveyed wanted to be professionals. Yet 28 percent of those were not taking a full college-preparatory program. More than 20 percent of the seniors surveyed, and 46 percent of the sophomores, reported no long-range planning sessions with their counselors, and 39 percent of the seniors' parents said they had never met with a school counselor.

Counselors described career planning as a low priority and admitted that they had minimal training in labor-market analyses or career guidance. Fewer than half had current information on the state's job market; a fifth said they had no information at all;

and many inaccurately described trends in the state's economy. Most had never received visits from employers with job openings for high school graduates.

Students who planned to work immediately after graduation fared the worst. Counselors in more than 60 percent of the schools surveyed estimated that these students occupied only 5 percent of their career-counseling time.

Many counselors had caseloads of 300 to 700 students each. They couldn't possibly know students well enough to give them advice. Moreover, their duties included everything from scheduling classes to enforcing discipline to monitoring the lunchroom. Supervisory and clerical chores consumed large portions of every day.

I have found the same thing in my travels across the country. In one Wisconsin high school that had a well-known youth apprenticeship program, school counselors were responsible for more than 400 students each. "It's very difficult to do serious career counseling," complained one guidance counselor. "We see every kid every year, and that's about the best we can do."

Orfield and Paul also found that counselors, students, and parents disagreed about the purpose of school guidance counseling. Given the option, counselors wanted to offer more assistance to students with personal problems. But three quarters of parents and students didn't want help with personal problems. They wanted ongoing assistance in making decisions related to the student's future.

The truth is that because we tend to think of high school students as too young to choose a career, we do little to help them explore their interests and aptitudes. But our noblesse oblige may be doing youths an extreme disservice. As Orfield and Paul argue, young people "must both dream and plan."

Another study found that acquainting students with basic job information in high school was associated with higher earnings in the future. Using data from a national longitudinal study of high school students, the researchers found that students who knew the steps necessary to find a job improved their average annual earnings three years later by about $850. Students who attended schools that regularly received and posted notices of job openings earned about $950 more than the annual average.

School-to-work systems represent a tremendous opportunity to improve career exploration and guidance. They can do so by sharing such responsibilities among a number of adults, including teachers, employers, counselors, and adult mentors at the workplace. To varying extents, this guidance was built into the structure of many of the sites that I visited. At Rindge, for example, all tenth-graders take a course known as Pathways that is co-taught by an academic teacher and teachers from the various technical areas. Through a combination of job shadows at local businesses and career-oriented projects, students are able to explore a number of career options and learn about their requirements.

At Howard High School of Technology in Delaware, tenth- and eleventh-graders participate in job shadows and short-term internships to help explore career options. Beginning in ninth grade, all students develop a binder that includes their best work, periodic reflections on their career plans and goals, and research on various careers. Students meet periodically with a teacher to talk about the things that go into their "Quest for Quality" notebook. The notebooks and the focused career exploration give students a sense of accomplishment and something to show to potential employers. Kiya Crippen, a dental student, says that when she looks in her binder, "It makes me feel good. I've talked to other friends that go to a regular high school, and you ask them what do you want to do, and they say, 'I don't know. I just want to graduate.' Before I got here, I never thought I wanted to be a dentist. But you start going through the program, and the job shadows, and you think, 'I can do this.'" Micah Goldston, a student in the information systems and services program, said, "I think it's real good that we have this because if you maintain your notebook and keep it up, then you can really see what you've done and get satisfaction from it."

Exploring Careers at Fenway

One school that has approached career exploration and planning with great care lies a subway ride away from Rindge. The Fenway Middle College High School occupies a few classrooms on the campus of Bunker Hill Community College in the Charlestown neighborhood of Boston. Only a small plaque near a stairwell distinguishes the school from the college at large. Begun in 1983 to serve dropouts and potential dropouts, Fenway does not operate like a traditional high school. Its 250 students in grades 9–12 reflect the diversity of Boston's neighborhoods. Many of Fenway's students are at least a year behind grade level, and others simply disliked the education offered in more traditional high schools. In 1994, Fenway became a "pilot school" within the Boston Public School system, which gave it greater independence from the centralized downtown bureaucracy.

Like the vocational-technical students in Delaware, Fenway students must take a solid academic curriculum. All Fenway students take four core subjects: humanities (which integrates language arts, literature, and social studies around a common theme), interactive mathematics (which teaches students to solve problems based on concrete situations drawn from the real world), science, and advisory. In advisory, each teacher is responsible for providing guidance to a small group of students who meet together several times a week.

Fenway works hard to relate the academic core to students' future career goals and to activities in the workplace. All Fenway students belong to one of three career- and service-oriented "houses," small units of teachers and students who stay together for four years. The houses give teachers a natural avenue for working together to design lessons. Each house also represents a strong commitment from the business community. There is the CVS Pre-Pharmacy program, which concentrates on science and pharmacy-based curricula; the Children's Hospital program, which introduces students to allied health careers; and Cross-Roads, which has a community-service focus. The business partner for Cross-Roads is the Boston Museum of Science, but students in this house can do internships in a variety of settings.

Through the houses, students are introduced to career options and gain exposure to the workplace. Fenway's oldest collaborative, with Children's Hospital, began in 1988. During the ninth and tenth grades, hospital employees visit the school to provide a general orientation to the health-care field and to teach classes on such topics as blood pressure. Students also visit the hospital in groups.

A specially designed curriculum helps connect students' experiences in the hospital with their activities in the classroom. In 1994, Fenway became one of three schools nationwide to participate in the "Working to Learn" project, funded by the Pew Charitable Trusts. Curriculum writers from the Technical Education Research Center, a Cambridge, Massachusetts, group that specializes in hands-on science and mathematics instruction, developed a series of units aimed at strengthening the academic component of students' work-based experiences.

Each unit has two strands: Classroom science materials use students' experiences in the hospital as a starting point for academic lessons. Materials for health-care staff suggest questions and activities they can do with groups of students who visit their hospital departments to promote hands-on learning and discussion.

Margaret Vickers, a transplanted Australian, conceived of the project after visiting a number of school-to-work sites. She found that although students were developing general workplace and occupational skills, there was minimal connection between their hands-on experiences at the work site and their traditional academic classes. Her goal was to create a "need-to-know" mind-set in students, so that they understand why they are learning essential concepts in science and how it will help them at work. "We actually teach core academics in the workplace," says Vickers. "So workplace learning is not an absolute subtraction from academic learning because we are dovetailing the two."

On the blustery December day that I visited Children's Hospital, Chris Dindy, a senior cardiographic technician, was preparing to teach students about the uses of an exercise-stress test. Dindy, a Boston native with a strong local accent, began by giving students a general tour of the department and describing what it does. Each student had a clipboard of questions to answer, such as "Describe the kind of work done by an EKG technician," and "What information can be obtained through an exercise-stress test?"

To help answer the questions, Dindy walked the students through a stress test, hooking one youngster up to the monitor while the other operated the equipment. Back in their high school biology class, the students had been studying the cardiovascular and respiratory systems. The object of the lesson at the hospital was to match hands-on experiences with such questions as "How do you know if something is wrong with your heart?" and "What does the heart's electrical conduction system do for you?"

In grade 11, Fenway students spend six weeks rotating among various departments in the hospital, so they can learn about a number of allied health careers. They work in paid internships over the summer. While at the work site, students keep journals that their supervisors read and annotate on a weekly basis.

During their senior year, students participate in the "Senior Institute," which consists of small-group seminars and advanced coursework. They also have a six-week full-time internship in a department that interests them. One student who was interested in architecture did an internship in the hospital's planning and development office to gain experience with building codes and blueprints.

Seniors also compile a series of graduation portfolios and participate in a portfolio defense. The portfolios include the best work from their academic subjects, the answer to a research question related to their work experiences, a senior project similar to that at Hodgson, a resume, and a statement of future plans. Perhaps as a result of this detailed focus on what they will do after they graduate, virtually every Fenway senior is able to articulate a career plan. "We graduate our kids with a direction, whether it's college or work," claims the program's codirector, Linda Nathan.

In a three-year evaluation of Fenway's program, completed in 1993, researchers found that students who participated in the internships exhibited among the lowest dropout rates and highest attendance rates of any students at the school. Student interns also completed more courses, earned more credits, and were promoted to the next grade at a higher rate than students who did not participate. That was why Fenway decided to expand the internships to all students.

Larry Myatt, the codirector of Fenway, says, "What really happened is a lightbulb went on for kids. 'This is why they're asking me to learn this.' Some of our kids are so much on the outside looking in, never getting a chance to contribute, never getting a chance to be accepted. Kids who couldn't take care of business at school could take care of business in the hospital. On a core level, it showed kids why you might want to do this, raised their standards of behavior, and raised their expectations."

Adults Who Care

Adult mentors provide another form of career guidance and support. Both Fenway's house structure and its advisory system are designed to bring teachers and students into close personal contact, so that each young person is known well by a group of adults. This contrasts sharply with the large, impersonal structure of many high schools, which at their worst may warehouse up to 5,000 young people. It is hardly surprising that in such environments, adolescents fall prey to peer pressure.

Work-based learning programs, like that at Children's Hospital, also foster close, personal ties between students and the adult employees who coach and mentor them. Over the past few decades, mentoring programs have sprung up around the country to link young people with caring adults who can help them make the transition into adulthood. Such programs developed, in part, because of a concern that students lacked traditional sources of support such as neighbors and extended families.

Stephen Hamilton, a professor of human development at Cornell University, has written extensively on the subject of mentors, particularly those in work-based learning programs. "Developmentally, this is a period in life when young people are confronted with choices that will shape who they will be as adults," he explains. "They have already taken about as much as they can get from their parents, and I mean that in a positive way. Their parents have stamped themselves indelibly on them for better or worse. And they need some other role models to know other ways of being an adult. Yet in our society we systematically separate young people from adults. Here's a place where they can come back together again."

Monica Swain, the administrative coordinator for the surgical unit at Children's Hospital, looks exactly like the mothering type: soft, jolly, and warmhearted. "They were my kids," she says of the three interns under her wing in 1994–95. "I think that they just need to know that somebody is out there for them, holding them responsible. It's not their parents, but it's somebody else who thinks that they can do whatever it is that they want to. I had that when I was younger, but they need it even more so now. Once you get to know them, once you find out what kinds of things interest them, they draw you in. You want to be involved and you can't let go. They feel like your kids. You wouldn't let go of your kids."

Mentors at Children's Hospital help develop a learning plan for each student. They monitor the student at the work site and take them under their wing. And they push and prod them to do everything from filling out college applications to finishing their science projects.

At least 40 students have obtained full- or part-time work at Children's Hospital after successfully completing the internship program. Jacqueline Concepcion, now 24, began working at Children's Hospital as a senior in high school. She is now a lead phlebotomist, earning $10.58 an hour. In the fall, she hopes to begin college part time, while she continues to earn money from her job. Today, she is a mentor to new students coming into the program. "When I look at them and I talk to them, it's like I'm seeing myself again," she exclaims softly. "I'm saying, 'Oh, my God, was I that bad?' They don't want to listen at times or do anything. I was always ambitious and I always wanted to learn. But when I see them, it's like I'm seeing me."

Comparable Trends Abroad

The assumptions that I have outlined in this chapter do not apply solely to schools in the United States. Most industrialized nations are moving in the same directions. They are seeking new combinations of academic and vocational education; upgrading the academic content required of students; and providing for earlier, and more intensive, career exploration. These nations also are encouraging students to participate in work-based learning that is related to their studies. They recognize the need to revise their education-and-training systems for a more knowledge-based economy.

"The training that we used to do was training for an occupation for a lifetime," explains Hermann Schmidt, the president of

Germany's Federal Institute for Vocational Training, "and that is over. The training for the future is to learn how to learn."

Many European countries are increasing the academic content of their vocational programs. Switzerland has expanded its school-based training for apprentices from one day a week to one and a half days. Apprentices also can choose to add another half day at their employer's expense so that they can qualify for admission to a technical college. Sweden has added a third year to the vocational programs within its comprehensive high schools. The extra year was designed to strengthen students' academic knowlege, add a substantial workplace component, and give young people greater access to higher education. In France, graduates of vocational programs can now complete another two years of schooling and earn an upper-secondary diploma. Students pursuing these diplomas must, by law, spend some time in the workplace. Germany also has begun to devote more of an apprentice's school-based education to the teaching of general academic subjects.

These European countries also are struggling to merge academic and vocational content and pedagogy. Historically, in these countries secondary schooling outside of the apprenticeship system has centered around the traditional academic disciplines, with little practical orientation. But now academic courses within the high schools are becoming more active and project based, and career exploration is being introduced at a younger age.

In 1994, Denmark's minister of education released a report calling for better career guidance in the primary and lower-secondary schools; more thematic teaching across subjects within commercial and technical schools; and a greater use of projects and workplace simulations. Upper-secondary vocational students in Denmark spend one third of their time on traditional academic subjects, like mathematics, and another third on practical and theoretical training in broad occupational fields. Only a third of the curriculum is devoted to more specialized training for specific occupations or companies. Denmark also has launched a program to integrate academic and technical subjects for some students in grade 10, so that more students are exposed to opportunities in the technical areas.

When I visited the German state of Baden-Württemberg in 1995, the same broad shifts were evident. A new state curriculum required that at least once a year, all schools teach a thematic unit that spans the traditional disciplines and encourages students to work in teams. The state also was increasing the career exposure for students in the *Gymnasium,* the secondary schools for university-bound students. These students would now spend a one-week orientation out in the workplace in grades 10 and 11, looking at an occupation that interested them. "It doesn't help if a student starts his university class and has no idea of what he wants to do later on," explained Karl Waidelich, the principal of the Königin-Olga-Stift-Gymnasium in Stuttgart. "This leads to the long time [many students spend] at the university. Also, pupils and their parents are more interested in finding jobs than they used to be, so there is more interest in making early choices."

Similarly, Scottish high schools began introducing more occupationally oriented courses into their curriculum in the 1980s, in part to respond to the large number of students who were choosing to stay on in school. In 1994, Scotland launched an initiative known as "Higher Still," which will further merge academic and occupational pedagogy and content in high schools and reduce the once-sharp divisions between the two. One of the goals of the "Higher Still" initiative is to create occupationally oriented courses that will have the same status, prestige, and intellectual rigor as the traditional academic, university-oriented curriculum.

Even Japanese schools can now offer an "integrated" curriculum that combines academic and vocational studies. Students in these programs have fewer required courses and receive more career guidance to help them design a course sequence.

More than 50 years after Dewey argued for the benefits of education through occupations, he may finally be vindicated, not only in the United States but abroad.

"Two Worlds"

Putting into action the building blocks I have described in this chapter, however, will not be easy. This is particularly true in large comprehensive high schools, where vocational and academic teachers occupy "two worlds" that rarely intersect.

Everything about the traditional high school works against the merger of vocational and academic studies. Teachers are organized into separate academic and vocational departments. They have little time to collaborate. Rigid, 50-minute class periods do not lend themselves to innovative teaching. Vocational courses and those who teach them carry low status. The complexities of scheduling thousands of students for individual courses discourage change. Furthermore, parents, students, and teachers are reluctant to make any adjustments that would threaten college admissions.

Many people still do not see the need to raise our academic expectations for all students. It is hard to discard traditional notions of what young people need to succeed in the economy. In New Castle County, Delaware, some vocational teachers think the school district has gone too far in stressing academic skills, which leaves less time for occupational courses. Carpentry teacher Dave Lutz complains that vocational education is "getting squeezed. . . . We still have to send kids out who can hammer and nail," he asserts. "Our job is to put people out into the trades or businesses. Maybe our job isn't to fill up the colleges." The English teacher Mary An Scarbrough thinks the school system has begun to recruit freshmen with stronger academic records, "so the shops where the kids want to get dirty are not getting filled up." This tension about how to balance academic and technical studies remains one of the fundamental unresolved dilemmas of the school-to-work movement.

Integrating learning at the workplace with activities in classrooms is equally difficult. Most school-to-work efforts start small because it is hard to find large numbers of slots for students out in the workplace. But that makes it hard to achieve the critical mass on the school side that would justify changes in curriculum and scheduling.

The intensive nature of some programs also limits their expansion. Teachers like Maria Ferri, at Rindge, teach fewer and smaller classes in order to spend more time at the work site, which means other teachers must carry an even larger teaching load. All of Rindge's internship programs combined served only 60 students in 1995–96, out of just under 2,000 students in the high school as a whole.

The greatest concern, however, is that many school-to-work systems have yet to demonstrate significant academic gains for students. One possibility is that incipient school-to-work initiatives are still too new to produce such results—which is not surprising, since many had their first program graduates in 1995 or 1996. Another possibility is that many of these interventions occur too late in young people's education. Many students do not enroll in school-to-work programs until grade 11 or 12, when they already have completed most of the academic courses required to graduate. If students have not taken a full sequence of mathematics and science courses by then, or have not mastered fundamental academic skills, it is often too late.

But another reason for the lack of academic progress among students participating in school-to-work programs is that some of these initiatives do not stress increases in both the number and rigor of academic courses. Some of the incipient school-to-work systems I visited had made only minimal changes to the school program. In a few cases, young people were sent off to the work site with no connections made to their academic classes. Often, the fragile reed that connected what young people were learning in school and on the job was a single vocational course. Without a clear focus on increasing intellectual content and rigor it is no wonder that these efforts do not produce immediate academic gains.

In too many high schools, the "shopping-mall" phenomenon so eloquently described by Arthur Powell and his colleagues still prevails, with the final decision about whether or not to engage in intellectual work left up to students. For example, of the three courses that Chris Scott-Martin took at Cambridge Rindge and Latin during his senior year, one was a study hall, one was a culinary-arts class, and the third was his internship seminar.

Throughout the rest of this book, I will be examining what can be done to connect learning on the job with the learning that occurs in school. One important factor is the role of higher education in school-to-work, which is the subject of chapter 4. Chapter 6 examines how school-to-work can contribute to the broader school-reform movement that has been growing over the past decade. But the first thing that needs to be considered is the role of the groups on the far side of the school-to-work transition: the business community.

CHAPTER 3

How Does Business Benefit?

W hy should U.S. companies get involved in school-to-work? The answer is both simple and complex. They should get involved because it is in their own self-interest to do so, as well as in the interest of society. But the benefits may be varied, long-term, and often subtle. To date, experiences suggest that school-to-work programs can help companies to:

❂ *Reduce the cost of identifying, screening, and training candidates.* Some companies have found that it costs less to prepare young people whose wages are lower and who can acquire some of their skills in school. Employers who work with young people can immerse them in the company's expectations and culture and select future

67

employees on the basis of a first-hand knowledge of their capabilities.

❧ *See immediate, short-term benefits.* Young workers can contribute to the bottom line. Employers who participate in school-to-work efforts describe their young people as productive and contributing employees.

❧ *Increase the pool of qualified applicants and fill labor shortages in high-demand fields.* Some of the earliest school-to-work efforts were in industries such as printing, metalworking, and health care, which were experiencing significant labor shortages. Participating companies decided to grow their own workforce, to the benefit of themselves and the industry as a whole.

❧ *Ensure that applicants meet their needs by working more closely with schools on education and training.* Through school-to-work, companies can directly influence the educational system and improve the lines of communication between educators and employers.

❧ *Increase the diversity of their workforce.* This is particularly true when companies recruit young women and members of minority groups into nontraditional fields.

❧ *Directly teach the work ethics and employability skills that they want.* Employers often state that social skills and competencies, such as the ability to work in teams or with customers, are as important as technical skills in today's workplaces. Many of these skills are best modeled on the job.

❧ *Enhance the skills and the morale of their existing workforce.* Employees involved as mentors and coaches for students frequently describe it as a generative activity that rekindles their own enthusiasm for work and learning. Human-resource directors and supervisors say employees become better leaders and communicators when they teach others what they know.

❧ *Help support education reform.* Corporations believe in philanthropy. But increasingly they want their giving to benefit the company's long-term strategic goals as well as the community's interests.

Today, many companies get involved in school-to-work to give back to their communities. This charitable impulse should not be discounted. But businesses that look upon school-to-work solely as a community service often consign it to the public relations or human resources arm of their company. As a result, they may not keep good figures on how much their investment costs or what benefits it produces. Then, when the economy turns sour, the programs are vulnerable.

Companies are making a mistake when they participate in school-to-work and do not tally the gains, or when they look upon school-to-work solely as an education-reform strategy and not as a workforce-development tool. There are also potential pitfalls for companies that participate in school-to-work, which I describe later in this chapter, and these need to be considered. But a serious accounting of what companies get from such partnerships could support their involvement and that of others and lift these initiatives out of the realm of corporate charity.

One study of participating companies by the National Center on the Educational Quality of the Workforce found a "wellspring of support both for the initiatives themselves and for the quality of the young workers they attracted." Employers were generally pleased with their students and believed the programs benefited themselves and the young people. Many said they would participate in such programs again and would recommend them to their peers. Similarly, a 1995 report by the U.S. Office of Technology Assessment stated, "Over and over again, the students, the school coordinators, and the employers told of how low-achieving and mid-achieving students had risen to the challenge of their work-based learning assignments."

Since the late 1980s, most national business organizations have endorsed the need for a better transition from school to work in the United States. These include the Conference Board, the Business Roundtable, the Committee for Economic Development, the National Alliance of Business, the National Association of Manufacturers, the National Employer Leadership Council, and the U.S. Chamber of Commerce. Corporate leaders also have championed the need for higher academic standards, most recently at the National Education Summit in 1996.

This chapter looks at several different companies and the benefits they have realized from bringing young people into the workplace. In Florida and a dozen other states around the country, the Siemens Corporation is investing in apprenticeships to produce the kind of skilled labor force it needs for the competitive electronics industry. In Wisconsin, the Serigraph Company, a high-tech printing firm, has successfully used apprenticeships to fill labor shortages and prepare workers who can perform multiple tasks. In Pennsylvania, Procter & Gamble has figured out that it can save money and increase the flexibility of its workforce by working with high school students. In Miami, companies in the travel and tourism industry are discovering that they can improve young people's employability skills before they come to work full time. The details of these programs vary, as do the payoffs the companies receive. Yet the experiences described in this chapter suggest that a more extensive collaboration with the schools is both possible and doable.

This chapter focuses primarily on apprenticeships because they are the most expensive, the most time-consuming, and the most difficult form of collaboration to implement. Stephen and Mary Agnes Hamilton, the founders of the Cornell Youth Apprenticeship Demonstration Project, state: "If we can learn how to create high-quality youth apprenticeships in the United States we will also learn how to create, expand, and strengthen other forms of work-based learning." Later in the book I will take a more detailed look at other ways in which employers can become involved in school-to-work.

First, however, this chapter looks at the experiences of a country that has long provided a model for school-to-work reformers: Germany. Although the United States would not want to adopt the German system intact, the latter provides useful lessons for developing a homegrown system and illustrates the forces that are changing education-and-training systems worldwide.

School-to-Work in Germany

In the fall of 1995 I visited Germany with a group of other journalists to see how Germans prepare their young people for work. German companies spend the equivalent of over $20 billion on their apprentices—an average of $12,000 in gross costs for every apprentice trained. After subtracting a young person's productive contribution to the company, employers still spend about $4,000 per individual. All of us wanted to know why German companies invest so heavily in the next generation.

I heard many explanations over the course of my trip. But the most succinct came from Wolfgang Breitmeier, who directs the Chamber of Commerce and Industry in Stuttgart. "German companies believe that schools alone can't provide the crucial subjects," he explained patiently. "Therefore, it is inevitable that companies commit themselves to use the learning potential of the workplace."

Breitmeier was oversimplifying a complex picture. But he wanted to hammer home a point: Companies in Germany view their education-and-training system as a vitally important partnership among employers, labor unions, government, and schools. Together, the four groups produce a highly skilled workforce that no one institution could develop on its own.

Young people in the Dual System, as the education-and-training system is called, spend three to four days a week at the workplace and one to two days at school. At work, they learn on the most up-to-date equipment under real-life conditions. They work under the supervision of a *Meister*, a master craftsman who also is a skilled teacher. At school, they continue to study such academic subjects as mathematics and German, while gaining a more solid theoretical and technical foundation for their careers. The broad outlines for young people's education-and-training cannot be changed unless all of the parties reach a consensus.

Is a German system appropriate for the United States? In many ways, no. As the early school-to-work reformers discovered, the cultural and economic conditions in Germany differ too greatly from our own to duplicate the German system intact.

Wage differences are one reason why the German experience does not necessarily apply here. Germany pays the highest wages in the Western world, the result of contract negotiations held at the national level. It is expensive and difficult to fire employees. In this context, apprentices offer a cheap source of labor. They typically earn about one half to two thirds the pay of a fully qualified worker. Particularly in small firms, where young people work as they learn, companies can make money on apprentices. "Why train?" asks Horst Locher, the chairman of the electronics guild for the Stuttgart region. "It's not an easy question to answer because an apprentice costs money. But a young person being trained in a craft . . . is already productive, which means the *Meister* can earn some money off his work." Apprenticeships enable companies to screen future workers and give them a dry run before selecting the best for long-term employment.

In contrast, wages in the United States vary widely even within industries, and a low minimum wage means that employers may not save much by hiring an apprentice. American companies also can hire and fire workers relatively easily, and worker mobility is high. This combination of varied wages, high worker mobility, and hire-fire companies makes it less attractive for companies to invest in the future labor force, according to Paul Osterman, a professor of economics at the Massachusetts Institute of Technology.

Germany also has an infrastructure to support the apprenticeship system that we lack. All German companies belong to a "chamber" (*Kammer*), an organization that represents employers in their industry. Although only 20 percent of German companies choose to train apprentices, firms that do not train still pay dues to the chamber to support the apprenticeship system. The chambers determine whether companies have the resources to offer training, help administer the apprenticeship exams, and issue certificates to those who pass. At the national level, employer groups, trade unions, and government collaborate to define the length and content of training and the material apprentices must master to succeed on their exams. As a result, employers can trust what graduates of the system know and can do, and apprentices earn a certificate—like a Good Housekeeping Seal of Approval—that is valued nationwide.

We have no counterpart to the German chambers. In the U.S., there are myriad sets of standards for occupations ranging from nursing to plumbers. But we have no common national framework for developing standards for specific industries that could be recognized nationwide. (Efforts are now under way to produce voluntary national standards, as I describe in chapter 5.)

Moreover, there are a lot of things we would not want to reproduce about the German system. It is too rigid and bureaucratic. In Germany it is hard for young people to change their minds in midstream without having to restart their apprenticeship training from scratch. Germany has standards for more than 300 separate occupations, at a time when job classifications are becoming more fluid. Employers in Germany complained to me that it can take up to seven years to alter training standards. It can take even longer to introduce the training framework for a new occupation. This is a drawback when technology and workforce needs are changing rapidly.

In recent years, the downsides of the German system have become apparent. In 1996, German unemployment hit 11.1 percent, more than double that in the United States. The excessive costs and heavy regulations involved in doing business have pushed many German companies to invest abroad rather than at home. As large German corporations downsize, they are offering fewer apprenticeship slots and are hiring only those needed to replenish the existing workforce. They also are trying to make apprentices more productive by reducing the time they spend in expensive training centers. In 1995, Chancellor Helmut Kohl raised the specter that Germany would not have enough training places for all the young people who want them, particularly in the former East Germany.

At the same time, greater access to higher education and high unemployment have led many young people to enter the university so they can keep their options open. In 1993, half of all Germany's school leavers sought to enter higher-level technical institutes or the universities. Many students now choose to complete an apprenticeship and then pursue a university degree to improve their job prospects.

These differences and dilemmas underscore the folly of attempting to reproduce another nation's education-and-training system in total. But businesses in the United States are discovering that a homegrown version of work-based learning can yield benefits. They are adapting the best of the European systems, tailoring them to American needs.

Developing the Core Workforce

It's hardly surprising that one of the premier examples of translating the European experience for the United States comes from a company with deep roots in Germany. The Siemens-Stromberg Carlson Apprenticeship Training Center is reached through the backdoor of a modest office building just off a major thoroughfare in Lake Mary, Florida, near Orlando. On a Thursday afternoon, groups of high school students in white lab coats with the company logo on the front are bent intently over their projects: filing metal, soldering circuit boards, analyzing blueprints. The room has the immaculate, antiseptic air of a hospital laboratory. A row of drill presses flanks one wall. The students' workstations, blue steel desks with Formica tops, dominate the center of the room. Near the entrance, a display case houses the projects built by previous graduates, ranging from miniature electronic pianos to a temperature-controlled voice-recording circuit. The air hums with quiet concentration. There's none of the slacking off easily spotted in most high school classrooms. A large sign on one wall reads: "Pay attention to details. Sweat the small stuff." Another sign states: "Perfection is our goal. Excellence will be tolerated."

In this unremarkable suburban community, Siemens has created a showcase apprenticeship program for electronics technicians. The high-profile venture has generated Siemens lots of community goodwill. But it is not rooted in a humanitarian impulse. Rather, Siemens is convinced that it can profit directly from even substantial investments in youth.

The program is based on the experiences of its parent company, Siemens AG of Germany. For more than 100 years, Siemens AG has trained German apprentices as part of the German Dual System.

Siemens is the sixth-largest electronics company in the world and the second-largest supplier of telecommunications switching equipment, the sophisticated relays that bring voice, video, and digital connections into homes and offices. In Florida, Siemens-Stromberg Carlson specializes in providing networking equipment to the telecommunications industry. In 1995 its clients included six of the seven Regional Bell Operating Companies, as well as some 400 independent phone companies.

In the early 1990s the company was having so much trouble finding precision toolmakers and technicians who could meet its quality standards that it was importing workers from Europe. The Lake Mary plant had a particularly high turnover among customer-service technicians, who spend most of their time on the road.

"We had thirty or so technicians a year leaving out of three hundred," says Gary R. Garman, the manager of training and professional development at the plant. "Some years, we had as high as twenty percent attrition. We had to do something to replenish that. We also found that the students coming out of vocational high schools were truly undertrained. They could pull a circuit board out and tell you it was broken, but they could do nothing prescriptively or diagnostically to tell you what was wrong and how to fix it." Community college graduates had a stronger theoretical background but no hands-on skills. It took the company a year to bring them up to speed.

So Siemens decided to adapt its German training program to the United States. Students in Lake Mary typically start the three-year program as high school seniors (although Siemens apprentices elsewhere in the country generally begin the programs in their junior year). Two days a week the students work at the training center after school and receive a stipend of $4.50 an hour. They also take an electronics class either at their home high school or at the local community college. If they perform well enough, they are accepted into the adult apprenticeship program when they graduate from high school. For the next two years they split their time between classes at Seminole Community College and 20 hours a week at the company. Part of that time is spent on the factory floor, where they learn to apply their knowledge in a real production environment. Graduates earn both an associate of sciences degree and a certificate that qualifies them to work as an electronics or installation technician for Siemens.

For Ryan Bouley, a senior at Lyman High School, it was a perfect match. Clean-cut and athletic-looking, Ryan had already completed geometry, algebra 2, physics, and three years of electronics before starting his apprenticeship. His dad, Dennis, teaches history at the high school. He says Ryan has been a tinkerer since childhood, endlessly curious about the way things work. At age eight, Ryan tore apart a broken television set and tried to reassemble it.

On the day I visited the training center, Ryan was poring over a blueprint for his final project of the year: an analog multimeter that allows a technician to measure voltages and currents in an electronic circuit and diagnose potential problems. Before he could build the electronics to go inside the equipment, Ryan had to build the casing from scratch. Starting with a flat piece of metal, he had to cut it, file it, bend and shape it, and drill the holes to assemble it. The blueprint was a flat, one-dimensional diagram. Ryan had to use his knowledge of geometry and trigonometry to calculate where to drill the holes so that when he bent the metal, they would be in the right place. On his first attempt, he was off by .5 millimeter and had to start the whole procedure over.

"Filing was so hard at the beginning," he recalled. "It was so much work, just to get that much metal down to perfect. I thought, 'Why are they having us do this when they can make it so much neater and cleaner by machine?' But I suppose when you're out in the field, and you've got to fix something, you're not going to have one of those machines around you. You'll have to know how that chassis was built to begin with, to certain specifications. I understand where they're coming from now, wanting us to learn it right from the start."

Ryan's experience reflects the German philosophy of apprenticeship. Students are with a company during their formative years, trained to the company's standards, and able to understand its culture and objectives. German apprentices learn their craft from the ground up. As a result, they understand the production process thoroughly, unlike many university-trained M.B.A.s in the United States. They also acquire the sense of pride in workmanship that characterizes the German system. Projects produced by trainees in the Siemens workshop must meet the same international standards for quality as those produced by veteran employees.

The standards for students are high. To be admitted into the program as high school seniors, students must have a 2.5 grade-point average, mathematics through algebra 2, and preferably physics. Siemens anticipates that of the 40 high school students who begin the program, 30 will make it through their senior year, and only 20 will be accepted into the postsecondary component. To graduate at the end of the three years, apprentices must complete a grueling five-day exam that tests their conceptual knowledge and asks them to build an intricate bidirectional electronic counter from scratch. The first group to graduate from the Lake Mary program in 1995 scored among the best in the world within Siemens AG.

At the heart of the German system lies the *Meister*, a master of his craft who is specially trained. A *Meister* in Germany must complete an apprenticeship, work for several years in a company, take additional courses, and then pass a rigorous series of exams. Only a *Meister* can train apprentices or operate a shop. Albert Hoser, the president of the Siemens Corporation in the United States, graduated from a Siemens apprenticeship program some 40 years ago, as did his daughter more recently; she is now studying for her doctorate in physics.

Chris Pierce, the U.S.-born *Meister* whom I met at the training center, was eloquent in describing the differences between the Siemens approach to training and that in other U.S. companies for which he has worked. "One thing I noticed right away is the breadth of the training," he explained. "Typically, U.S. companies upgrade a worker's skills by focusing on one narrow aspect of production: how to solder, how to assemble the components of a circuit board, how to repair a particular piece of equipment. No training class is longer than a week.

"Instead of teaching them a small piece of the puzzle," Pierce said, "we're teaching them everything a manufacturer or service technician would do. Where previously I was focusing on skills training, here in the apprenticeship center we are training these students in how to be an employee. It's more than just technical skills. Instead of building a circuit board by themselves, we'll give them a complete system that their group has to build as a team. I'm used to one-shot, stand-up presentations. Here, I'll talk fifteen minutes, and then the students will have to do more of the thinking themselves. We're developing their ability to think inductively, which is not something that's done very well in America."

Dmetra Campbell, a senior at Lake Mary High School, noticed the difference in expectations immediately. "We always say, 'It's good enough,'" she explained. "Mr. Pierce always says, 'There's no such thing as good enough.' But good enough at school, that's what we're used to." Charity Watson, another senior at Lake Mary High, said, "I work harder here than in school. Not that I don't work hard in school. But this is basically my future. And the only way you can get into the rest of the program is if you work hard here."

By 1996, Siemens had launched 25 apprenticeship programs for young people or adults in locations in 13 states, including Alpharetta, Georgia; Raleigh, North Carolina; and Franklin, Kentucky. In Georgia, Siemens helped develop the manufacturing curriculum taught in the high school. Students also spend three hours a day working at the plant and eight hours a day during the summers. In North Carolina, Siemens provided about $350,000 to equip and renovate the facilities at a regional vocational-technical high school and train its instructor. Siemens worked with teachers at the school to develop a curriculum that combines physics and electronics. Students in the program also work at the plant for six weeks during the summer, moving through all of the departments and doing hands-on assembly work.

The cost of the different apprenticeship models ranges from more than $8,000 per student each year at the Lake Mary training center to just $2,185 per student each year in North Carolina, where most instruction is provided at the high school and students are paid to work only during the summer. Nevertheless, Siemens views the expenditures as a good investment, just as companies in Germany believe in the bottom-line benefits of their own apprenticeship programs.

"It's not altruistic," explains John Tobin, the director of vocational training for the Siemens Corporation in the United States. "It's not to make America look better or to make people happier. It's the bottom-line business sense that it is good for the company."

Tobin estimates that Siemens will recoup its investment within the first five years that a former apprentice works for the company. (Apprentices must commit to only one year of employment after the training period ends, but Siemens hopes to make their jobs attractive enough to keep them.) In some cases, the payback has been immediate. One young woman, Nelsy Leyba, had just completed her apprenticeship training and was working in a Siemens manufacturing facility when she noticed that some chafing on a cable next to an expensive piece of equipment was causing the machine to shut down frequently. Ms. Leyba suggested putting a bracket or a barrier between the cable and the spot where it entered the machine. That one recommendation essentially paid for the entire cost of her training within the first few days of her graduation.

Siemens also has used the lessons learned in its apprenticeship programs to reap much broader cost savings. In 1995, for example, the Raleigh facility took two of the modules that Siemens had developed to train its apprentices—one in schematic and blueprint reading, the other in electrical wiring and components—and taught them to 48 workers on the assembly line. The result: a 42 percent increase in productivity and a 70 percent decrease in errors or deviations. In one year, the company saved $458,000 by training those 48 people.

"Apprenticeship is contagious," asserts Barry Blystone, the director of training and development for Siemens Energy and Automation in Raleigh. "We're showing it's a business decision. Not a publicity thing. Not a community service. All that stuff happens. But the corporate strategy for this is to develop the core workforce."

Filling Labor Shortages

Siemens began an apprenticeship program in the United States largely to satisfy its need for highly skilled, flexible employees. But often the demand for workers is felt across a whole industry and not just within a single company. That was certainly the case in Wisconsin, where labor shortages propelled the printing industry into a new relationship with the schools.

In the early 1990s, Wisconsin's printing industry was booming. But it had a problem. Older workers were retiring and companies couldn't find enough qualified entrants to fill their places. Young people were available, but they were being attracted to more glamorous occupations.

John Torinus, the owner of the Serigraph Company in West Bend, was feeling the pinch. Torinus had bought the company several years earlier and turned it into a competitive, international business. Under his guidance, the company had grown from a $40 million venture to a $110 million concern, doing three times as much volume with about the same number of workers.

Serigraph specializes in multicolor printing on plastics, producing everything from the panels on automobile dashboards to pogs, a popular children's toy. Companies such as Honda, Xerox, and TRW are its customers. To meet their exacting standards, Torinus had introduced new quality-assurance mechanisms, advanced technologies, and work teams that took responsibility for a product from beginning to end. Torinus knew he needed skilled, flexible employees who could adapt to this changing environment.

"Almost everybody here has to be flexible and able to do five or six different jobs, so that as the work mix changes and new people are added, we can stay competitive and stay efficient," he explained to me. "The toughest, most high-quality companies are our customers, so we have to be operationally excellent. And to get there, you basically have to trust your employees."

As a member of the Governor's Commission on Workforce Excellence, Torinus had made the pilgrimage to Germany and had come away impressed. So did Wisconsin's Gov. Tommy G. Thompson and the then superintendent of public instruction, Herbert Grover, the driving forces behind Wisconsin's efforts. When Wisconsin passed a youth-apprenticeship law in 1991, modeled after the German system, Torinus wanted a part of it. But as the discussions in Madison dragged on, Torinus grew restless. Finally, he approached West Bend High School and suggested they launch one of the state's first pilot sites.

With the help of the state and the printing industry's trade association, Torinus and a group of Wisconsin printers hammered out a curriculum. In under six months, they had a program up and running. By the second year, it involved six businesses and 23 students in two communities. The largest number of apprentices, a dozen that first year, worked at Serigraph.

The students, who are high school juniors and seniors, take a graphic-arts class together along with an applied academic curriculum in the morning and spend the afternoon at the work site. In both their classrooms and the workplace, they work through a series of 107 competencies developed by the state in cooperation with the printing industry. Students who complete the program receive a skills certificate along with their high school diploma. It qualifies them to enter the workforce directly, receive advanced standing in a technical college, or join a registered apprenticeship program.

Jeff Kannenberg, a slim teenager with dishwater-blond hair that falls over his eyebrows, is the second person in his family to work for Serigraph. His brother graduated from the apprenticeship program in 1993 and is employed as a screen printer. On the day that I visited Jeff, he was hunched over a drafting table in image assembly, correcting imperfections on the film negatives for a five-color job. His rotations through the company had already taught him how to operate a screen press, as well as the rudiments of electronic publishing. Next semester he planned to work in image transfer, where he would learn how to take the films and plates he had made and print a finished product.

Once a week his mentor at Serigraph, Paul Gouvian, met with Jeff to review what he had accomplished and deal with any problems. Gouvian, a planner who helped determine how products flow through the plant, was responsible for Jeff throughout his stay at Serigraph and worked closely with his trainers within the different departments. Every six weeks Gouvian met with Jeff, his parents, his trainers, and his teachers over lunch to talk about Jeff's progress.

A college graduate, Gouvian wished the program had been around when he was a student. Jeff was learning about the latest technologies and production methods in a real business environment, compared to the outdated equipment that Gouvian remembered working on in high school and in college. "This is an awesome program," he told me. "I took graphic-arts in high school, but you never really got into the plant to see what was being done."

Jeff agreed. He said the instruction at the plant was both more individualized and more exacting than in the high school. "Here, it's more one-on-one," he explained. "You're in the work area, so you get a better idea of how it should be. They go through it with you. They explain it first and give you something easy to start with. Then they watch you. You have to have better quality. You have to work harder. Like in school, the graphic-arts class is kind of easier. They're not as strict, really. It doesn't have to be so perfect."

It was also harder for students to fall through the cracks. Torinus recounted how one young man decided that he might forgo his high school diploma and just obtain his skills certificate. "Everyone was all over him," Torinus chuckled. "We were all over him at work. The educators were all over him. We called his parents. His parents were all over him. And, finally, the youth apprenticeship council changed the rules so that you can't get your certificate if you don't get your high school diploma. By this time, the student was floundering in his English course. So we offered to have his mentor in the workplace sit down and work with him. Anyway, he got the message that he had to get serious, and he did."

Serigraph also has worked to raise standards at the high school to reflect its needs. When four out of five students in the first group of youth apprentices failed the company's tests on statistical process control, "we got really upset about it," said Torinus. "You've got to have that knowledge to work here. This isn't just a test you take and then forget about it." Serigraph's quality-assurance engineer tutored the students until they passed the tests. He also reviewed the math curriculum with an instructor at the high school to ensure that the right basic concepts were being taught and provided the school with concrete examples from the work site that could be used in the classroom. The next six students to take the exams all passed.

What benefits does Serigraph get from all this work? "We used to have a lot of kids come here unskilled just out of high school," explains Torinus. "They didn't know if they wanted to be in printing or not. So we'd give them six months of training and they'd decide, 'This isn't for me. I'm out of here.' We don't have that problem with youth apprentices. They know they want to be in the printing business. Not only that, they have some kind of long-term goal beyond the job that they're starting in. So we avoid the misfits."

Serigraph also saves money it would have spent recruiting and retraining adults. Bill Wollin, who works in screen press, says, "There aren't people on the street that you can hire to do this job. So here, we're producing our own resources."

Another, unexpected benefit of the apprenticeship program has been to spur Serigraph's existing employees to request more training. Serigraph invests about 2.3 percent of its payroll in worker training. Three of its four plants have on-site learning centers where employees can take advantage of computer-based, self-paced instruction. Serigraph also pays workers a cross-training bonus of 25¢ an hour if they learn how to operate a new piece of equipment. But after seeing how broadly trained the apprentices were, employees began to press for even more. So in 1994 the company designed a 48-hour customized training program in screen printing for its existing workforce.

For every apprentice, Serigraph spends about $3,500 over two years and receives about a $1,000 reimbursement from the state. Torinus calculates that the apprentices, who are paid $4.25 an hour, spend about half their time learning and half producing. The young people get priority for summer and holiday jobs and have between 10 and 20 technical-college credits under their belt by the time they graduate. They also have entree to the company and a credible, portable certificate. If they stay with the company, Serigraph will pay their technical-college tuition while they work. "The kids come out [ahead] every which way," maintains Torinus, and so does the company.

By 1995 the Wisconsin Youth Apprenticeship Program in printing had expanded from its initial 2 pilot sites to 11 sites around the state, serving 66 juniors and seniors. A two-year evaluation of 5 sites, including West Bend, that compared apprentices with students in regular cooperative education programs or in vocational classes concluded that the youth apprentices received broader work-site training that covered more aspects of the printing industry, had greater opportunities to apply their printing skills at the work site, and were more likely to use on the job such academic skills as chemistry, communications, mathematics, and computing.

Six to eight months after they graduated from high school, 94 percent of the apprentices were employed by the industry, most by the firms that had trained them. Compared to other students, they were more likely to work full time, had better salaries, and used more skills on the job. Although they did not enroll in college at higher rates, those who did had more concrete career and educational plans than other students and were more likely to be getting employer assistance. Their employers highly valued the young people's training. And they perceived them to be equally or better prepared than other entry-level employees in a range of technical and social skills.

"The reaction we got from the employers was they really valued this as a way of getting to know the kids and train them. And then they really liked the product that they had trained and they took the kids in," says Margaret Terry Orr, a professor of education at Teachers College, Columbia University, who conducted the study. "I think the employers really bought into the product."

Of the first 11 apprentices to graduate from its program, Serigraph hired 9. The 2 others decided to go to college full time. Six of the apprentices hired by Serigraph decided to attend the local technical college part time while they worked. "Someday, twelve or fifteen years from now, I would guess that a good percentage of our employees—or at least of our high-skilled employees—will be from this program," predicts Torinus. "If we find a career employee, it's certainly worth the investment. If the guy is just twenty percent better than his coworker, and his pay is twenty-five thousand dollars a year, we get that money back in the first year. So I think you can make the economic argument. But you have to have a long-term view."

The success of the apprenticeships in Wisconsin is catching on. By 1996, Wisconsin had standards for 13 apprenticeship occupations, ranging from printing to banking and finance. That year, apprenticeship programs enrolled more than 730 students and attracted the participation of more than 595 employers. State officials claimed that there were more companies interested in setting up apprenticeships than their small staff could handle. "We've got the German system in Wisconsin," said Governor Thompson, in typical bulldog fashion. "We modeled it after Germany. We changed it and modified it. But it is basically the German apprenticeship program here in Wisconsin, and it's working."

But What If They Work Somewhere Else?

One of the concerns most often cited by employers about school-to-work programs is that they might never see their investment realized. They fear that they'll invest thousands of dollars and several years of effort in a student, only to see that student go to work someplace else—or, worse, for a competitor.

It's a legitimate concern. Over one third of U.S. workers change their employer or job status each year. Job tenure in the United States also appears to be declining modestly, primarily because of company downsizing and restructuring rather than worker choice. Although younger and less educated workers have suffered the greatest loss in job stability, there have been significant increases in job loss for older, more educated, and white-collar workers as well.

"High rates of job turnover are a major disincentive for employers considering training investments," writes the Cornell University economics professor John H. Bishop. "The job turnover of American workers has increased over the last twenty-five years, making it more costly for firms to provide training. The proportion of the workforce with fewer than twenty-five months of tenure at their company rose from twenty-eight percent in 1968 to forty percent in 1978 and has remained high since."

But he notes that occupational mobility, the rate at which people switch careers, actually has decreased. "Occupational mobility fell by thirteen to twenty percent between 1978 and 1987 and this has raised the social returns to occupational skill development."

This suggests that the advantages of apprenticeships and other education-and-training programs may accrue more to the workers and to an industry as a whole than to individual firms. In general, the more companies engage in school-to-work systems, the better off everyone is because it increases the overall pool of skilled labor. In Wisconsin, for example, about 15 percent of the state's printing firms now participate in the apprenticeship program and statewide skill standards ensure that what apprentices learn will be valuable at more than one company. This is where public goods become private goods. It's like collectively building an infrastructure that benefits everyone.

One reason Siemens promotes school-to-work so actively among employers nationwide is to prevent other businesses from stealing its graduates. Of the first 15 graduates of its Lake Mary program, four left the company. John Tobin, the director of vocational training for Siemens in the United States, notes that these were older adults with family and financial responsibilities. They had not begun the program as high school students. He argues that if companies focus their efforts on high schools, they will suffer less turnover in the long run and produce workers of higher quality at reduced cost. "If you get most of the local employers to train together," adds Tobin, "they all benefit by having a trained workforce and no one company is funding the employees of the other companies."

Given the high rates of job turnover in the United States, however, skills training is likely to remain more school based than in Germany and other European countries. Individual companies will have to weigh the risks and benefits carefully before deciding whether to participate. In a country that traditionally has not invested heavily in the training of its front-line workforce, that may be a hard sell.

Early results indicate that a surprisingly high percentage of young people who participate in school-to-work efforts are remaining in the field for which they were trained. Of the first 38 students to graduate from Project ProTech in Boston, a youth apprenticeship program that began in health occupations, 28 entered postsecondary education in the health-care field. In Kalamazoo, Michigan, about 90 percent of the students who graduated from the health-occupations program in 1994 continued their education in allied health, and about 83 percent of those who graduated from the law-enforcement program continued their education in a related field.

But other results are mixed. During their second year after high school, half of the graduates of the Cornell Youth Apprenticeship Demonstration Project in upstate New York (18 young people) had made progress toward a college degree in a field related to their apprenticeship. Another 5.6 percent (2 young people) had a job related to their training. But 44.4 percent (16 young people) of the program graduates were not working or learning in a field related to their apprenticeship. Apprentices from both the Kalamazoo and Cornell programs who attempted to secure occupationally related work immediately after high school also were less successful. This raises troubling questions about whether apprenticeships can improve the work transition for young people whose education stops at high school in an increasingly knowledge-based economy.

Improving the Bottom Line

Corporate executives at both Serigraph and Siemens told me that investing in young people required their companies to take a long-term view. They accepted more responsibility for developing a highly skilled workforce than is common among U.S. firms and in return they got better employees who stayed with the company and made their employers money. Procter & Gamble, a U.S. company that traditionally has invested heavily in human capital, exemplifies this lesson.

P&G is one of the largest consumer-products companies in the United States, with over $30 billion in annual revenue. On an overcast day, billows of steam hang suspended over the Procter & Gamble paper plant in Mehoopany, Pennsylvania, about a half hour's drive south of the New York State border. Twenty-five years ago, farms dominated the rolling hillsides around the plant, but today, there are few working farms left. The plant and its surrounding acreage stretch as far as the eye can see. The facility operates 24 hours a day, seven days a week. Giant logs roll into one end of the sprawling plant—82 acres under one roof—and roll out the other end as finished products. From here, a steady stream of trucks dispatches Luvs, Bounty, Pampers, Charmin, and other familiar brands up and down the East Coast.

Built in 1965, this is the largest P&G manufacturing facility in the world, employing almost 2,500 people, and is one of the largest employers in the region. It was the first Procter & Gamble plant based on the concept of work teams, in which front-line employees control many of the decisions about how to schedule their work and improve productivity.

Like most large companies, this Procter & Gamble plant has not routinely hired recent high school graduates. Until 1993, it did not have much use for recent high school students—period. Then Peter Butler, a quiet, no-nonsense engineering manager for the facility, began to crunch a few numbers: The typical new hire at the plant is about 30 years old. Over 10 years, Procter & Gamble invests $100,000 in training that technician, who on average stays with the company for 17 years.

Butler calculated that if Procter & Gamble could hire some-one at age 20 who stayed with the company for 27 years, the company would dramatically reduce its retraining costs. If young people already had some training behind them and were familiar with P&G's culture, the company would come out even further ahead.

Moreover, educating a high school student was much cheaper than training an adult to whom the company had to pay full wages and benefits while he or she was being trained. At $5 an hour, it would cost just $15,000 to employ and train a youth apprentice for 18 months, spread out over a four-year program, compared to $34,800 for an adult technician. The company also could shape a well-educated, flexible pool of employment candidates who could hit the ground running. Even if half the apprentices dropped out, Butler figured, Procter & Gamble remained ahead. "From a business standpoint," he told me, "I don't have any trouble saying this is nice to do *and* it saves money."

Pennsylvania had already taken the plunge into youth apprenticeships before Butler began making his calculations. In the 1980s, the state had developed an aggressive economic-development strategy to support key industries. State officials were particularly concerned about the fate of 250 small and medium-sized metalworking companies clustered in the Erie, Pittsburgh, Lancaster, and Philadelphia regions. A survey of these employers, sponsored by the Pennsylvania Department of Commerce, had identified a critical shortage of skilled labor and an aging work-force. Companies anticipated needing more than 450 new machinists and tool-and-die makers each year during the coming decade.

At the urging of the Pennsylvania Commerce Department, representatives of government, industry, and education began to wrestle with the problem. In 1991, Pennsylvania's Governor Robert P. Casey launched the Pennsylvania Youth Apprenticeship

Program with over $1.5 million in funding from the state, the U.S. Department of Labor, the Alfred P. Sloan Foundation, and the Heinz Endowment. A dozen eleventh-graders in Williamsport, Pennsylvania, made up the first graduating class.

At a state conference, P&G's Butler heard a presentation by one of the Williamsport students and came away sold. In 1993 he teamed up with other area businesses, schools, and colleges to form the Northern Tier Industry Education Consortium. Its goal was to create a highly skilled workforce for the Susquehanna Valley, where P&G is located. By May the consortium had a state grant, and by September, P&G and four other companies had enrolled the first 10 high school students. By 1996, 40 companies and 16 school districts had joined the effort, with 115 apprentices in the six-county area, and growth remained strong. The Mehoopany plant had 20 apprentices that year.

The four-year program begins in the last two years of high school and continues through two years of technical or community college. High school students work at the plant two days a week and attend their home school three days. At the plant they spend most of their time in a work team on the factory floor, where they learn entry-level technical skills and how to function in a team environment. About four hours a week they spend in classes in the company's training facility. Every student has a mentor to provide personal support and guidance.

The work-based curriculum combines basic machine skills with the cognitive reasoning and social skills needed to succeed in a modern manufacturing environment. The students learn about safety, leadership skills, the characteristics of high-performance workplaces, quality processes, presentation and communication skills, and priority setting and time management. On the floor they have a list of learning objectives that cover the basics of manufacturing. Most of the teaching is hands-on and immediately applicable. "We wanted to make sure, when they had classroom training, they could go right out onto the floor and use it," says Beth Lunger, the site trainer who developed the curriculum.

Over the course of the four years, their instruction becomes more sophisticated. The curriculum expands to include hydraulics, basic pneumatics, electronics, and statistical process control. By the time they finish the program, the apprentices will qualify for at least "technician 2" status out of six technical levels within the company, and they will earn a starting salary of more than $12 an hour. Although P&G does not guarantee them employment, it promises them preference for any job openings.

"We have a good pool of candidates that, when we turn around and hire them, I think are going to be very effective here," says Lunger. "One of the things that they learn very quickly is that there's not going to be anyone here rescuing them. I'm not going to baby them in the process."

For Joseph LaRue, it was the perfect opportunity to do some growing up. A tall, thin, 17-year-old farm boy dressed in a Harley-Davidson T-shirt and jeans, he fairly burst with pride in his job. Together with the 16-year-old apprentice Dan Trivett, Joe took me on a tour of the factory and described the intricacies of turning pulp into paper. In the control room, they ran a sample of the paper through its paces, checking its weight, thickness, strength, speck and hole count, and other quality features. Outside the control room, about a half dozen men and women in safety glasses and ear plugs monitored the operation of a three-story paper machine the size of a ship.

"I can't wait for Thursday and Friday," Joe told me over the noise. "I want to come down here and work. I find myself sitting in English class, thinking about a problem down here and how we can solve it." Joe's father, who has worked for Procter & Gamble for 23 years, couldn't believe the change in his son's attitude. "He was a good student. He'd get B's. He just didn't care about school," explained Arnold LaRue. "I think he was pretty focused on the fact that he wanted to go to work somewhere, that he wasn't thinking about college, although he really didn't know what he wanted to do."

But after talking to people at the plant, Joe began to buckle down. "It's my observation that a majority of people here have gone to college at least four years, and some even six," Joe told me. Now he was thinking about becoming a mechanical or electrical engineer.

The program has not been without some bumps. The first year, the company was so anxious to expose apprentices to every aspect of production that it raced them from logging operations in the forest to inventory control at breakneck speed, without more than a week spent in any area. By the end of the year, both the apprentices and their mentors were exhausted. Now the students get a brief tour of the facility and an overview of its operations before settling into one area for their first rotation. Of the nine high school students who enrolled in the P&G program in the first two years, three dropped out—one because of poor grades, one because of personal problems, and another because he lost interest.

But for the students and the mentors who stick with it, says Charlie Coppola, a project engineer and coach, it has been tremendously rewarding. "For me, it's hard to put into words," he explains, "just seeing the kids mature, becoming part of the workforce, becoming successful. It's not something you can hold in your hand. I personally haven't found any of it hard, it's been so damn interesting. It makes you feel young again."

Indeed, many of the companies that I visited described how their employees had become better coaches and leaders as a result of working with teenagers. Many coaches and mentors, like Charlie, have taken great pride and satisfaction in their work. Unfortunately, coaches and mentors typically do not receive extra pay or external recognition for their work with young people, and they often are expected to remain just as productive as before. One way that P&G has tried to counter that trend is to recognize its coaches and mentors once a year in a companywide ceremony that honors both the adults and the apprentices.

The Basics Plus

One of the most noticeable aspects of the P&G program is the emphasis that it places on employability skills, reasoning, and teamwork—the same qualities that the company looks for in its regular job applicants. Prospective apprentices go through the same application procedure as all new hires. Multiple-choice tests assess their mechanical, technical, and problem-solving skills; their mathematical problem solving ability; and their proficiency in basic mathematics and algebra. Candidates watch a videotape of a work situation unfold and answer questions about what they would do at key moments; this helps evaluators to predict their ability to work in teams. They also complete an application essay about their previous experiences, which is used as evidence of qualities like persistence and initiative. Those who do well on the tests complete formal interviews.

When I asked the apprentices what they needed to succeed at P&G, they replied: You have to be open-minded, be able to do a lot of problem solving, be able to think. Jackie Dymond, a short, sandy-haired girl from Tunkhannock High School, said, "I've learned a lot about the mechanical aspect of things, computer skills, quality control, a lot about working with other people. You don't get the experience in school of working in teams, you usually work as individuals. I guess I've matured a lot over this past year because of all the responsibility and priority setting."

In designing the program, says P&G's Butler, "We're really talking about a very broad, high-performance work system. . . .

Sure, we expect people to have good mechanical skills. But we also want them to be problem solvers, to be self-directed, to lead improvement efforts, to exhibit shared leadership, to give presentations. I don't know if [most] high school kids get as high a level of expectation . . . as they get when they walk through the door and talk to our technicians, who are working under high expectations."

Butler's perceptions of what employers want coincide with the conclusions of a national commission appointed in 1991 by the U.S. secretary of labor. The Secretary's Commission on Achieving Necessary Skills (SCANS) was asked to examine how changes in high-performance workplaces would affect educational requirements. The commission's report stressed that basic skills in reading, math, writing, listening, and speaking were essential. It also identified a list of competencies that it said rivaled technical expertise in their importance. These included the ability to collect, analyze, and organize information, identify and use resources, work with others, use technology, and understand and design systems. Tomorrow's workers, the commission stated, must be able to think creatively, make decisions, solve problems, visualize things in their mind's eye, and continue to learn on the job. They also need to display such personal qualities as responsibility, integrity, and honesty.

Since then, other national reports have stressed the need for these kinds of personal and cognitive attributes. Peter Cappelli, the codirector of the National Center on the Educational Quality of the Workforce at the University of Pennsylvania, suggests that a lack of these core attitudes, rather than of technical knowledge, lies at the heart of the employee "skills gap." He notes that employers identify problems stemming from inappropriate work attitudes or behaviors as the primary cause of poor job performance. In a 1991 survey, businesses identified a lack of dedication to work and discipline in work habits as the biggest problem among high school graduates applying for jobs.

Skills in the Service Sector

These soft skills are important in the manufacturing sector, which has shifted most noticeably toward new forms of work organization. But they are equally essential for the nation's burgeoning service industries—and that's where much of the action is in modern economies. Service jobs now account for 77 out of every 100 jobs in the United States. By the year 2005, the percentage of service jobs in the economy likely will exceed 80 percent.

The growing importance of the service industry is especially apparent in a place like Miami. In the high-rises and barrios of Miami Beach, the small shops of Coral Gables, and the teeming bustle of the Caribbean Market Place, the old and the new coexist in an uneasy partnership. You are as likely to hear Spanish spoken here as English. As the country's traditional bridge to Latin America and the Caribbean, Miami International Airport has more foreign travelers than any other American airport except John F. Kennedy in New York.

In the late 1980s the American Express Company, in collaboration with the Dade County Public Schools, launched one of the first Academy of Travel and Tourism programs here at Miami Springs High School. The program was designed to deal with two challenges simultaneously: the explosion of the travel and tourism industry—which is now one of the largest industries in the world—and the poor academic and workforce preparation of young people coming into the field.

Elvis Vasquez's parents, like many of the recent immigrants to Miami, came to the United States seeking a better life. They immigrated from Cuba 15 years ago, stopping first in Panama. Elvis's mother is a nurse. His father, a former worker in a glass-manufacturing plant, never completed college. But Elvis is the epitome of an ambitious first-generation U.S. citizen. In elementary school he joined the Boy Scouts and later the Miami-

Dade Police Cadets. In high school he worked more than 40 hours a week to earn the money to buy a car. Eventually, he'd like to be a businessman, preferably in the tourism industry. That's why he enrolled in the Academy at Miami Springs High School. The magnet program attracts students from 10 surrounding middle schools who want to pursue a career in one of the fastest-growing industries in the United States.

"In the Academy," says Elvis, "we're treated as adults. When our teacher doesn't like something we do, he tells us. He says, 'You're acting immature. I don't like how you're acting. That's not you.' And we don't walk out of the class, like most people do. We can take criticism because it's strict.

"In a way," he adds, "it's like an acceleration of growing up. And I like that. If I can skip two steps, I'll do it."

The Academy here in Miami is affiliated with the National Academy Foundation and follows the same general design as other programs around the country in the fields of finance, travel and tourism, and public service that are affiliated with the foundation. In 1989 the American Express Company created the foundation in New York City to help spread the use of the Academy model nationwide. Today, the independent foundation provides technical assistance and support to more than 200 Academies across the country.

Students usually choose to enroll in the Academies as juniors. The Academies typically are small programs within a larger high school. Students take a sequence of two or three specialized courses together each semester. For travel and tourism students these include "Physical Geography and Destinations," "Tourism Marketing and Management," and "Economics for Travel and Tourism." These supplement their core academic courses, which are taken with the rest of their classmates in the regular high school.

Students' work-related experiences are much less intensive than in an apprenticeship program. They focus primarily on career exploration and work-readiness skills. Students go on tours of local companies, have frequent interaction with business partners, and participate in paid internships during the summer, doing real entry-level jobs for real wages. During their senior year, in addition to their other Academy courses, they are encouraged to take a college-level course at their high school or a nearby college and are eligible for college scholarships sponsored by the business partners.

Because the Academies' courses are developed by teams of teachers and industry experts, they are more likely to reflect existing labor-market needs than many traditional vocational education programs. In each city a project director oversees the program in coordination with the school district and an advisory board of local businesses. The curriculum helps connect basic academic skills with a student's career goals. Specific courses teach students about such industry sectors as mortage banking or the cruise industry, while stressing the general acquisition of skills.

The program also emphasizes the kinds of generic workforce skills emphasized by the SCANS commission. In Elvis's classes, for example, students were frequently asked to make oral presentations; plan and organize public events; analyze and critique public tourism policies and marketing strategies; and work in cooperative groups. Students also belong to a travel-and-tourism club that emphasizes leadership skills and community service.

I first met Elvis during the summer of 1995, when he was an intern in the Latin American office of the Florida Department of Commerce's tourism division. Elvis's responsibilities were pretty mundane: to type up labels, keep the shelves well stocked with brochures, send out faxes, and answer the phones. But his exposure to the tourism industry extended beyond his actual job description. During the summer he attended La Cumbre, the largest computerized trade show for Latin American countries in the United States, an unusual experience for a high school student. He also had to develop short-term goals for himself every week and evaluate his job performance at the end of the summer. And he completed weekly homework assignments such as describing the career ladder in his office, the workplace policies, and the management style.

Gina Hartmann, his boss, said having an extra pair of hands during a busy period relieved a lot of pressure on her office and, in the long run, would benefit the industry. "We want people educated in this industry, who understand the industry," she explained to me. "I've been in this industry for thirty years, and I learned the hard way. I came up the ladder from the secretarial pool. These kids will have an overview of the market. They will get a view of what a professional should be like, and they will get it from working people."

The Academy that Elvis attends is a magnet school that draws students from all of northern Miami, beginning as early as their freshman year. Some NAF Academies are located in comprehensive high schools; others operate out of vocational schools. Since 1984, when the first Academy of Finance was launched in New York City, more than 6,000 students have graduated from NAF programs. The annual graduating class was expected to reach 3,000 in 1996.

According to the foundation, more than 90 percent of Academy graduates attend postsecondary institutions, most of them four-year colleges, and the majority pursue a major in a field related to the Academy. In one study of participating employers in New York City, the vast majority rated the quality of their interns' work as good or excellent, and about one third rated their knowledge of travel and tourism as better than that of other entry-level employees.

Compared to the costs of a youth apprenticeship program, which can be substantial, the cost per student for an Academy affiliated with the National Academy Foundation is about $550 per year. This primarily covers the cost of program materials, including industry-specific textbooks, the salary of a program director, special events, and teacher training. It does not include teacher salaries or the cost of a student's summer wages, which average about $5.50 per hour for seven weeks, or about $1,540 in direct costs to employers.

The development of a core set of work-readiness skills is not unique to the Academies. Many school-to-work programs place a strong emphasis on SCANS-type competencies. In 1994, for example, Kalamazoo officials surveyed local employers to find out what skills students needed to be productive in the workplace. In addition to basic academic skills, the employers stressed these "workplace know-how skills." Today, all Kalamazoo students in work-site learning programs are rated on their interpersonal skills, their ability to communicate, their teamwork, their productivity, their critical thinking and decision-making skills, their contribution to quality-improvement processes, and the extent to which they assume responsibility and initiative for their own learning.

Similarly, the Cornell Youth Apprenticeship Demonstration Project in upstate New York stresses a core set of personal and social competencies that students at all work sites must master. These include the ability to understand organizations, adhere to professional norms and standards, cooperate with others, communicate clearly, take initiative, assume responsibility for continued learning, and exhibit motivation and self-confidence on the job.

James C. Witte and Arne L. Kalleberg, two American professors who have studied the German apprenticeship system, argue that its primary benefit may lie in teaching these generic employability skills. "Graduates of the dual system are particularly likely to acquire attitudes and general skills that retain much of their value even if an individual changes occupations," they write. "Participating in an apprenticeship leads to a sense of control and competence, the tendency to view employment as a team endeavor, and an ability to learn flexibility and to execute tasks." Supporting their hypothesis, they found little difference in earnings among German men who had completed apprentices and found jobs in their field and those who found jobs that did not match their training. "The insignificance of fit indicates general skills and worker socialization are the primary benefits received by male graduates of the German vocational education system," they write.

Problems and Pitfalls

The profiles in this chapter demonstrate that school-to-work can benefit both young people and employers. But these are admittedly best-case scenarios. There are also problems and pitfalls in designing a school-to-work system. Any honest calculation by a company must take these potential barriers into account.

Applicability

Intensive school-to-work experiences, such as apprenticeships, are not for every student. They require a substantial commitment on the part of a young person. Some students will drop out, for a variety of reasons. These can range from a loss of interest to an inability to do the work, from competing demands on their time to a lack of maturity. Students who have no exposure to career options ahead of time may discover that an apprenticeship is not for them only after an employer has invested time and money. One study of school-to-work programs found that about 30 percent of students withdrew early in their experiences. Of these, about a third were dissatisfied with the program or lacked interest in the career field.

In Lake Mary, Florida, I talked with several academically able students who had withdrawn from the Siemens apprenticeship. "I just wanted to try it," said Jeff Alderson, a senior. "To me, it wasn't worth it. I had a lot of scholarships I was being offered to go to the University of Central Florida. I really wanted my four-year degree, instead of just two years." Another student, Natalie Martin, also withdrew from the program to attend a four-year college. In addition, she said, "I wasn't good with the hands-on stuff. It's not for me." Siemens builds an attrition rate into its design and does not anticipate that all students will finish. P&G also lost three of nine students in the first two years of its program for reasons ranging from poor grades to lack of interest. Of the 100 apprentices in the Cornell Youth Apprenticeship Demonstration Project, 15 dropped out of the program during high school. Better career guidance and exposure to real workplaces ahead of time could help reduce the attrition rate from intensive work-based learning experiences.

A related problem is that programs based in vocational schools may have trouble attracting students, both because of the stigma attached to vocational education and because many students want to retain a postsecondary option. Traditionally, vocational schools have focused on jobs that do not require higher education. One way to overcome this obstacle is to design programs that include numerous postsecondary and career options so that they can attract a broader range of students.

Time Investment

Apprenticeships are very labor-intensive. The cost of adult time is real and substantial. Stephen and Mary Agnes Hamilton, the founders of the Cornell Youth Apprenticeship Demonstration Project, note that this includes time spent supervising students, communicating with schools and parents, planning and coordinating the program, training and supporting mentors and coaches, designing learning plans for students, and assessing their performance. "We have records of 251 different adults in 11 firms who worked extensively with our 100 apprentices, many of them with more than one apprentice," they write. "This is a low estimate of the ratio of adults to apprentices because we know many other adults were also involved."

Such time pressures may diminish somewhat as start-up programs become more established. But companies will have to decide if the payoff is worth the effort. And some may choose to participate in less intensive forms of school-to-work.

It may be particularly difficult for small firms to provide highly structured and intensive work-based learning experiences. This was the case with an appliance-repair curriculum written by the Sears Corporation and the National Alliance of Business. In the three sites where the program was piloted, the service-repair industry was dominated by very small independent firms, often consisting of a single technician. These technicians often had an unpredictable schedule and spent most of their day driving from one job to another, making it difficult to plan for students to accompany them. The volatility of their earnings also made it hard for them to deal with the liability concerns raised by employing a student.

One way that printing companies in Wisconsin have overcome some of these difficulties is by rotating students among firms to teach them all of the necessary skills. In Germany, small firms also may send apprentices to an inter-firm training center for part of their time. These centers provide education and experiences to apprentices that the individual companies cannot.

Too-Narrow Focus

Programs that rely on a single employer, or prepare students for a single occupation, may be vulnerable to changes in the economy and have trouble attracting students. For one thing, the economic fortunes of companies change. The Rindge School of Technical Arts lost its partnership with the Polaroid Corporation when the company moved its headquarters to the suburbs. In Kalamazoo, Michigan, restructuring and downsizing at two area hospitals during the 1995–96 school year placed severe strains on the health-occupations program. The Sears Corporation had to scale back plans to provide part-time employment for students at one of its sites after corporate restructuring resulted in the lay-off of hundreds of employees and a moratorium on hiring. Job insecurity also diminished the enthusiasm of existing workers to train high school students. And in the three pilot sites, the demand for appliance-repair technicians was weaker than expected. An evaluation of the program suggested that such problems could be avoided in the future by working with more than one company and by designing programs that prepared students for a broader range of occupations within an industry.

In addition, school-to-work initiatives designed for narrowly defined occupations or industries may fail to attract students. In Pennsylvania the number of students participating in apprenticeships in metalworking has remained essentially flat in many communities since the program began in 1991–92. Rob McIlzaine, the director of workforce development for the south-central region of the state, said parents and students perceive manufacturing in general, and the metal trades in particular, to be dying. Although there are good, well-paying jobs to be had, the programs have failed to surmount that perception.

In Philadelphia, where the program was expanded to encompass engineering, manufacturing, and electrical-mechanical technologies, it has managed to attract more young people. Also, students now receive a broader preparation in pneumatics, blueprint reading, computer-assisted design, and data processing, which will serve them better as the economy changes. Although the program has lost some participating companies as a result, it has gained others.

Uneven Commitment Level

Companies often discover that the capacity and interest of individual schools to work with employers differ. In some schools, teachers and administrators are eager to cooperate. In other schools, adminis-trators barely acknowledge that a work-based learning program exists, except to let young people leave their campus. They may not provide support for teachers to change their curriculum, to collaborate, or to work with employers, and they may not recruit students very actively. Under these circumstances, work and school compete for young people's attention, and coordinating learning between work and classrooms can be extraordinarily dif-ficult. Companies that work with students from more than one high school also may find it difficult to coordinate their efforts across sites, unless they are part of a larger consortium that ensures some consistency among all program participants. Companies can avoid this problem, in part, by working only with schools or school systems that provide evidence they want to change.

Perception of Benefits

If students do not benefit from school-to-work efforts, neither will com-panies. Today, many school-to-work programs are not good enough. A study by Mathematica Policy Research of 15 early-youth appren-ticeship programs found that the intensity of work-based learning varied widely. In some cases, employers offered carefully structured, sequenced training opportunities but no real work experience. In other cases, students gained real work experience but only informal on-the-job training and only as much as they needed to get their work done.

As I traveled around the country, I saw wide variations in the kinds of tasks that students were asked to perform on the job. In some health-related programs, students were drawing blood sam-ples and functioning as EKG technicians. In others, they were lim-ited to folding bedsheets, setting up examination rooms, and filing medical records. These kinds of experiences can hardly substitute for the acquisition of real technical and intellectual skills.

Lack of Clear Standards

Ensuring the quality of work-site learning remains a huge challenge—particularly in the absence of any widely recognized credentials or certificates that would attest that young people have learned certain skills. It is also unclear what level of return employers will need to justify such a substantial investment of time, people, and resources. Most of the employers with whom I talked were confident that their investment would pay off. But they expressed the greatest concerns about the time it takes for workers to supervise and mentor high school students.

Stephen and Mary Agnes Hamilton from Cornell University have thought deeply about how to create high-quality apprenticeships for American youth. In the late 1980s, Stephen Hamilton, who is the chairman of the Department of Human Development and Family Studies at Cornell, received a Fulbright Senior Research Fellowship to spend a year in West Germany studying the apprenticeship system. Hamilton told me he was particularly impressed with the "skill level and the knowledge level of ordinary kids in Germany. Kids in our society who would be school dropouts or marginal students were working hard. They took their education seriously. Young people in the European countries that have apprenticeships know what it is they have to do in order to achieve a goal. And all of that just seemed constructive and positive for the young people and for the economy."

In 1991, the Hamiltons launched the fledgling Cornell Youth Apprenticeship Demonstration Project in upstate New York, based on the German system. In its first four years, it trained 100 youths in 11 companies. On the basis of their experiences, the Hamiltons have a number of suggestions for creating high-quality apprentice-ship programs. They recommend that participating companies:

- ❀ Design a multiyear sequence of learning activities for apprentices, with yearly rotations that enable them to gain high-level technical and personal skills.

- ❀ Design a learning plan for each apprentice that deter-mines what the apprentice does and for how long.

- ❀ Formally assign adults to work on the program, with the performance of those roles written into their job descriptions and included in the overall assessment of their own job performance.

- ❀ Clearly spell out the expectations for apprentices and regularly assess their progress.

- ❀ Assign someone in the firm to take responsibility for coordinating the program so that it does not become a patchwork of incoherent placements.

- ❀ Place more stress on ensuring that students achieve high academic standards. Studies of early school-to-work ini-tiatives found that absent changes in schools, students' grades and attendance did not improve. Simply provid-ing work-based learning was not enough.

Another study of designing and implementing quality work-site learning activities, by Jobs for the Future and the Manpower Demonstration Research Corporation, identified 10 elements of a high-quality program. These include goals to which all partners for-mally agree; a structured learning plan at the work site; experiences that promote the development of broad, transferable skills; school-based activities that help distill and deepen what students learn at work; and learning at the work site that is documented and assessed.

The American Federation of Teachers also has identified steps to ensure that learning in the workplace enhances, rather than impedes, students' academic progress. These include explicitly stating the academic goals of work-based learning, limiting the number of hours that students work, and maintaining a central role for schools.

Piecemeal Development

Attempting to build a school-to-work system company by company and school by school is painfully slow. Today most programs serve fewer than 100 students. Procter & Gamble officials would like to hire about 15 youth apprentices a year at a plant with 2,400 employees. The Siemens Lake Mary facility would like to recruit 40 high school students each year but expects only 20 of them to complete the entire program. Out of the 2,400 students in West Bend's public high schools, only 26 were in apprenticeship programs in 1995–96. Most communities have dealt with the small number of students who can participate in any one program by expanding into other industries and taking on new employers.

On the basis of its survey of 15 relatively intensive school-to-work programs, the U.S. Office of Technology Assessment concluded that on average, programs recruited about six additional employers per year, and the median number of businesses participating in any single program was 35. "Because there are only about two students per employer, this growth translates into an increase of about a dozen students per community per year," the researchers concluded. "Other studies have revealed similar findings. Unless the rates of growth improve significantly, it will take a long time before more school-to-work transition systems can serve substantial portions of students in their communities."

Slow and Steady

In the United States, the costs and benefits of work-based learning for employers are only now being documented. Most participating companies cannot provide an adequate reckoning of how much they spend and what they get in return. And we do not know how much their costs could be reduced through greater economies of scale or lessons learned from experience.

Most companies expect to see a return on their investment down the road. But many are content to balance their long-term self-interests with some measure of civic-mindedness. Striking the appropriate balance between the two is not always easy, but employer interest in such initiatives is growing steadily.

❖ In 1993 the McDonald's Corporation began to develop a youth-apprenticeship program in consumer-service management in collaboration with Robert Sheets of Northern Illinois University. McDonald's is the largest employer of entry-level workers in the United States, and students account for half of the company's workforce. The new program is meant to put young people in the retail and hospitality industries on a fast-track to management careers. National business partners include Walgreens and Red Lion Hotels. Students who graduate from the program will earn an associate's degree and a certificate based on national industry standards. In 1996 the program was scheduled to operate in five pilot sites, including Austin, Texas; Chicago; and Portland, Oregon.

❖ In 1995 the General Motors Corporation launched GM-YES (for Youth Educational Systems) to create a pool of qualified service technicians for GM dealerships. The program combines structured learning in school with paid, hands-on experiences at the work site. "Now, when an automotive student is studying [antilock] brakes in school, he will work on brakes at the work site," said Donald Gray, the director of the program. "The school and the dealership will work together to coordinate what is studied and when. And the student graduate will have a high school diploma and a mastery certificate from GM." By the year 2000, GM's CEO, John F. Smith, expects the program to expand from about 10 initial sites to 110 locations nationwide:

❁ Since 1990 the Boeing Company, the world's leading aircraft manufacturer, has worked with school districts and community colleges throughout Washington State to prepare young people for technical fields and expose their teachers to the workplace. It helped develop a new associate degree program in manufacturing technology that students can begin in high school. Students in the program participate in three progressive summer internships, starting after their junior year in high school. The 160-hour, paid summer internships began in 1993 with 25 students. Plans were to expand the program to 300 students by 1997. The company also provides summer internships for educators. In late 1992, Boeing was a founding member of the Manufacturing Technology Advisory Group, a statewide consortium of educators and employers working to define a common core of standards for preparing a highly skilled labor force in manufacturing technology.

❁ A state survey conducted by the National Governors' Association in the spring of 1996 found that reported levels of employer involvement in training were higher than one year earlier. Thirty-nine states had solicited individual employers or employer groups to help expand the number of slots available to students for work-based learning, and about half of these states also had reached out to labor groups. Three fourths of the states had implemented, or were planning to implement, incentives to increase employer involvement. These ranged from providing training to workplace mentors and supervisors to tax credits for the wages paid to school-to-work participants. Several states also had changed workers' compensation, tax, or child-labor laws and regulations to make employer involvement easier.

Today, most American companies are not deeply engaged in preparing young people for careers. Unlike Germany, we seem content to leave the responsibility for educating the next generation to the schools—even if we are unhappy with the results.

It is too soon to tell whether enough employers will step up to the table to create a school-to-work system in this country capable of serving large numbers of young people. What is clear is that without strong business involvement, school-to-work will fail. Only employers can identify the skills and knowledge needed in the workplace. Only people experienced in business can help develop curricula that reflect the world of work. Only the owners and managers of companies can open up their workplaces to students and teachers for learning or provide business mentors and coaches.

Chapter 5 looks at ways to build school-to-work systems more comprehensively than one company or one school at a time. It describes how some communities have targeted clusters of employers, rather than individual companies, to expand their school-to-work efforts, and lays out a number of less intensive options for employers to become involved, ranging from job shadowing to summer internships.

CHAPTER 4

The Link with Higher Education

$\mathcal{M}$ost people think about school-to-work as a way to reform high schools, with little role for higher education. This couldn't be further from the truth. Higher education must be a central player in the school-to-work movement. If higher education is not involved, school-to-work will not succeed.

First, the education requirements for employment are rising. College graduates stand a better chance of being employed than those with only a high school education, and they are much more likely to earn a decent wage. In 1994, male college graduates earned on average over 50 percent more than those with a high school diploma and nearly twice as much as high school dropouts. While some college graduates have struggled in the labor market, overall they have better job options and earnings than their less-educated peers. In the future, the majority of well-paying jobs—perhaps the majority of all new jobs created—will require some education beyond high school.

Second, high school students overwhelmingly see themselves as going to college. To convince them otherwise is like pushing water uphill. In a 1992 survey, 95 percent of high school seniors said they planned to continue their education, and 84 percent expected to earn *at least* a four-year degree. Today a record 62 percent of high school graduates are enrolled in colleges the following fall. Unless school-to-work systems include strong options for postsecondary education, they will have few takers and even less support.

Third, high schools are not the appropriate site for most career-specific training. They lack both the facilities and the resources. Postsecondary institutions have a better track record of designing programs that match labor-market needs and place their graduates in jobs.

The need to prepare students for the workplace is not lost on the nation's colleges. In its 1996 guide to America's best colleges, *U.S. News & World Report* reported that colleges increasingly are providing experiential learning for their students.

"Realizing the educational value of learning by doing and growing by doing, many schools now offer college credits for participation in off-campus internships, independent study and research projects, volunteer service and undergraduate teaching assistantships, and for enlisting in local community development activities," the magazine reported.

President David Shi of South Carolina's Furman University told the magazine: "We have found that undergraduates who are involved in real-world experiences like internships take more responsibility for their own education and develop greater self-confidence and sharper communication skills." Furman graduates, he added, frequently develop off-campus contacts that help them land their first job.

Similarly, an article in *The New York Times* of December 4, 1996, described the surge in corporate internships now available to college students. In 1996, the newspaper reported, an estimated 40,000 student internships were available nationwide, a 30 percent increase in just three years. "These corporations are ever more competitive," Peter Likins, the president of Lehigh University, was quoted as saying, "and they're saying, 'We can't afford to hire someone and then take two years training them how to function— you have to do it.' I've been in higher education a long time, and I've never seen such fundamental change in undergraduate education as what I'm seeing now."

Students at the baccalaureate level also are paying more attention to applied fields of study than to a general liberal arts education. In fact, many students with B.A. degrees are returning to community colleges to receive job-specific training.

The question is not whether young people should expect to pursue some form of higher education to get or keep a well-paying job. Many should. But are students making the right choices among postsecondary institutions? Are they adequately prepared for higher education? And are they likely to reach their career goals? For all three questions, the answer is often no.

Many students harbor career and college aspirations that bear little resemblance to reality. The majority of high school students expect to become highly paid professionals, such as doctors or lawyers, even though only about 20 percent of employment is in the professional ranks. And consider the numbers. Each year, medical schools in the United States have 16,000 openings. U.S. law schools have about 40,000 slots. Only one of every 60 high school graduates will become a doctor or a lawyer.

In contrast, only about 6 percent of high school seniors express a desire to become managers or technicians. Yet that is where the jobs are. Since 1950, the number of technical workers has increased nearly 300 percent, according to *Fortune* magazine— triple the growth rate for the workforce as a whole. The Bureau of

Labor Statistics forecasts that careers in technologies, crafts, or specialized repair fields will represent a fifth of total employment within a decade.

Moreover, many students are woefully unprepared for the college education they claim to want. A shocking number of young Americans show up at college unable to do college-level work. About one third of college freshmen now expect to take at least one remedial course. This weak preparation pressures colleges to lower their standards and reteach high school material.

Weak preparation also contributes to the lengthy time young people are taking to graduate. The average college graduate now takes more than four years to earn a B.A. For 26 percent, it takes more than six years. Changing schools or majors, attending college part time, working long hours in outside jobs, enrolling in remedial courses, temporarily dropping out, and having difficulty enrolling in required classes all may delay graduation. This can be costly to students, who must pay additional tuition and postpone their entry into the labor market.

But the most shameful aspect of higher education is that many young people never graduate at all. Only about half of those who start a baccalaureate degree ever finish. In many cases, students would be better served financially by earning a two-year associate degree in an occupational field than by dropping out of a four-year institution with no degree and no career direction.

In a longitudinal study of the high school class of 1972, the researcher Clifford Adelman found that the only feature that distinguished the most from the least satisfied adults was an earned degree of *any* kind. According to his analysis, a higher percentage of students who earned an associate degree landed in professional occupations than students who dropped out of four-year colleges. Other analyses suggest that earning an associate degree in a professional field will not raise a person's lifetime earnings to that of a four-year college graduate. But it can result in higher earnings for young workers just starting out.

"Students who drop out of a four-year college are not receiving education of any kind," writes James Traub, a well-known journalist and the author of a book on City College of New York. "They need to be helped; and if a two-year degree or vocational training will help them to get a good job and lead a decent life, then it isn't to be denigrated."

When Congress passed the School-to-Work Opportunities Act in 1994, it specified that school-to-work systems should establish linkages between secondary and postsecondary institutions; enable most students to complete at least one or two years of postsecondary education; and establish mechanisms for young people to transfer to higher education. Local school-to-work partnerships also are required to include representatives of postsecondary institutions. But the role of two-year and four-year colleges in building a school-to-work system was not clearly spelled out. Furthermore, the initial focus on the "non-college-bound" discouraged many higher-education officials from becoming involved.

This chapter focuses primarily on the role of two-year colleges, rather than four-year colleges, in preparing young people for work. It does so for several reasons. Many of the skills required for tomorrow's technical workforce can be gained in two-year institutions, and the proportion of technical workers with at least some college education is rising. Students who earn two-year degrees in such fields as radiology technology, automotive technology, computer science, and industrial engineering can step immediately into well-paying, career-ladder jobs.

Second, preparing students who currently do not continue their education beyond high school to earn an associate's degree would be a major step in itself. In 1994, only 25 percent of males age 25 or over had completed four years or more of college.

Third, two-year institutions have shown the most willingness to become involved in building school-to-work systems. In part, this stems from the creation of tech-prep programs during the early 1990s. These prepare students for technical careers through courses of study that combine the last two years of high school with two years at a community college. Such programs have fostered collaboration between high schools and two-year institutions and provide a foundation on which school-to-work systems can build.

Community colleges also tend to have stronger ties to businesses than do either high schools or four-year institutions. The majority already provide workforce training for companies in their region. Most also embrace economic development and education for work as a central part of their missions.

Finally, two-year colleges have proved to be among the most flexible and dynamic parts of the education system. Their number has nearly doubled since 1947. They now serve about 5.5 million students, compared to 9 million on four-year campuses. They also have taken on a diverse set of roles: from preparing students to transfer to four-year colleges to providing continuing education for adults.

This chapter focuses on three institutions that have built bridges back to high schools, on the one hand, and out to employers, on the other. In New England, Maine Career Advantage places high school students in apprenticeships that include a year of postsecondary education and give credit for work-based learning. In Ohio, Sinclair Community College sponsors a more traditional tech-prep program that also includes an extensive work-based learning component. In South Carolina, Tri-County Technical College has supported curriculum development and professional training for high school teachers to better prepare all students for both careers and college.

Community colleges are not without their problems. Too many place barriers in the way of students who want to transfer to four-year colleges. Their attrition rates generally are even higher than the rates at four-year institutions.

Also, in focusing on two-year institutions, I do not mean to downplay the role of four-year colleges and universities. Given students' aspirations and the data on lifetime earnings, the route to four-year institutions must remain open. As the Cornell University economics professor John H. Bishop has argued, "Everyone who is capable of handling college should be encouraged to do so."

A high-quality school-to-work system would provide students with access to a full range of postsecondary options at two-year and four-year institutions. And it would smooth the transition between the various sectors. Four-year colleges, for example, determine whether students who earn technical degrees can transfer many of their credits if they later decide to pursue a baccalaureate. They also determine whether students who take nontraditional routes through high school, such as participating in apprenticeships or taking applied academic courses, will be at a disadvantage when they apply to college.

Finally, as noted in chapter 1, some of the strongest and best-known work-based learning programs already exist in four-year colleges and professional schools. No one questions the value or the wisdom of these arrangements. What is good for the most accomplished students should be good for all students.

Whether bound for two-year or four-year colleges, almost all students eventually will work. Many will cycle through education and employment and back again. For many young people, a more accurate concept than "school-to-work" would be "school-to-college-to-work" or some combination of the three. Colleges and universities are inextricably tied up in the nexus of education and employment. Indeed, the vast majority of young people already work while they are in college. To assume that institutions of higher education have no role to play in the school-to-work movement would be a grave mistake.

Maine's Technical College System Takes Charge

One person who believes in the role of higher education in preparing a skilled workforce is John Fitzsimmons, the president of the

Maine Technical College System. The *Maine Times* once affectionately referred to Fitzsimmons as the state's "blue-collar academic." When he was state labor commissioner in Maine during the 1980s, Fitzsimmons spent most of his time helping adults who had been blindsided by the new economy. His constituency included workers who had been thrown out of their jobs by downsizing, welfare recipients who had never graduated from high school, and assembly-line workers who lacked the skills or knowledge to transfer to new jobs. For some of these workers it was too late. They drifted away into lives of declining incomes and shattered expectations.

These days, as president of the state's technical college system, Fitzsimmons is practicing some preventive medicine. He has become a strong proponent of creating a school-to-work system in Maine that would enable young people to hit the ground running.

Like many educators, Fitzsimmons traveled to Germany and Denmark in the early 1990s, along with the then governor John R. McKernan, Jr., to get a first-hand view of European apprenticeships. The governor and Fitzsimmons were so impressed by what they saw that they plotted the outlines for a Maine initiative on paper napkins on the transatlantic flight home. In February 1993 the Maine Youth Apprenticeship Program—now called Maine Career Advantage—accepted its first 12 students. By 1996 the initiative had spread to 276 students, 108 high schools, and 197 businesses. An additional 850 students were involved in career-preparation activities such as job shadows, developing portfolios, and summer internships.

"I really believe, in my state, the future lies in the quality of the skilled workforce," Fitzsimmons told me in 1994, a strong Rhode Island accent still lingering in his voice. "We will not compete with a North Carolina Research Triangle or with Massachusetts's Harvard and M.I.T. and their ability to be international research areas. We will be the producers of goods. And I take great pride in that because if we're able to produce high-quality products, it will mean high-wage jobs for our people."

Maine Career Advantage is designed for students who do not plan to go directly from high school to a four-year college, yet want to gain the education and skills necessary to secure a good job. The two-year program begins at the end of the junior or senior year in high school and includes tuition-free classes at a technical college subsidized by the student's work site. Students can choose from placements in a variety of career fields, including manufacturing, health-information services, computers, customer service, and banking and finance.

During the school year, students alternate time between work and school and earn a stipend starting at $80 a week. They work full time during the summer, earning stipends of $170 a week. Participating companies pay the program about $500 a month for each student, to cover the stipend, liability insurance and workers' compensation, and tuition at the technical college. The students are employees of the program rather than of the companies.

Program graduates receive a skills certificate listing their technical competencies and a one-year certificate in "workplace technology" from the technical colleges. Sample competencies in banking and finance, for example, include the ability to understand loan policies, prepare loan documents, and order and analyze credit reports. The certificate represents about half the credits needed toward an associate's degree and includes some credits for students' work-based learning.

"What we're doing is opening up the whole world of postsecondary education for these kids," McKernan told me. "It is very hard to give youngsters the foundational education that they need and the additional skills necessary for a quality job in the modern economy in twelve years. And that's the problem with not having a postsecondary component.

"Since we have spent fifty years urging people to go to college if they want to be a success," McKernan added, "I do not believe that the general public will ever support the idea of promoting any educational pathway that does not include at least some form of college learning."

By locating responsibility for Maine Career Advantage in the technical colleges, McKernan hoped to give the colleges an incentive to make it work. The headquarters for the program is a modest red brick building on the campus of Southern Maine Technical College in South Portland at the end of a paved parking lot that looks out upon Casco Bay; military fortifications remind visitors that the campus is the former site of Fort Preble, which served the nation from the War of 1812 until the early 1950s. To Fitzsimmons and McKernan, Maine Career Advantage is the new beachhead in a war for economic survival.

In 1994, Maine officials estimated that the state had about 6,000 openings a year for people with two-year, college-level technical degrees, far outpacing the supply of qualified workers. Nine of the top 10 fastest-growing occupations in the state now require education or training beyond the twelfth grade.

One of the primary purposes of Maine Career Advantage is to create a pipeline of these qualified workers that will stretch far into the future. Fitzsimmons also hopes that a steady stream of such students will reduce the need for remedial education at the colleges and enable them to move young people through their programs faster and more effectively.

Most community colleges pride themselves on being "open admissions" institutions, meaning that anyone can enter. But individual degree programs often have admissions requirements, particularly programs that train for the more high-skill occupations such as nursing or industrial engineering. "For the first time," said Fitzsimmons, "we have a systematized approach for our faculty to sit down with the secondary school system and say, 'If you're going to come into our nursing program, you must have this course of study.' What we usually get is somebody who graduates from high school, who says, 'Gee, I want to be a nurse.' And then you go back and check, and they haven't taken the courses."

Since 1994, the state has contributed nearly $3 million to support Maine Career Advantage. The federal government has provided another $4 million, over 70 percent of which has gone directly to secondary schools and technical colleges. Most of the money has been spent to develop standards, evaluation tools, and curriculum materials based on what students should know and be able to do within particular career fields, as well as to train teachers and work-site supervisors.

By championing the program, the technical colleges have garnered political stature and marketability. They've also broadened their ties to the business community.

Diane Wescott, the mother of a Maine Career Advantage graduate, Matthew Burr, initially had some concerns about the program. "I had reservations about his missing his normal senior-year activities with his classmates," she said. "I also was afraid that it was seen as a program for kids who were not going on to college or were not capable of doing that. I'm thrilled with it now because he has grown so much with it, and he's matured so much, and he's been given lots of opportunities I don't think he would have had in a normal setting."

Matt, who attended Gorham High School, admitted, "I wasn't a very hard-working student. I didn't do very much homework, but I got okay grades. I just wasn't putting in any extra." When he became an intern at D&G Machine Products Inc., Matt switched from general-track courses to advanced English, precalculus, and physics. By 1996, Matt had graduated from the program and had been promoted to an assistant engineer at the company. He had a skills certificate in metals technology. And he had been accepted into the four-year industrial engineering program at the University of Southern Maine, where he hoped to transfer many of his credits. He also had started his own business on the side, building model automobiles for slot-car racing.

Of the eight interns who graduated from the program in 1995, two chose to study for their associate degree full time. Seven have continued working, five for their original employer. In 1996, six of the original interns either had finished or were close to completing their associate degrees, and two more students in addition to Matt had been accepted into four-year institutions.

"In our colleges, and across the country, we take great pride in the new average age of the returning student," said Fitzsimmons, which in the Maine Technical College System is 29. "What it means is that people have been in dead-end jobs for a decade. And they're finally having to reengage in education to find anything that they and their families can survive on."

Sinclair Community College: "An Incredible Relationship"

Another person who understands the link between higher education and high-paying jobs is David H. Ponitz, the president of Sinclair Community College in Dayton, Ohio. A tall, imposing figure, Ponitz has presided over the growth of his institution from 7,000 to 20,000 students in the past 20 years. He also has made Sinclair a prominent player in the business community. Its advanced manufacturing center helps local industries adapt to changes in technology and reduce costs. Each year, more than 500 mostly small and midsize companies take advantage of the seminars and training offered through the college's corporate and community-services division. "Sometimes it seems as if every other person in Dayton is either enrolled at Sinclair, taking a class there, or planning to do so," wrote Sara Rimer in *The New York Times* in March 1996.

Dayton embodies all of the contradictory elements of a national economy in transition. The once prosperous automobile town has hemorrhaged manufacturing jobs over the past 15 years. In the mid-1970s, the National Cash Register Company, a producer of computerized cash registers, shed 20,000 jobs during its retrenchment and takeover by AT&T.

But today Dayton demonstrates many signs of economic revival. Advanced-materials, software, and information-services companies are all thriving, and though many large corporations have downsized, a lot of smaller, newer ventures have sprung up (although the *New York Times* article notes that many of the new jobs do not pay what the old ones did). In 1996, unemployment in the region fell below 4 percent for the first time in years. Suddenly, many employers were finding it difficult to recruit workers who had the skills and attributes they wanted.

"We have in this community about ten thousand scientists and engineers," Ponitz told me. "They're working at Wright-Patterson Air Force Base [the largest in the nation], they're working at General Motors, they're working in small spinoffs from research at the base. And for every scientist and engineer, you need at least five or more technicians."

So in 1994 the community college joined with the University of Dayton, 100 business partners, and 64 high schools to form the Miami Valley Tech Prep Consortium. Its goal is to increase the pool of well-prepared young people in such technical fields as allied health, computer-support technology, automotive technology, and industrial and electronic engineering. By 1996 the program had enrolled about 460 students in 64 high schools. Students begin the program in their junior year in high school and complete the program after two years spent at Sinclair, when they earn an associate's degree. In many cases they have the option of continuing on for a baccalaureate at the University of Dayton.

The seeds of an economic recovery have put down strong roots at the Greene County Career Center, a public vocational school on a long country road about 20 minutes outside Dayton. On a warm spring day, about 20 high school juniors and seniors are working at computer terminals or on industrial equipment in a renovated laboratory facility. One student is programming a robotic arm; another is writing the instructions for a computer-operated lathe; a third is working on the motor controls for a work cell that the students are building from scratch. The students here are part of a new tech-prep program in Industrial Engineering Technology that was jointly designed by area high school teachers, representatives from business and industry, and faculty members from Sinclair Community College and the University of Dayton. In 1995–96 the program was operating in four high schools, with more scheduled to come on board.

Ohio follows the original tech-prep concept developed by Dale Parnell, the former president of the American Association of Community Colleges. In his 1985 book, *The Neglected Majority*, Parnell accused public schools of ignoring the needs of the middle 50 percent of students. These young people were not benefiting from traditional lectures and abstract materials, he argued. They were bored and turned off by schooling and were graduating unprepared for either work or college.

Parnell recommended creating a high-quality alternative to the traditional college-preparatory curriculum, which he called the "tech prep/associate degree" program. It would use new methods to teach traditional academic subjects and equip young people with technical skills. Such programs also would build bridges between high schools and community colleges, so that students entered higher education better prepared and graduated with a two-year degree in a technology field.

One of the primary features of tech prep is the use of "applied academics" curricula. These classes teach English, math, science, and social studies concepts by using real-world examples, hands-on demonstrations and activities, and problems drawn from the workplace and the community. In a life-sciences class, students might learn to take their vital signs before and after exercise, chart their recovery rate, and determine which individuals had the steepest recovery slope. A physics teacher might use an everyday event, such as an automobile accident, to teach the concepts of momentum and impulse. In a history class, students might trace the development of labor unions in the United States and then interview employers, workers, and parents to compile opinions about the current status of unions in America.

In 1990, Congress seized upon the tech-prep concept. As part of revisions to the Carl D. Perkins Vocational Education and Applied Technology Education Act, it provided funding for states to create local tech-prep consortia between high schools and community colleges. Each partnership was to develop, in consultation with business and industry, programs that began in high school and culminated in a two-year associate degree. Each program was to include a rigorous sequence of mathematics, science, communications, and technology courses.

The idea spread rapidly. Today, there are more than 1,058 tech-prep consortia nationwide, serving well over 500,000 students. Most consortia were started in the early 1990s.

But tech prep in many communities consists primarily of "articulation agreements." These agreements between high schools and higher-education institutions stipulate what each institution will do to connect their coursework and the conditions under which students can receive college credit or advanced standing for work completed in high school. Often, the actual changes to the curriculum at either institution are minimal. This is probably not very effective.

In contrast, more ambitious programs, like those in Dayton, define courses of study, change how content is taught, engage employers in identifying learning outcomes and developing the curriculum, and provide learning in the workplace. At the Greene County Career Center, a public vocational school, a team of four high school teachers—in English, mathematics, science, and technology—try to integrate what they are teaching across subjects. Students might learn how to calculate resistance in their mathematics class; design an electronic circuit board on the computer in the technology lab; and then build the board in their science class, using mathematics formulas to calculate how much voltage it produces. They might write the results in their English class and prepare a report.

"It's a lot more interesting," says Brett Cottle, a junior at the high school. "You get to actually work with things, hands-on, instead of just working in books and stuff like that. The academic classes are more understandable because it relates to what you're doing."

The Ohio program is a classic tech-prep model because it focuses explicitly on the middle 50 percent of students—young people who either don't go to college after high school or have difficulty when they do. To get into the program, students must have passed algebra 1 with at least a C average and be on track to graduate. Once accepted into the program, high school students complete a core sequence of applied academics and technology courses. In college they are expected to take more advanced course work than the typical community college participant.

Ohio has viewed the involvement of community and technical colleges in tech prep as critical. It also has encouraged community colleges to rethink the way they do business. A very few, like Sinclair, have upgraded the content of their courses and changed their own pedagogy in preparation for the incoming group of high school seniors. For example, Sinclair has created a brand-new program in computer-support services. It has added courses in its industrial engineering and automotive divisions that teach more advanced skills. It has opened two new satellite labs on campus— one in industrial engineering technology, the other in allied health—where high school students and their teachers can come to take courses using equipment that is not available in their home high schools.

The college has reached out to area high schools in other ways. Community college faculty teach courses at the high schools. They have supplied high school teachers with textbooks and college-placement tests to give them a better sense of what is expected of high school graduates. "It's an incredible relationship," says Bill Holden, a high school instructor who teaches industrial engineering at the Greene County Career Center. "Their lab facility is basically my lab facility. Anytime I need to use anything down there, those machines and materials are at our disposal."

In perhaps the strongest sign of support for the program, Sinclair has created an endowment that guarantees free tuition to any tech-prep student who graduates from high school between 1995 and 1997 and chooses to enroll full time at Sinclair. So far, this is a tiny fraction of Sinclair's 20,000-strong student body: By March 1996, there were only 31 tech-prep graduates on campus. But that number was expected to grow to about 500 in the next two years.

Why would Sinclair bother to make such an effort? Tom Carlisle, the chairperson of the Industrial Engineering Technology Program at the college, had both a pragmatic and a philosophical reason. On a philosophical level, he liked the idea of having students apply what they were learning in their academic classes to real-world, manufacturing problems. On a practical level, he needed more graduates.

Companies in the area were so desperate for technicians that his division was offering a night program for existing workers from 10 P.M. to 7 A.M., five days a week. Starting salaries averaged $22,000 a year for machine-tool operators with no experience— and still Sinclair couldn't meet the demand. Sinclair's three-year placement rate for graduates of its electrical engineering program is 80 percent. Its eight-year record for graduates of its manufacturing technology programs is 100 percent.

Carlisle hoped that the tech-prep program would change the trickle of incoming full-time students to a steady flow. "I'm expecting that within the next two or three years, when all these high school programs fill up, they'll be graduating a hundred to a hundred twenty students a year," he said. "If I can just recruit half those students and bring them to Sinclair, my full-time enrollment is probably going to be close to tripled."

It's not just the number of students that Carlisle expects to improve. It's also the quality. About 80 percent of all Sinclair freshmen entering degree programs need to take at least one remedial course in either mathematics or English. Only about 14 percent eventually make it through to graduation. That's an incredibly low percentage and far worse than that for four-year institutions—but not unusual for community colleges in urban areas. By spelling out exactly what students need to know and be able to do in high school before coming to Sinclair, and by attracting better-quality students, Carlisle hopes to see those numbers change dramatically.

In 1995, 86 percent of the high school students who graduated from Miami Valley tech-prep programs enrolled at Sinclair the following fall, and only 10 percent of them needed remedial coursework. Of the 17 students who enrolled in Carlisle's division that first year, seven dropped out—still a higher number than program organizers want. But the remaining 10, Carlisle claims, "are very good. They're just probably the best group of full-time day students I've ever had."

Studies have found that in most tech-prep consortia, changes in curriculum and instruction have been limited to the high schools. Community colleges appear to be waiting for a better class of students to appear on their doorstep before they begin to change the way they operate. But that is not true at Sinclair.

In the 1990s, Sinclair began to experiment with multidisciplinary courses for its students, such as one on the history of technology in Dayton. The college also has developed "capstone" courses—projects that require students to demonstrate what they know and can do by applying knowledge from several fields. In one case, students had to design and start a fictitious business based on their knowledge of plant layout, materials handling, and budgeting. More recently, the college has begun to experiment with products whose design and manufacture the students carry out over several semesters.

The Miami Valley Tech Prep Consortium also is trying to add a work-based component to each of its tech-prep programs, starting in high school. This remains largely a rarity in tech-prep initiatives nationwide, although in the mid-1990s the situation was changing in response to the federal School-to-Work Opportunities Act.

In automotive technology, for example, the consortium has set up a mentorship program in collaboration with the Dayton Area Automobile Dealers Association. In their junior year, high school students begin a series of job shadows at area dealerships. In their senior year, they work at a car dealership making repairs about 20 hours a week, from noon to five P.M. The internships continue while the students are at the community college. Sinclair faculty members provide mentorship training for the technicians who work with the students. Community college faculty also teach a class on "dealership principles" to high school students to prepare them for their experiences in the workplace.

As in engineering, one of the primary motivations for college faculty in the automotive department was to improve the number and preparation of their students. In 1974, an automotive technician needed to be able to read and understand about 5,000 pages of service manuals. Today, he or she needs to understand about 500,000 pages of material. In many new vehicles, computers control as much as 82 percent of the car's functions. "We're finding it more difficult, as time goes on, to find individuals who are prepared enough to take on the curriculum that we give them," says Stephen Ash, the automotive department chairman at Sinclair. "We just don't have a lot of time to teach them how to read, how to analyze, how to do math."

Today Sinclair is one of the few places around the country that have really taken hold of school-to-work from the postsecondary level, although the number of students involved remains small. "It's such an incredible opportunity," says Karen Wells, the vice-president for instruction at the college. "I don't know anyone with just a high school diploma who feels that they have enough education to sustain a career anymore."

When Ponitz looks into the future, he likes to envision an army of technicians marching out of Sinclair, diplomas in hand, who can help fuel Dayton's economic recovery. "Our experience has been if we wait for industry to do some of these things, it won't happen," he asserts. "So we have to be the cheerleaders. And when industry gets involved, we give them lots of cheers, too."

Tri-County Technical College: "If There're No Jobs, There're No People"

Pendleton, South Carolina, nestled in the foothills of the Appalachian Mountains, bears little outward resemblance to Dayton. While the Midwest is still struggling to overcome its Rust Belt image, this northwestern corner of South Carolina is booming and accounts for 50 percent of all manufacturing in the state. In recent years, Michelin, BMW, Robert Bosch, and other foreign companies have established a foothold here, drawn by the state's right-to-work laws, low taxes, and strong technical-college system. A drive south along I-85 from the Greenville-Spartanburg International Airport resembles one endless construction project.

But when it comes to philosophy, Don Garrison, the president of Tri-County Technical College, and David Ponitz are soulmates. Both are tall men who fill up a room with their booming voices, and both see themselves as unabashed champions of economic development. "The reason [this college] was created was economic development," says Garrison, in a deep Southern voice. "That was the need, and that's our birthright. If there're no jobs, there're no people, and if there're no people, there's no community to be served. You don't need a community college unless there's a community to be served. It's that simple."

Sinclair has focused on creating high-quality tech-prep programs starting with a small number of students. In contrast, Tri-County Technical College has worked to instigate changes for all students, based on the assumption that they all will end up in the labor market. Its experiences demonstrate what can happen when higher education gets behind a broad array of school-to-work initiatives, developing curriculum materials, providing technical training and assistance, and cajoling and working with school districts.

In 1985, when Dale Parnell published *The Neglected Majority*, the upstate area of South Carolina was already beginning to feel the pressure for more highly skilled workers. Low-skill jobs in textile factories were disappearing, to be replaced by fewer but more high-skill jobs in a diversified manufacturing base. Garrison had lived in the community all his life. He saw himself as deeply attuned to its needs. He had even begun his career as a high school teacher. But Garrison also was a personal friend of Parnell's. And he knew that Parnell's condemnation of the weak linkages between high schools and community colleges was justified.

"We really stand guilty," Garrison remembered thinking of the relationship between his own college and the surrounding school districts. "I'm going to tell you right here, we weren't fighting, but we really didn't know each other."

So in 1987 Tri-County Technical College created the Partnership for Academic and Career Education (PACE) with seven surrounding school districts and the National Dropout Prevention Center at nearby Clemson University. Its goal is to change instruction across the board—in both high schools and colleges—so that students can see the connection between the classroom and the real world. Tri-County pays for the partnership's full-time executive director, provides a small institutional budget, and gives it free office space. The consortium also has secured nearly $2 million in government and nonprofit grants, and it has attracted more than 50 business partners.

PACE views its role almost totally as technical assistance. "We are a service organization," states Diana Walter, PACE's first full-time executive director. "We impose no policy. We are the support people. In the schools, we have really great people, but sometimes they have no curriculum or instructional materials to work with or the stuff they have is too cumbersome for them to use. So part of what PACE does is to develop materials for seven school districts that are ready to go, easy to use, and the training comes with it."

A small resource room on Tri-County's campus is stacked to the ceiling with curriculum guides, books, training manuals, and articles that PACE has written or acquired for teachers. Teachers also can enroll through PACE in courses that will earn them graduate credits at Clemson University, many of which are taught by local educators.

Wayne Frady, the school-to-work coordinator for the Hamilton Career Center in Oconee County, one of the vocational schools involved in the consortium, says, "Tri-County has been instrumental in guiding or directing the emphasis for our community. While we all, as individual districts, could do very little, by having them and their credibility and their support, we've been able to get a lot done."

Most of the local middle schools now expose students to careers through business speakers and visits to companies. High school students can select from a variety of applied academic courses in addition to a more traditional college-preparatory curriculum. With the consortium's help, most high schools are moving to replace less demanding "general education" classes with applied academics in mathematics, science, and English—a shift now required by state law. Depending on the school district, students also can choose among career academies, community-service projects, internships, apprenticeships, and job-shadowing experiences that put them into the workplace. Many of these initiatives still are not available throughout the PACE system; others are available only to small numbers of students.

In 1992, Pickens County began a youth-apprenticeship program in electronics in collaboration with four local employers, one of which was Ryobi Motor Products. Both college and high school students spend about 20 hours a week at the work site. Tri-County and high school faculty collaborated with employers to determine the competencies that students will learn on the job. In 1993 the program was expanded to include business and automotive technologies. About 16 business partners now provide placements for about 20 young people.

The Robert Bosch Corporation also sponsors a two-year apprenticeship program in general engineering technology. High school seniors take all of their courses at Tri-County Technical College. The students are paid for a full 40-hour workweek, whether they are in school or at work, and earn both an associate degree and a journeyman's certificate within one year of high school graduation.

Tri-County also has begun to modify its staffing to support students who participate in work-based learning at the postsecondary level. Within each technical division, it has assigned a faculty adviser who monitors students at the work site and keeps track of their progress. Butch Merritt coordinates work-based learning for the college and also identifies high school students who are in work placements, such as coops and apprenticeships, and helps ease their transition to the technical college. Merritt helps them apply for scholarships, works out their class schedules, keeps in touch with them during their first few months on campus, and meets with them several times a year to offer seminars on work-related topics.

Dale Campbell, a first-year college student in engineering graphics technology, first met Merritt during his senior year at Palmetto High School. He had begun taking classes at the vocational center during his junior year because "I was mainly interested in finding out how things work." During his senior year, he began a cooperative-education placement with the Torrington Company, a manufacturer of car suspensions and steering components. He worked there about 20 hours a week and received high school credit.

Merritt helped Dale apply for a scholarship that enabled him to attend college, and he met with him regularly during the first few months of class. He also devised a schedule that would enable Dale to continue working for the Torrington Company about 25 hours a week while he attended school. "I'm always on the go, but it's neat how it all works together," Dale told me. "What I learn at work, I turn around and carry back to school. And what I learn here, I carry back there. My goal now," he said, "is to finish up college and get my degree and do drafting and design as a career, and possibly go back to school and become an engineer one day."

But Dale's experiences also highlight the drawback of the consortium's broadly focused, systemwide approach: In some instances, change has been wide but not deep. Dale's high school has yet to implement all of the changes that others have made within the consortium. And Dale took many of the low-level academic courses that PACE and the state of South Carolina would like to replace: He stopped taking science after a general science course in grade 10, and his most challenging mathematics class he described as "business math." Not surprisingly, Dale had to enroll in a remedial mathematics course when he arrived on campus.

Like Sinclair, Tri-County is teaching more advanced skills to students who do arrive on campus better prepared. But it has not created separate, advanced courses for tech-prep students, as Sinclair has done. Instead, students who arrive on campus with some community college credits under their belt can graduate early. Or they can earn "advanced technology certificates," additional credentials beyond the regular associate degree that provide them with more specialized training. These certificates also are available to adult students and are identifiable on college transcripts.

"This approach addresses our need for advanced skills in a cost-effective and less traumatic manner than redesigning associate degree programs," says Walter. "It helps us deal with the fact that the number of high school graduates entering with advanced standing often is not high enough in any given curriculum, or consistent enough from one year to the next, to justify and sustain a major overhaul of associate degree programs."

By 1993–94 more than 5,700 students were enrolled in applied academic courses across the PACE consortium. A June 1995 evaluation of PACE found that, compared with students in other area high schools, students in schools that had been active in the consortium had better attitudes about high school; rated their courses as more structured, challenging, and relevant; and described less lecturing and rote memorization. Students in these schools also were more optimistic about their chances of succeeding after high school. But the study found no evidence that PACE had led more students to secure mid-level technology jobs or to attend Tri-County Technical College.

Walter, the former executive director, says that a higher percentage of high school graduates in the Tri-County area attend technical colleges within one year after graduation than in any other region in the state. She credits this, at least in part, to PACE's efforts. Ironically, only 50 percent of these students initially choose to attend Tri-County instead of one of the other technical colleges in South Carolina. Within four or five years after high school graduation, however, Tri-County enrolls nearly one third of all local high school graduates. This suggests that some students are working for a few years prior to entering college.

The Barriers to Greater Involvement

Maine, Ohio, South Carolina—these three very different communities all demonstrate the potential role that higher education can play in preparing young people for the workplace. But there also are substantial barriers to forging stronger connections between high schools and postsecondary institutions.

First, like businesses, colleges want to see a return on their investment. In this case, that translates into higher student enrollments or better-prepared students as a result of closer collaboration with high schools. So far, there is little evidence to suggest this is happening. A number of school-to-work programs—including the Cornell Youth Apprenticeship Demonstration Project, the Kalamazoo Education for Employment Consortium, the National Academy Foundation, and ProTech—report college-going rates above 80 percent for their graduates. But these young people are going off to a wide variety of colleges and universities, not just those that have participated actively in the program. Higher-education institutions that want to attract these graduates may have to provide more direct incentives, such as the free tuition offered by Sinclair and the Maine Technical College System.

Second, many tech-prep programs have focused on signing articulation agreements between local high schools and community colleges. Through articulation agreements, students can earn college credit for courses taken in high school that cover the same content as college courses. The agreements are meant to avoid duplication between high school and college curriculum and to give students the option of graduating from college in less time.

But most articulation agreements are reached on a course-by-course basis, in dozens of individual negotiations between local high schools and a neighboring community college. This time-consuming procedure does not result in coherent programs of study, such as those at Sinclair. Moreover, colleges have few incentives to encourage students to use the credits to graduate early, since the institutions then lose tuition. Studies suggest that few students actually use articulation credits gained from individual high school courses. One problem is that students don't know they can because the option has been so poorly publicized. Another problem is that community colleges have required students to jump through numerous, often complicated hoops to gain such credits.

Rather than focusing on expanding articulation agreements, community colleges and high schools need to focus on more ambitious strategies that would cause their teachers, counselors, and students to interact in more substantive ways. These might include bringing high school students onto community college campuses, getting college staff out into high schools, and arranging joint staff development for their faculty.

Third, college presidents may have even less leverage than high school principals or district superintendents to promote school-to-work within their own facilities. Many decisions within community colleges and universities are made by individual departments and their faculties. University professors cannot be mandated to work with high schools or employers or to change their teaching methods. In the colleges that I visited, some department chairmen were very enthusiastic about and engaged in school-to-work initiatives, but other faculty members were barely aware that the efforts existed. Very few places have committed the additional resources and incentives that would encourage college faculty to engage in such work.

"If you're going to do it right," says Tom Carlisle of Sinclair Community College, "you ought to have college faculty going out to the high schools every once in a while, and you ought to have high school students coming to the colleges for projects and demonstrations. . . . It takes a lot of work. It's not easy. And it's not cheap. It's like anything else. It's an investment. The colleges have to put some money and time and facilities into it."

Fourth, the flexibility of community colleges may work against the creation of carefully sequenced, rigorous school-to-work programs, a point made by Richard Kazis, the vice-president for policy and research at Jobs for the Future. On two-year campuses, more than two thirds of students and over half the faculty are part time, making it hard to design coherent programs. Colleges also get the lion's share of their funds from student enrollments, not the quality of education students receive. So colleges have an incentive to create large, introductory lecture classes and a disincentive to create smaller, more advanced classes in the technical areas that cost more.

It's also important to note the vast differences among institutions of higher education in size, quality, and emphasis. Although some two-year colleges, like Sinclair, have vibrant technical-training programs, others are primarily small transfer institutions with few occupational offerings and weak ties to local companies.

Finally, admission to college is only the first step toward getting a degree. One of the biggest problems in postsecondary education is not getting students in but keeping them. Many community college students drop out within their first six months, and their course taking reflects the same lack of focus as in high school.

School-to-work initiatives have taken a number of steps to improve the transition to higher education. Many require high school students to take at least one college-level course before they graduate, so that they become familiar with college-level expectations. A number—including the Kalamazoo Education for Employment Consortium, ProTech in Boston, Maine Career Advantage, and Tri-County Technical College—also provide support groups or advisers to students during their first year in college to help them make the transition.

In the 1980s, School & Main, a department of the New England Medical Center's Health Institute, designed a successful national initiative known as Career Beginnings. It helped low-income and underachieving high school students set career and academic goals and work to attain them. Local consortia of high schools, colleges, and employers provided these young people with adult mentors, summer job experiences, and workshops focused on academic skills and college planning. Over a 10-year period, 95 percent of Career Beginners graduated from high school, and of these, 80 percent went on to postsecondary education.

But it soon became apparent that, once in college, Career Beginners ran into difficulties that could compel them to drop out. So in 1990, School & Main launched an ambitious initiative to improve college retention rates for young people called Higher Ground. Over four years, eight colleges and universities in six states began projects based on the Higher Ground model. The model includes a college orientation the summer before the freshman year, individual and group tutoring, faculty and peer mentoring to help students develop one-on-one relationships at the college, and career exploration and planning. The latter ranges from job shadowing and community service to paid career internships.

By 1996, more than 800 primarily poor and minority students had participated in such activities. An evaluation of Higher Ground found that the participants were less likely to drop out of college than carefully chosen comparison groups. The approach increased retention by about 15 percent over what it otherwise would have been. In the spring of 1993, for example, 84 percent of Higher Ground participants who had entered college in 1990, 1991, or 1992 remained in college compared with 67 percent of the comparison groups. In the spring of 1994, 63 percent of Higher Ground students were still in college, compared with 48 percent of the comparison groups.

Parental Resistance

The biggest obstacle to creating closer linkages between high schools and community colleges may be parents.

In many ways, community colleges suffer from the same image problems as vocational education. About one third of high school graduates who proceed directly to higher education enter community colleges. Yet few aspire to a two-year degree. The majority intend to transfer to a four-year institution. "Two-year and community colleges are looked at as a safety net," complains Diana Walter of PACE, "but rarely as something one would choose purposefully."

Particularly in South Carolina and Ohio, where the tech-prep initiative has been heavily associated with vocational schools, it has been hard to shatter that image. This is true even though the programs have tried to sell themselves as another form of preparation for higher education, rather than as options for the non-college-bound. "Another way to go to college," trumpets the brochure for the Miami Valley Tech Prep Consortium, "a technical program plus college level academics taught the applied way."

PACE calls tech prep "the *other* right choice" and stresses that students will have the chance to earn college credit while still in high school, giving them a leg up on their college careers. "We have avoided like the plague calling this a vocational program," says Tom Carlisle, of Sinclair in Ohio. "We call it a college-level, college-preparatory program, because it is. We are preparing students to go into a college curriculum."

But do these programs really keep the pathway to a four-year degree open? That is a harder question to answer. Many high school tech-prep programs encourage students to take "applied academics" courses in mathematics, science, and English in place of traditional college-preparatory curricula. Theoretically, these classes teach equally rigorous content by using more concrete experiences, problems, and projects drawn from the workplace and the community. But it is not clear that the classes are always challenging. Many four-year institutions do not yet recognize applied courses as meeting their admission requirements. This means that if students change their minds and decide to attend a four-year college immediately after high school, they could have trouble getting accepted or would have to take additional course work.

In 1994, South Carolina passed a law requiring institutions of higher education to recognize applied academic courses as meeting their admission requirements, unless they could provide a valid reason not to do so. The University of Wisconsin system and the Oregon state system of higher education have gone one step further. They are working on performance-based standards for college admission. These would base admission on what students know and can do, rather than the course titles they sat through in high school. If such efforts succeed, they could give students more flexibility—and recognition—for participating in work-based learning and other nontraditional programs without worrying that they had jeopardized their chances to attend a four-year college. Such standards also could help reduce the need for remedial education in college by ensuring that students have actually learned the content of their high school courses.

To really deal with the concerns of parents and students, however, school-to-work systems will have to ensure that young people who begin their technical training in two-year institutions can transfer to four-year programs. It must be absolutely clear what these young people will have to do to enter the university, and that option must remain open.

At present, many technical degrees are dead-end. The technical credits that students earn will not transfer to a four-year institution. In 1996, Wisconsin's Gov. Tommy Thompson was lobbying hard for the University of Wisconsin system to recognize a technical degree from a two-year college as equivalent to the first year of a university education, so that students would not have to start their college education over again if they decided to pursue a B.A.

Another effort, spearheaded by Johns Hopkins University and five community colleges, is trying to ensure that the degree young people earn from a community college is recognized by employers hundreds or even thousands of miles away. With the support of the National Science Foundation and the Alfred P.

Sloan Foundation, employers from the manufacturing sector and educators from community colleges have been trying to devise a two-year associate degree in high-performance manufacturing. The goal is to equip students with broad-based competencies that will continue to be useful as the technology evolves or as the graduates change jobs and employers. The curriculum includes an eight-week work-based experience. The core of the degree will be constant across all of the community colleges that offer it and will prepare students to continue to a B.A. Each community college must work with a local four-year college on the effort.

European Parallels

The movement to combine technical training with postsecondary studies is occurring worldwide, not just in the United States. As employers demand higher skills, students everywhere want access to a university education.

In Germany, more young people are choosing to combine a university education with an apprenticeship. Between 1985 and 1994 the proportion of university students who also had completed apprenticeships grew from 21 percent to 30 percent. Many students are choosing to earn an *Abitur*, a diploma that qualifies them for the university, before they enroll in an apprenticeship program. As a result, the average age of apprentices is rising.

To maintain the attractiveness of the Dual System, Germany is trying to make it easier for apprentices to make the transition to higher education. At a Mercedes-Benz plant that I visited in Stuttgart, for example, most of the second-year apprentices in industrial mechanics were attending school on Saturdays so that they would be able to continue their postsecondary education after their apprenticeships ended. In 1995 the government officially recognized a new form of postsecondary education, a three-year program known as a *Berufsakademie*, or professional academy.

Students must have an *Abitur* diploma to enter one of these programs, which alternate months spent at the workplace with months spent in school. The graduates will earn the equivalent of the bachelor of science degree now provided by a *Fachhochschule,* or technical university, but with even more firm-based training.

Great Britain recently has created General National Vocational Qualifications (or GNVQs) for students in upper-secondary school. These are designed to be the equivalent of A-level exams, which are required for university entrance, but in a broad career area. They are currently offered or planned in 14 fields ranging from leisure and tourism to science.

In Denmark the fastest-growing programs combine theoretical and technical studies. In 1990 Denmark passed legislation creating two new pathways through upper secondary school. Students who pass a higher technical exam or a higher commercial exam qualify for admission to engineering or advanced commercial courses or to a university. But they also receive more practical training than young people who attend a traditional "*gymnasium.*" "Yesterday, we told young people it's very important to be a skilled worker—a smith, and so on," the vice-chairman of one technical-college board told me. "Tomorrow, I think we will tell them that you can become an engineer, a dentist, a doctor. The *first step* in your career could be to become a skilled worker."

Creating Opportunity

We can no longer afford to tell any student that a high school education is sufficient for a lifetime. We need to tell students: Sure, you can enter the workplace right after high school. But at some point, probably sooner than you think, you will need to continue your education. Today all students need to master the academics that will permit them to go on to college if they choose, pursue further education and training beyond high school, or re-educate themselves for new careers in the future.

There is abundant evidence that the skills demanded by the new economy are rising. It is true that most new jobs created in the past decade have been in low-wage industries, especially in the booming service sector. And this trend is expected to continue at least through 2005. But this overall pattern misses the upskilling *within* occupations and industries.

John H. Bishop, an economics professor at Cornell University, argues that Bureau of Labor projections during the 1980s consistently underestimated the growth of managerial and professional jobs and overestimated the growth of lower-skill jobs. That's because low-wage classfications such as "services" include waitresses and janitors, but they also include such new positions as computer-network administrators. Bishop asserts that the most rapidly growing occupations require above-average skills and training. Managerial, professional, technical, and high-level sales jobs accounted for 67 percent of the 6,728,000 jobs created between November 1989 and November 1994, he notes. These occupations now account for 37.6 percent of all workers.

According to the Bureau of Labor Statistics, in 1990 more than two thirds of the 30 fastest-growing occupations had a majority of workers with education and training beyond high school. The same was true for nearly half of the 30 occupations adding the most jobs in absolute numbers. Studies of well-paying technical jobs also have found that the educational requirements for those jobs are rising.

In addition, there is evidence that workers with higher academic achievement, as measured by test scores, earn more. According to the U.S. Department of Education, 28-year-old workers who scored in the top quartile on a battery of tests in mathematics, science, and reading comprehension had a lower unemployment rate and higher earnings than other workers.

Richard J. Murnane, an education professor at Harvard University, and Frank Levy, an economics professor at the Massachusetts Institute of Technology, analyzed longitudinal data for two sets of high school graduates. They found that young people with higher basic mathematics and reading skills earned more in the labor market. Moreover, the wage advantage associated with higher basic skills increased significantly between 1978 and 1986. "These results demonstrate that in the economy as a whole, mastery of basic cognitive skills plays a larger role than it did twenty years ago in determining which high school graduates are able to find jobs by their mid-twenties that pay middle-class wages," they concluded.

Many economists believe that changes in technology, often related to computer use, have shifted the demand for labor away from unskilled workers and toward those with relatively high intellectual abilities. People who use a computer at work, for example, now earn on average 10 to 15 percent more than those who do not. Some economists attribute much of the rising wage inequality in this country to the shift in favor of the most skilled workers. Although we can argue about the degree of upskilling in the economy, the past two decades have shown a steady but clear trend in this direction.

It's also clear that no job is safe for the lifetime of a worker. Everyone has to be prepared to find a new job—or at least to acquire brand-new capabilities within their existing job—to remain employed. This suggests that learning, at work and in higher-education institutions, will become a lifetime endeavor. In the future, says Rosabeth Moss Kanter, economic security will not come from being employed but from being "employable": "No matter what changes take place, persons whose pool of intellectual capital or expertise is high are in a better position to find gainful employment with the current company, with another company, or on their own."

Finally, there's a moral argument to be made. Improving the knowledge and skills of young people certainly does not guarantee that the jobs will come. But no educator or parent wants to consciously prepare a young person for a low-wage, low-skill occupation. If education is to benefit the individual and to change society, not just to reproduce it, then educational institutions must be on the side of upskilling.

Instead of thinking about school-to-work as a single transition that happens at age 18, we need to think about school-to-work as creating stepping stones for students, in which one step can always lead to another, as long as students are willing to put in the time and effort to learn. In structuring school-to-work systems, therefore, we need to be careful that we are expanding students' opportunities for further education, not limiting them. I particularly worry about state laws that require students to choose between "college-prep" and "tech-prep" pathways at age 16. Unless we are vigilant in ensuring that the content and the expectations in both pathways are rigorous—and that colleges and universities recognize this—we could end up reinventing a new and better sorting machine without retaining the flexibility for students to change their minds. In the future, much, if not most, technical training will take place in community colleges and other postsecondary institutions, not in high schools. And many students will want to pursue their education beyond that point.

"The fact is that effective education for 'work' and for 'college' is best conducted in much the same way," says Theodore R. Sizer, the chairman of the Coalition of Essential Schools, "and therefore we need not make wrenching decisions about career paths for any students during the high school years."

Particularly in a democratic society such as ours, the decision about who goes to college must remain firmly in the hands of students and their parents. And the fundamentally democratic vision of education as the avenue of opportunity must remain intact.

CHAPTER 5

The New Frontier: Regional School-to-Work Strategies

$\mathcal{I}$ ndividual schools and companies have demonstrated that school-to-work can offer a powerful new way of educating young people in America, one that combines a rigorous academic education with learning on the job. But even large companies have started school-to-work small, employing only a handful of students. Moreover, when a business pulls up stakes or downsizes, an entire program can wither overnight.

Preparing large numbers of young people for tomorrow's workplaces requires that far more employers participate. It also necessitates looking beyond a sole focus on apprenticeships, which will never serve more than a fraction of American youth, to a more broad-based definition of school-to-work. What is needed is a system rather than a handful of programs limited to a small number of schools and companies.

The numbers are daunting but not insurmountable. Today there are somewhat more than 5 million juniors and seniors enrolled in public high schools. Not all of these students would be involved in work-based learning even if the movement spread like wildfire, but many would. That's a lot of students. But there are over 20 million businesses in the United States. If a large fraction of companies were involved in school-to-work initiatives of various kinds, there would be plenty of opportunities for students at varying levels of intensity. In Germany, only 20 percent of companies provide apprenticeship slots. Yet these companies provide apprenticeships for 70 percent of German young people. In all the European systems, 80 percent of the learning opportunities in the workplace are provided in small and medium-size firms.

Getting a large fraction of companies involved, however, will require a fundamental change in business attitudes. Instead of waiting on the sidelines until young people finish their formal education, employers will have to take greater responsibility for shaping what that education looks like. They will have to define what they want young people to know and be able to do, accommodate student placements on a regular basis, and recognize and reward employees who spend time teaching and working with young people and schools.

There is a huge gap in organizing the employer community in the United States. In European countries like Germany and Denmark, all employers must belong to "chambers," industry organizations that help, among other things, operate the apprenticeship system and ensure that it meets industry's needs. Nothing similar exists in this country. Our local chambers of commerce are voluntary organizations. They typically focus more on lobbying and on business recruitment than on preparing the future workforce. There are over 20,000 trade and industry associations in the United States, representing much of industry. But education and training are rarely their top priority.

This chapter looks at one of the most promising approaches for bringing more employers to the table. It focuses on regional or community-wide strategies that reach out to employers as a group and give them a unified voice in education and training. Each of the communities profiled here has begun to make changes in schools necessary to accommodate a larger role for business. Each has gone beyond serving a few dozen students, although they still reach only a fraction of the total student population. Each has a strong intermediary organization that can connect educators with employers and troubleshoot when problems arise. This chapter discusses three regional alliances—in Tulsa, Oklahoma; Boston; and Austin, Texas—to highlight the similarities and differences between their approaches. The final part of the chapter describes the various ways in which companies can become involved in school-to-work and some of the lessons learned thus far.

Tulsa: Supporting Champions

Tulsa has always been a private-sector town. It was built on oil—the black gold that in the 1920s made this city the "oil capital of the world." Even today, its wide downtown streets feature ornate turn-of-the-century buildings erected by private philanthropists who pumped their money from the ground.

When the oil industry collapsed in the 1980s, Tulsa was hit hard. But since then it has been making a comeback. The town has rebuilt its economy around aerospace, telecommunications, and manufacturing. One of its largest manufacturing subsectors is a combination of the old and the new: metalworking.

By the late 1980s, some metalworking companies were having trouble finding employees skilled enough to operate their increasingly sophisticated equipment. That was certainly true of Hilti Inc., a multinational company specializing in products for the construction industry, including hand-held electronic tools;

high-load fasteners for attaching walls, floorboards, and ceilings; and devices for shooting nails into steel and concrete. Hilti's managers noticed that nonsupervisory workers in the United States could be trained to operate individual pieces of machinery, but they lacked the broad foundation skills that would enable them to move easily from one piece of equipment to another or to troubleshoot problems as they arose. Moreover, Hilti could see itself plagued by labor shortages far into the future.

The company's headquarters are in Liechtenstein, a tiny principality sandwiched between Austria and Switzerland. So for Hilti's top management, an apprenticeship system was second nature. In the spring of 1990, Hilti officials invited the mayor of Tulsa and a group of local businessmen affiliated with the Metropolitan Tulsa Chamber of Commerce to tour its Liechtenstein facilities, including its training center. The outcome was that a group of manufacturers, spearheaded by Hilti, agreed to work with the chamber to develop a metalworking apprenticeship modeled after those in Europe.

They found their champion in Wayne Rowley, who was then the director of new business development for the chamber. Short and barrel-chested, Rowley is feisty as a game hen, with a studied Oklahoma twang. But his good-ole-boy mannerisms hide a keen sense of opportunity. He saw in the proposal from Hilti a chance to do more than establish a few metalworking apprenticeships. He spied a chance to develop the kind of workforce that would attract many different businesses to Tulsa—and keep them there.

Rowley devoted most of the next two years to nurturing the project. In 1992 the chamber created a separate, nonprofit entity to coordinate the apprenticeship program. Known as "Craftsmanship 2000," its board included representatives from six manufacturing companies and American Airlines. It also included representatives from all of the key stakeholders in Tulsa: the chamber, the office of the mayor, the city's public schools, the Tulsa

Technology Center (part of the state's separate system of vocational education), and Tulsa Junior College. In 1992 the U.S. Department of Labor gave the program $250,000 as one of 10 youth apprenticeship grants nationwide.

The program began with a structure much like a tech-prep program, but with a strong work-based component. It prepared young people for the metalworking trades through a four-year apprenticeship that began in the eleventh grade and culminated with an associate's degree. Every year except the first included some in-plant training.

At the beginning the program was a Cadillac model. Employers paid students for their time at work and in school—at a cost of more than $10,000 per student each year—and students could earn additional bonuses for good performance. Working with industry, educators designed a new curriculum that was co-taught by a team of academic and occupational teachers. Instruction took place at the Tulsa Technology Center, which serves both teenagers and adults, instead of at the high schools. At the request of employers, apprentices attended school for 220 days a year, instead of 175. The school day also was extended until five P.M. and individual classes could run as long as four hours.

By 1993 the program was beginning to show some success. Ben Boren, a big, easygoing student, was one of the original apprentices. "I really didn't have anything going for me in high school," he told me. "I just saw no future in it." Boren played football—but not very well. Other than that, he knew a little about drywalling from helping his father on the job. At school, he was struggling to maintain a C average. School subjects just didn't interest him.

By his second year in Craftsmanship 2000, Ben was making straight A's. "Out here," he told me in the laboratory at the Tulsa Technology Center, "I can see how physics, algebra, trigonometry relate to the machine shop. The courses were applied and they related to my skills. That made it a lot easier for me to understand."

In 1996 he graduated from Tulsa Junior College with a 3.0 average in his academic subjects and a 4.0 average in his technical classes— and a full-time job at Hilti.

The program was a good start, but Rowley saw it only as a prototype—and an expensive one at that. To attract more employers, Craftsmanship 2000 reduced the apprenticeship from four years to three, so that students earn only one year toward their associate's degree. Employers no longer pay for the time students spend in class; academic instruction in mathematics, English, and science has been moved back to the high schools; and the program has been broadened to include industrial maintenance and welding. By 1996, Craftsmanship 2000 had reduced the cost to employers to less than $5,000 per student each year, essentially the cost of hiring a part-time worker and paying for insurance.

Even so, the program remained small, limited to 16 new students a year. Only four additional employers agreed to sponsor apprentices between 1992 and 1996. For Tulsa to provide school-to-work experiences for large numbers of high school students, something else was needed.

In 1994 the chamber decided to use the same basic infrastructure to expand into other industries. It rechristened the non-profit corporation "Career Partners Inc.," to reflect its new focus, which was to expand school-to-work to at least 10 industries by the end of the decade. Like Craftsmanship 2000, each industry cluster has its own partnership of businessmen, community leaders, and educators to develop the curriculum and design the program. The board of Career Partners Inc. includes representatives from each educational institution and a business representative from each of the industry clusters. The board sets policy, raises funds, promotes school-to-work, and serves as the employer of record for the students.

The goal of Career Partners Inc. is to make some combination of school-based and work-based learning available to all 6,000 Tulsa seniors by the year 2000. "We're saying to business, we don't want you griping anymore about the schools," Rowley told me. "You'd better communicate what you want now or forever hold your peace."

By 1996 the strategy had succeeded in significantly expanding the scope of school-to-work in Tulsa. In addition to metalworking, Career Partners Inc. had launched programs in health care, small business and entrepreneurship, and transportation. Additional programs in international studies and telecommunications were on the drawing board. In total, these programs served about 460 students and involved about 50 local companies. It was still a tiny piece of the pie, but it was a significant step forward in scaling up the school-to-work effort.

"What the chamber did initially was serve as a catalyst," explained Jenny Auger Maw, the vice-president of organizational development at Hillcrest Medical Center and the chair of the health-care partnership. "They found people willing to be champions, and then they supported them."

"Hilti probably would have had a tough time to make a program like this happen without the chamber," agreed Karl-Heinz Gaertner, the vice-president for manufacturing at Hilti. "There would have been no community or school involvement. We probably would have been on our own to design the program, but never with the impact we had together as a group."

The staff at Career Partners Inc. schedule meetings, take the minutes, distribute school-to-work materials, provide clerical and secretarial support, and serve as a buffer between businesses and the schools. Participating employers pay the partnership once a year. The partnership purchases workers' compensation and liability insurance, which reduces the bureaucratic burden on participating companies.

Even so, getting the various programs started was not without its difficulties. In 1993 Tulsa's school superintendent asked the chamber to work with McLain High School, one of the lowest-performing schools in the district. After some initial discussions, the school system agreed to create a career academy in health and biological sciences at the school. By 1994 the committee had launched a pilot program with a hand-selected team of teachers. It had secured a federal grant to develop the curriculum, installed thousands of dollars of new computer equipment, and provided teachers with training. About 200 students in grades 9–12 signed up for the academy for the following school year. Then a change in leadership at the high school threatened to bring the program to a screeching halt. By the fall of 1995, scheduling difficulties had enabled only 65 students to enroll in one health-related class, and only a handful were participating in internships. It was only after Career Partners Inc. intervened and scheduled a series of meetings between the superintendent, the chamber president, the school principal, and Auger Maw that a compromise was reached for keeping the academy at McLain. Without the chamber's intervention, Auger Maw says, businesses would have walked. "The school system operates very differently from business," she explained. "What the chamber does nicely is act as translator."

The chamber also has tapped its existing networks to reach out to employers, particularly small businesses. Of the chamber's 2,800 members in 1996, approximately 86 percent had 50 or fewer employees. The chamber has an active small-business council, as well as a small-business hotline. When Career Partners Inc. decided to create a program in "American Business" that would focus on entrepreneurship, it went first to the small-business council and asked for help. Lynn Martin, the owner of Gourmet on the Go, a local catering company, agreed to chair the committee and recruited about a dozen other companies to participate.

"Our philosophy is to let business tackle business," said Rowley. "If I am going to have to go out there and sell every businessperson on this, I can't do it. There's not enough of me to go around. But if I can line up the first eight or ten companies and then say, 'Okay guys, this is your responsibility,' then I can make this work."

Boston: Beyond Pilot Programs

In Boston the driving force for school-to-work has been the Private Industry Council. For more than 15 years, the council has been working with the school system to improve the prospects for the city's young people. In the past few years, it has tried to move from a handful of model programs to the creation of a school-to-career system that would be available to all youth.

"It's not just about pilot programs anymore," Neil Sullivan, the executive director of the council, told the *Boston Globe* in 1994. "What we're talking about is taking the entire district system and working with area employers to create education and job experiences for thousands of young people."

To understand school-to-work in Boston, you have to go back at least to 1982. That was the year that the business community, dismayed at the poor academic achievement of local high school graduates, negotiated a quid pro quo agreement with the Boston public schools. The schools agreed to reduce the dropout rate and improve daily attendance. The employers pledged to provide summer and after-school jobs for young people and to give priority hiring to public school graduates. Known as the "Boston Compact," the agreement was hailed as a national model for school reform. It stated in clear, measurable terms what all parties were committed to achieve for Boston's youths.

William Spring, the vice-president of the Federal Reserve Bank of Boston and one of the visionaries behind the Compact, said, "In 1982 the business community in a newly reprosperous Boston came to understand that Boston's future would never be any better than Boston's public schools. Make no mistake. While the Compact is famous for getting kids jobs, the reason the businessmen are at the table is because they want the schools to improve."

That initial agreement, which has been renegotiated twice since 1982, has produced concrete results for area students. The first was a summer jobs program that by 1995 employed more than 3,300 Boston youths. The second was a commitment by the Private Industry Council (PIC) and the school system to place a "career specialist" in each high school, who would prepare students for the workplace, help match them with employers, and troubleshoot when problems arose. The third was ProTech, a youth apprenticeship program that began in health care in 1991 and has since expanded to five other fields.

Students in ProTech begin as juniors in high school and can continue through two years of postsecondary education and training. For example, juniors in the health-care program participate in a series of unpaid clinical rotations at one of 12 area hospitals. Beginning in the second semester, they are eligible for part-time jobs during the school year and full-time jobs during the summer. Teachers are urged to relate class material to students' experiences at the work site, and ProTech has contracted with a curriculum developer to help teachers and hospital supervisors write sample lessons. If students enroll in college, many employers provide scholarships. Students who complete a postsecondary degree in a health-care field receive priority hiring when they graduate.

To make the program doable for employers, the PIC hires program coordinators, based in participating schools, who serve as the liaison among the school, the students, and the companies. The coordinators also work with students on basic work-readiness skills. The PIC also employs career and college counselors who work with ProTech students to ease the transition to college. In 1996 the combined cost of these efforts was $1,200 per student per year, supported almost entirely through government and foundation grants. This does not include the employers' contribution to the program, which can be substantial. In 1995 one report estimated that a local hospital contributed $8,892 per student each year for student wages, staff coordination and supervision, and other in-kind contributions.

To sell employers on such a sizable investment, ProTech has stressed employers' long-term self-interests. Hospitals can directly influence the preparation of their entry-level workforce, recruit qualified minority candidates, and help shape school programs. In the late 1980s and early 1990s, this message resonated with area hospitals, which faced such severe labor shortages that they were recruiting nurses and technicians from out of state.

Like many new ventures, ProTech has had a steep learning curve. An initial evaluation of the program published in 1993 found that only a small fraction of Boston's public school students met even its modest admission requirements, namely, a C average and good attendance. During the first year, 40 percent of the students quit the program or were terminated, in part because of academic difficulties. Many were unprepared to function in a work setting, where they would have to follow hospital rules and procedures for everything from dress codes to conduct. The students also complained about the quality of the job rotations, which did not offer enough chances for hands-on learning. The three participating high schools had made minimal changes in curriculum or instruction.

Rather than give up, the program developers began to learn from these mistakes. Working with the participating hospitals, ProTech developed rotation guides, individual training plans, and case studies based on fictitious patients to structure students' on-the-job learning. The PIC hired a curriculum development group to help teachers write instructional units that would integrate health-related material with science, mathematics, and English instruction.

A second evaluation, in March 1994, reflected these slow and steady improvements. ProTech students were taking more rigorous mathematics and science courses than their peers, although their grades were not substantially better. In 1992–93, all 38 ProTech graduates enrolled in postsecondary education, most in a health-related field. Many continued to work in area hospitals while they attended school.

In the fall of 1993, ProTech launched a second program in financial services. In 1994, it expanded into the utilities and communications fields. In 1995, it added environmental services.

By the 1995–96 school year, ProTech was substantially larger than Craftsmanship 2000 or any other youth apprenticeship program nationwide. The program had grown from three high schools to six, from 6 employers to 40, and from 75 students to 450. But it was still reaching only a fraction of the 16,000 students in Boston's public high schools. Moreover, it had failed to penetrate very deeply in the schools. Instructional changes were limited and uneven, and educators largely viewed the program as an add-on.

Like Tulsa, Boston needed to move beyond a pilot program to a system that was capable of serving large numbers of young people. It also needed to help employers make sense of what had become a confusing array of school-to-work initiatives in the city. In addition to ProTech, Boston had several career academies affiliated with the National Academy Foundation, a career-awareness program for middle-school students, and the collaboratives with Fenway Middle College High School described in chapter 2.

When the Boston Compact was renegotiated for the second time in 1994, it included a new challenge to the business community. Employers were asked and agreed to support a school-to-career system. The timing was fortunate. In 1993 the state of Massachusetts passed an education-reform law that abolished the general track and required high schools to develop career pathways organized around broad occupational themes. The act also empowered 16 "regional employment boards," led by the private sector, to develop and help implement local school-to-work plans. In 1994, Boston received a $1.2 million school-to-work implementation grant from the federal government.

As in Tulsa, the PIC's strategy is to organize employers by industry clusters—as it first did in health care—and to pair each industry with a particular group of schools. Each cluster has its own executive committee composed of the vice-presidents of human resources for the participating companies and the school principals. These groups meet quarterly to set policy and evaluate progress. Within each cluster, a committee of work-site supervisors, teachers, and ProTech coordinators meets monthly to hammer out program details. The clusters are responsible for developing a sequence of work-based learning activities for students. These range from paid work experiences to career education, such as job shadowing and mentorships, to full-blown apprenticeships.

A systemwide school-to-career steering committee reflects the power structure in Boston. It is chaired by Thomas W. Payzant, the superintendent of schools, and Dr. J. Richard Gaintner, the chairman of the Conference of Boston Teaching Hospitals. It also includes the presidents or vice-presidents of several local colleges and universities, a representative from each industry cluster, the mayor's chief of staff, and representatives of organized labor and community-based organizations.

The recruitment of companies combines planning and pragmatism. The state has targeted 10 critical or emerging industries in which to develop career pathways in high schools. These employ large numbers of state residents and have a high concentration of well-paying, midlevel jobs. But Boston has also taken a utilitarian approach, often going where opportunity knocks in the search for partners. For example, neither utilities nor environmental services are among the largest employers in the city, but both were ready to work with the schools.

Lois Ann Porter, the original director of ProTech, moved from Alabama to Boston in 1988 to work on Gov. Michael S. Dukakis's presidential campaign. A tall, fast-talking southerner whose accent still lingers despite her years in the north, Porter does not suffer fools gladly. She brought the same hard-driving, pragmatic campaign tactics to school-to-work that she once applied to politics.

"There's no one cut-and-dried reason why we selected these clusters," she told me. "You've got to be flexible. You've got to be realistic. You've got to go where there's a certain level of interest."

In 1996 the PIC decided to step up its recruitment efforts. It hired a team of people with business experience to aggressively recruit new employers for work-based learning experiences. That winter, Boston kicked off a job-shadowing experience for more than 400 students on Groundhog Day. "Come See Your Shadow," the public service announcements enticed employers.

Initially, ProTech had focused on large companies that could employ more students and carry some of the administrative burden for coordinating the program. But it realized that to serve the majority of Boston's young people, it would have to expand its efforts to small and medium-size companies by working with the Greater Boston Chamber of Commerce. Recruiting these small employers has not been easy.

Tom Bryan, a retired Bank of Boston executive hired by the PIC to enlist companies, beat the bushes for three months to recruit 15 small companies for a program in environmental services. To find enough companies to start a program in business services, he predicted, "I'll probably make about 1,100 telephone calls and try to make 80 visits to companies to get the 25 slots that we need." Most small companies hire only one or two students at a time, if they hire at all, and they don't have a human-resources department to help coordinate a program.

The PIC also has worked with the Boston Public Schools to deepen its efforts in the schools. It now focuses only on schools that want to change. In 1994 the school system designated school-to-career coordinators at four high schools that were willing to create smaller units organized around career themes. This structure enables students to take at least some of their core academic courses together, making it easier for teachers to track students' progress and to plan lessons that integrate school-based and work-based learning. The coordinators are all experienced teachers who are responsible for working with their colleagues to develop new curriculum and programs. In 1995 the Boston Public Schools agreed to institutionalize the costs of these positions as part of its budget, signaling its commitment to school-to-work.

Some of the needed changes in the schools are emerging at Madison Park Technical Vocational High School in Roxbury, the only public vocational technical high school in the district. The entire high school has been restructured into three career academies in commerce, allied health, and craft and technical fields, along with a separate academy for freshmen. The building, which takes up a full city block, now houses about 2,000 students, who are almost lost in its cavernous recesses.

Senior Kwesi King, an apprentice in utilities and communications, works in fiber-optics technology at NYNEX, New England's regional telephone company. His job as a special-services technician entails working on the installation, maintenance, and repair of high-tech fiber-optic wires in downtown Boston. "It was a great opportunity for me to get started in my life," Kwesi told me one day in December, as he led me around the banks of high-tech equipment at NYNEX's downtown facility, a tool belt slung around his waist. Before becoming involved in ProTech, Kwesi was just a regular student, he says, with ideas about becoming an electrician. By his senior year at Madison, he was pulling down straight A's and applying to college, where he planned to major in computers. Kwesi's mentor at NYNEX, Steve Campbell, had become a close personal friend, who attended Kwesi's sporting events, kept in touch with his teachers, and frequently lectured Kwesi about the importance of his schoolwork.

NYNEX's program has the strong support of the International Brotherhood of Electrical Workers Local No. 2222, an affiliate of the AFL-CIO. But gaining that support was not a foregone conclusion. At the time the program began, NYNEX was in the midst of a bitter four-month strike and massive reductions in the workforce. Joan Rahavy, NYNEX's director of market-area human resources for Massachusetts and Rhode Island, said, "It was not a situation where someone would stand up and say, 'I would really like to take students into my environment.'"

Nonetheless, union leaders were able to look beyond the immediate circumstances and into the future. They saw an aging union membership and no new blood coming in. So they agreed to sit down with management and jointly craft a program. Edward B. Carle, who has been a union representative for 25 of his 27 years at NYNEX, was put in charge of coordinating the program for the union. "Here was an opportunity where we could not only give back to our union but give back to our community," Carle said. The union agreed that student interns would work alongside a mentor to help complete his or her job assignments, so that there would be no risk that students would replace existing workers. Students would be paid the starting wage for whatever job position they held. And once they began working full time, during the summer, they could join the union and pay union dues of about $3.40 a week. "All of our students are union members," says Carle, "and we don't force them to be union members." In addition, the mentors meet once a month on company time to iron out any problems, and they are able to visit the schools during their work day to collaborate with teachers.

By 1994, NYNEX was hiring again, adding 100 nonmanagement workers to its payroll. In 1996, it hired 600 new technicians and expected to hire several hundred more. NYNEX officials viewed ProTech as an ideal recruitment strategy. Company officials were particularly interested in diversifying their workforce, which was under 3 percent minority, even though NYNEX served many predominantly minority communities.

Karen James Sykes, NYNEX's associate director of human resources for the region, devotes about 20 percent of her time to ProTech, an investment that the company believes is worthwhile. "There is no shortage of people applying for NYNEX positions," she explains, "but there's definitely a shortage of people of color who apply. Many of our operations are in urban areas, where we think it's important to have diversity both for business reasons, for marketing reasons, and because we think it's the right thing to do."

Plus, she adds, "we've had a difficult time attracting young people with the right skill sets for these positions, which are very technical. These are people who actually install telephones, service equipment, work on the network, and are in customer contact positions. The students are learning about the actual job: what the requirements are, what the expectations are. The curriculum is very integrated with the work requirements so that the school is really developing the skills that we need."

In the past, studies of ProTech had criticized the uneven quality of students' work-based placements and the often weak connection back to the school curriculum. Now, through career academies like those at Madison Park, the PIC hopes to deepen the quality of what students are experiencing at school and at the work site, even as it greatly expands their numbers.

Of the seven students in the first graduating class from NYNEX, six planned to enroll in postsecondary education while continuing their connection with NYNEX and one hoped to work for the company full time. Joan Rahavy hopes that eventually all seven will come to work for the company, whether as technicians or managers. "We have always looked at this as a long-term strategy," she explains. "It is also desirable to have management employees who understand the craft and who come up all the way from the entry level." Kwesi had been accepted at Northeastern University. He planned to continue working for NYNEX as a cooperative education student, for which he would gain college credit, and NYNEX would help pay for his education.

Boston's goal is to have 50 percent of the school system's juniors and seniors participating in a structured program that combines work and learning by the year 2000. To monitor progress, the PIC is developing clear, measurable goals for school-to-work. These include increases in business participation; targets for how many students will be served in any given year; implementation by schools of career pathways and school-to-career plans on schedule; targets for the number of teachers involved; and long-term changes in student achievement and employment.

Boston still has a long way to go to create rigorous and meaningful school-to-work experiences for the majority of the city's youths, but it has begun to build an infrastructure that could take it beyond the model-building stage. In doing so it has demonstrated what can be accomplished through a sustained and focused partnership between educators and employers.

Austin: Providing the Glue

Both Tulsa and Boston began with small, high-intensity programs that evolved over time to embrace more employers and industries. In contrast, Austin started by cutting a broad swathe through the world of work.

Like Boston, Austin in the early 1990s suffered from high youth unemployment, low high school graduation rates, and abysmal student test scores. Several influential community groups were prodding city officials to make youth development a top priority. In the spring of 1991 the Greater Austin Chamber of Commerce created a committee to study how to improve the transition from school to work.

Two researchers from the University of Texas at Austin, economist Robert W. Glover and mathematician Kenneth W. Tolo, helped the committee develop a plan. Known as "Bridging the Gap," it proposed creating a school-to-work system in Austin that would be driven by industry needs and organized around industry clusters. Glover speculated that if industry had a primary voice in shaping the system, it would be more likely to participate and would stop waiting on the sidelines until students graduated.

In designing their strategy, Austin officials were heavily influenced by their sister city of Koblenz, Germany. In 1993, Mayor Bruce Todd made a visit to Koblenz to view the German Dual System first-hand. He came back determined to create an American version of apprenticeship and made school-to-work one of the top priorities of the newly elected Austin City Council. In 1993 the city and the chamber helped launch the Capital Area Training Foundation, a nonprofit, industry-led group whose primary mission was to promote school-to-work in the region.

The city pledged to provide about $200,000 a year in seed money for the foundation as well as free office space. Although the chamber maintains close ties to the foundation—its president is chairman of the foundation's board of directors—the foundation is a separate entity. This allows it to receive government grants without exposing the chamber to conflict-of-interest or open-meeting laws.

The mayor challenged the foundation to increase work-based learning opportunities for Austin's youths steadily over the next 10 years, until about half of all 12,500 high school students could be served. He personally convened the CEOs or site managers of area companies in the health-care, high-technology, and hospitality industries to enlist their support. In the fall of 1994, with over $1 million in federal school-to-work grants, the foundation hit the road.

Researcher Robert Glover felt that Austin was ideally suited to launch a school-to-work effort. In 1995 its unemployment rate was near 3 percent, and the number of new jobs was growing twice as fast as the population. In 1993 the Austin area accounted for nearly one quarter of all gains in manufacturing statewide, with much of that growth concentrated in high-tech industries. Texas Instruments, International Business Machines, Motorola, and Advanced Micro Devices all had major plants in and around Austin. Samsung had announced that it would construct a $1.3 billion wafer-fabrication plant that would hire 1,000 workers by 1998.

By 1996 the Capital Area Training Foundation had steering committees under way in health care, high-tech electronics, construction, metalworking, insurance, and consumer-services management. The foundation was working with 14 of the 55 high schools in the region. Employers had provided summer jobs for 218 youths the previous summer and contributed more than $2.5 million in cash and in-kind contributions to the schools, including student wages. In the summer of 1996 the consumer-services management group launched an apprenticeship program in collaboration with the McDonald's Corporation and Northern Illinois State University that initially served about 20 young people, placing them in jobs in area hotels, grocery stores, and restaurants. Thirteen Austin youths also had journeyed to Koblenz to participate in German apprenticeships.

The foundation provided staff liaisons, many of them retired businessmen, to each of the industry clusters to help them develop school-to-work plans. It also assigned staff people to work with individual companies that wanted to launch a program.

Some of the most enthusiastic business partners have come from high-tech industries. Austin has become an international magnet for the semiconductor industry, drawn in part by the region's high concentration of colleges and universities, network of secondary suppliers, and relatively low living costs. By the early 1990s there were more than 800 high-tech companies in the area, employing 85,000 people.

For these companies, quality was everything. If they could not keep pace with the latest innovations, they would disappear. Many of the largest companies already were involved in school-business partnerships. Motorola, for example, provided summer internships for teachers and had experimented with internships for high school students. IBM had adopted the entire Austin Independent School District in the late 1980s as part of a 10-year education-reform initiative launched by the Business Roundtable.

Together, these industries formed a large and active steering committee.

One of the biggest success stories involved Advanced Micro Devices, or AMD. In 1996, AMD was Austin's third-largest high-tech employer, with 4,000 workers. The previous year it had finished construction of a $1 billion wafer-fabrication plant. It anticipated building another new plant every two years. Almost overnight, AMD found itself recruiting around the country for qualified workers. "That had never been done before," recalled Kathrin Brewer, a chemical engineer who at the time was program manager for computer-systems integration. "We had never moved people, and it was very expensive." AMD also was spending millions of dollars on in-house training, including the construction of a computerized training center where employees could come to take self-paced courses while earning an AMD paycheck. Even so, Brewer saw a huge gap between the skills of the existing workforce and what AMD needed.

Then several events converged. Brewer discovered a computer-based training program in first-year electronics. She approached the director of human resources with the idea of installing it in the local community college and hiring students who took the course to work at AMD over the summer. As it happened, the director of human resources had gone on one of several trips to Germany to view the Dual System. He, too, had come back favorably impressed. He put Brewer in touch with the foundation, which was anxious to get something large and visible off the ground in the high schools. AMD's community affairs office also was anxious to refurbish its corporate image after a bruising and unsuccessful campaign to secure a tax abatement from the city in 1994. The result was the "Accelerated Careers in Electronics" program, which began with summer internships for 32 students from Johnston and Del Valle high schools in 1995.

The students participate in paid internships during the summer and part-time work during the school year. Juniors and seniors in high school take 16 hours of college-level credit in industrial electronics at Austin Community College. They also take a principles of technology course at their high schools. In addition to paying students' wages, AMD funds lab equipment and materials for the high schools, instructor salaries, and transportation to and from the community college.

The Capital Area Training Foundation helped the high schools apply for a grant from AMD; it was funneled through the foundation, which contributed $20,000 in matching funds and helped design the program and recruit and screen students.

Allyson Peerman, the director of community affairs for AMD, said, "I would call the foundation the glue, or maybe the catalyst. As a company, when we started looking into this, we were overwhelmed. We were spending an inordinate amount of time sending people to different meetings and not knowing what was going on. The way we made sense of school-to-work, basically, was through the Capital Area Training Foundation."

The program had some growing pains. Because of its rapid start-up, the initial group of work-site mentors had only a vague idea of what they were supposed to do. They received no compensation or recognition for the extra duties that they had taken on, and the prior preparation—and commitment—of their student interns varied widely. Some mentors and students had a very positive experience, but other mentors were overwhelmed by the time and energy that it took to work with a high school student.

Yet despite a bumpy first year, most students were engaged in productive work. They took bacteria samples to measure water quality, conducted statistical analyses of the surface impurities on plant equipment, and analyzed wafers under the microscope to check for defects. Some mentors found the students' work invaluable and were anxious to expand their participation.

Students experienced less success in their academic classes— particularly in the college-level electronics course, where many of them were struggling. As in Boston, this underlined the extent to which students' prior academic preparation needed to be strengthened.

By late 1995, AMD was working with the foundation and the schools to fine-tune the program. It had developed a list of workforce-readiness objectives to teach students before they began working at the company. It planned to schedule regular meetings for mentors and interns during the summer. The company also hired an outside evaluator to assess the program and offer recommendations. Despite weak profits and slow sales in early 1996, the company's commitment to the program remained strong.

AMD also began working to craft a full-fledged apprenticeship program in three areas where it was having difficulty recruiting qualified technicians: ultrapure water, ultra-high-purity piping, and instrumentation and control. The program, which would be limited to high school graduates and incumbent workers, was scheduled to begin in 1997.

The Capital Area Training Foundation has had more difficulty getting school-to-work initiatives up and running in other industries. For example, early attempts to organize the financial community were not successful. In February 1995, Robert Egloff and his wife, Ruth, two experienced apprenticeship consultants from Zurich, Switzerland, moved to Austin to help local companies structure work-site apprenticeships. Egloff, a tall, bearded man with an easy laugh and an outgoing personality, had graduated from an apprenticeship program in banking back in Switzerland. He had worked with financial institutions most of his life. So when he settled in Austin, he immediately contacted some of the local banks to talk about creating an apprenticeship program in the financial sector. "The banks were very impressed," he told me more than a year later, "but nothing came of it. Nobody got back to me. It made me think, why did that happen?"

Egloff concluded that three characteristics were needed for industries to embrace apprenticeships: a deep concern for quality, preferably generated by international competition; a desperate need for qualified people; and enough prosperity to invest in their future workforce while still meeting their current hiring needs. In retrospect he realized that none of these conditions applied to Austin's banks, which in the mid-1990s were caught up in the general wave of mergers and downsizing.

The foundation also had underestimated the amount of time it would have to spend working directly with schools to improve the academic component of school-to-work systems. Initially the foundation anticipated that most of its time would be spent providing technical assistance to companies. But by 1995, much of its technical assistance was school-based. The foundation funded a dozen new career centers in high schools, where students could come for career guidance and counseling. It hired "career specialists" to work in six high schools. Their job was to help develop career pathways in the high schools, staff the career centers, and help schools reach out to industry. The foundation also provided professional development for teachers, purchased textbooks and supplies for classrooms, and revived a defunct program in industrial electronics within several Austin public schools. In addition, it helped the Austin Independent School District structure a grants competition to expand the number of career academies within the city.

Despite these efforts, the foundation made more progress in some of the smaller, outlying school districts than within Austin itself, where a large, urban bureaucracy was slow to embrace school-to-work. In 1995, however, the central office began an initiative to create a career academy in each of the city's 10 high schools. Administrators also mandated that all counselors participate in industry field visits that were arranged by the Greater Austin Chamber of Commerce and the Capital Area Training Foundation. Discussions between the school district and Austin Community College about sharing education and training facilities also got under way.

Lessons Learned

The experiences in Austin, Boston, and Tulsa arose from the unique circumstances and histories of each city. But all three regional initiatives share a number of common strategies that point toward the future of large-scale business involvement in school-to-work:

❧ Each initiative had an independent employer organization that could bring large numbers of businesses to the table.

❧ Each initiative focused on industries that had a clear labor-market need, based on local conditions. For example, the financial community proved to be a strong player in Boston but a reluctant participant in Austin.

❧ To the extent possible, the programs worked with existing business networks and associations. This enabled them to reach more employers simultaneously, particularly small and medium-size companies.

❧ Intermediaries proved invaluable in recruiting schools and employers, raising funds, developing programs and curricula, and coordinating the initiatives. The importance of such third-party players has been emphasized in other research on school-to-work.

❧ The intermediaries provided full-time staff members who were available to work with employers as a group and to provide targeted, technical assistance to individual companies. The Boston PIC placed a ProTech coordinator within each participating high school. In Austin the Capital Area Training Foundation hired Robert Egloff to work with interested firms.

❀ Companies were engaged in ways that went far beyond advice and consent. In each community, employers helped design the programs from the start. They focused on concrete, short-term initiatives as well as long-range planning.

❀ Each community organized employers by industry clusters. The clusters helped recruit businesses, created the critical mass needed to start programs, and provided work-based learning opportunities for students. They also gave industry an organized voice at the table. Even so, the process of organizing and recruiting within these clusters could be quite slow.

❀ Each community set measurable goals for increasing the number of students, companies, and industries involved in work-based learning. Though these goals sometimes had the effect of emphasizing quantity over quality, they resulted in substantial forward movement.

❀ Each community treated its efforts as a work-in-progress. They learned from past mistakes to make their programs better, even as they strove to deepen their connections with the schools.

One danger of industry-led groups is that they will be perceived as yet another band of outsiders telling the schools what to do. This is a very real risk, and it accounts for some of the initial resistance in both Boston and Tulsa. If schools feel their own roles and responsibilities are being usurped, they will not cooperate.

It is no more productive to think about school-to-work as "industry led" than it is to think about it as "school led." All stakeholders must have a voice if it is to be a true partnership. This includes parents, students, and the incumbent workers themselves—whose voices are noticeably absent in shaping many school-to-work initiatives. At the same time, participating businesses need a way to come together and hash out their concerns in a separate forum so that they can approach the schools with a unified voice.

Another obstacle to keeping these efforts alive is money. As much as anything, the intermediaries described in this chapter have been consummate fundraisers, generating more than $2 million each in government financing for their efforts. But government and foundation grants are only a temporary recourse. Somehow, these connecting activities must become self-sustaining.

Innovative ways of funding intermediary activities are beginning to emerge. In 1996, Massachusetts passed a law to provide an ongoing state revenue stream for connecting activities related to school-to-work. If businesses agree to pay student wages and provide mentoring and instruction in the workplace, the public sector will assume the cost of preparing students for the work site and funding connecting activities. To receive state funds, each local partnership must show at least a 2:1 match from the business community in the form of student wages.

Neil Sullivan, the executive director of the Boston Private Industry Council, explained, "You want each player to have a role in creating the funding stream, so that any one player has the power to pull out and destroy everything. That's how you create ownership in a collaborative environment. So you need the school system, you need government agencies, and you need the private sector. And everyone needs to know exactly how much everyone else is committing."

Austin has found another way to provide ongoing funding for school-to-work initiatives. In the spring of 1995 the city of Austin and Travis County approved a tax-abatement plan to attract the construction of new wafer-fabrication plants. The incentives are limited to companies that invest at least $50 million in new plants and equipment and at least $250,000 for each new job created. The agreement calls for 20 percent of a company's property taxes to be set aside for training local residents for up to 10 years.

School-to-work activities, as well as adult training initiatives, are eligible for the new monies.

Tulsa, however, has yet to devise a long-term solution to financing Career Partners Inc.

The Various Faces of Employer Involvement

These three regional partnerships illustrate the many ways in which employers can become involved in school-to-work, beyond just apprenticeships. Employers also provide job shadowing for students; work with teachers to develop school-based projects; and provide work-based experiences for educators during the summer. They have helped develop curricula and have contributed instructional materials and advice. Each community has created industry-led committees that can help set policy and evaluate progress.

In 1996 the National Employer Leadership Council, a non-profit group committed to expanding employer participation in school-to-work, unveiled a new "employer participation model" based on the experiences of its member companies. The model outlines 56 ways in which employers can become involved in school-to-work partnerships, including the following:

❀ They can work directly with students by providing them with information and on-the-job experiences. This can range from one-hour visits to the classroom to talk about their company to formal apprenticeship programs.

❀ They can work with teachers in high schools and colleges to improve their understanding of the workplace and to support classroom activities. Employers can help evaluate school-based projects, serve as consultants for student-operated businesses, and work with educators to develop instructional materials and curricula. Many companies, such as the Boeing Company and Procter &

Gamble, now invite teachers and students into their work sites over the summer to learn about their culture and expectations.

❧ They can change company practices to support new relationships with educators and recognize schools as suppliers of their future workforce. For example, employers can develop a "skill profile" of their workers; share information with schools about the performance of their graduates; consider an applicant's academic transcripts when making hiring decisions; look toward educational institutions as a source of job applicants; and provide recognition and incentives for employees to work with schools and young people.

❧ Employers also can support the development of a school-to-work system through their business and industry associations, their participation in state or regional partnerships, and their collaboration with government to help develop incentives for employer involvement.

Employer incentives also can affect whether students enroll in school-to-work programs and continue their education after high school. In one study of 15 such programs, students reported that the guarantee of continued work-site placements during college, the availability of tuition assistance, and the knowledge that they would likely have a job if they finished their postsecondary education and training all influenced their decisions to enroll in school-to-work programs and complete their education.

One of the founding members of the National Employer Leadership Council is the BellSouth Corporation, the regional phone company for nine states in the Southeast. The company's human-resources staff estimates that BellSouth could reduce its initial selection and training costs at least 20 percent by working with the schools to increase the work readiness of the average job applicant. The corporation has been involved in school-to-work initiatives on a number of fronts. It has created formal internship and apprenticeship programs for students and enabled them to shadow employees on the job. Employees also serve as mentors and go into the classroom to share case studies of how academic subjects are applied at the work site. BellSouth also provides opportunities for teachers to participate in work-based learning.

Lee Doyle, the director of external affairs for BellSouth, said, "I think the largest barrier [to employer involvement] is that the commitment people ask for first is, 'Will you take an apprentice?' They're starting on the wrong end. You don't ask somebody who's never bought a camera before to buy the world's most sophisticated camera. You start them out with something that's real easy and simple and has instant rewards, like a half-day job shadow for students."

Skill Standards

Another way in which employer organizations can help strengthen preparation for work is through the development of skill standards. Skill standards spell out what workers within an industry or cluster of occupations should know and be able to do to succeed on the job. They indicate to employers the skills of job applicants and provide workers with a widely recognized credential. They could improve the quality of career information available to schools, employers, and young people. For example, they could help improve the match between what is learned in school and what is needed on the job by clearly communicating the expectations of employers. They could provide guidance for keeping education-and-training programs current and evaluating their performance.

One of the most obvious distinctions between the United States and its European counterparts is that European countries have national systems of skill standards and certificates. Young people in these nations know what they must learn to enter an occupation, which provides them with the motivation to study hard. Those who succeed receive a national certificate that signals their accomplishments to employers and that they can take from company to company. The development of skill standards provides a forum for educators and employers in these countries to communicate their needs on an ongoing basis.

In contrast, the United States has dozens of individual skill standards and certificates—for everything from auto mechanics to architects—but no system. Our standards-setting efforts are not coordinated at a national level. They frequently differ from one state to another. And they do not cover the full range of industries and occupations.

Many people view the creation of *voluntary* national skill standards and certificates as the first step toward developing an education-and-training system in the United States, as opposed to a collection of fragmented programs. But this will not happen without the participation of employer organizations and industry groups at the state and national level. Toward that end, in 1992 the federal government funded 22 pilot projects to test whether industries in the United States could develop voluntary skill standards. The projects covered industries ranging from printing, metalworking, and electronics to retail, hospitality, and tourism. Of the 22 pilot projects funded so far, the vast majority are led by trade associations or industry groups.

In 1994 the Congress created a National Skill Standards Board to help promote the development of such voluntary efforts. The board is charged with clustering occupations or industries into broad groups that would cover most of the workforce in the United States. In addition, it is supposed to develop a common national framework in which skill standards could be developed.

There is very little research to suggest whether skill standards and certificates will work in the United States. So far, the pilot projects have varied widely in quality. Most have relied upon traditional methods for analyzing jobs, by breaking them down into long lists of discrete skills. Thomas Bailey and Donna Merritt of the Institute on Education and the Economy at Columbia University argue that this approach may not reflect the needs of high-performance companies, whose employees are typically assigned broader and more complex responsibilities. Studies also suggest that many employers do not understand the skill requirements of their non-managerial workforce well enough to communicate them to others.

Moreover, one of the strengths of the U.S. economy is its flexibility. There is a risk that skill standards could diminish this flexibility, by creating barriers to employment and locking in current job practices and descriptions.

Many European systems also are concerned that narrowly defined skill standards will become quickly outmoded and will channel students into rigid job classifications. They are streamlining their standards to focus on broad occupations or industry clusters. In 1991, Sweden developed 14 occupational clusters (plus two university-oriented clusters in the social and natural sciences) around which all school-to-work preparation would occur. Denmark has moved from about 360 clusters down to 86. Scotland has developed a system of skill standards based on modules that young people can mix and match to earn awards in broad industry clusters or to meet the specific needs of employers. Even Germany has reduced the number of metalworking occupations from 37 to 6, with much broader descriptions of responsibilities. Still, employers complain about the glacial pace at which German skill standards change.

Finally, no one knows whether employers in a labor market as decentralized as the United States will really make use of skill standards in hiring workers or in designing their education-and-training programs. Some case studies suggest that in local communities where there are strong relationships between employers and educators, such formal mechanisms may not be needed.

In the absence of national standards, however, many states and communities have been forced to come up with their own skill standards—a repetitive and time-consuming procedure. Patricia Stone, the former manager of corporate education programs for the Bank of America, helped develop skill standards for the banking industry in California. "Companies don't see state lines," she argues. "They do business in regions, which sometimes can be multistate regions. They do business nationally and internationally. So I think that skill standards are best done across an industry, which is a multistate affair. And I think they can be adopted or adapted by a state or a region. I think to reconstruct them region by region or state by state is a waste of money and time and effort. I don't think that it creates the kind of portability or understanding of workforce development that is really global in nature. So it is my hope that industry skill standards continue to be developed nationally, by industry associations. Voluntarily, for sure. But benchmarked against world-class standards."

National Initiatives

Tulsa, Boston, and Austin were fortunate to have a strong chamber of commerce or employer group to act as a broker between the schools and companies. This is not the case in every community.

One question is whether national employer organizations could spur more companies to participate in school-to-work initiatives, in part by encouraging greater activism on the part of their local affiliates. One such effort has been the National Employer Leadership Council. The council was formed by 18 of the nation's leading corporations shortly after passage of the federal School-to-Work Opportunities Act in 1994. Its goal was to further school-to-work efforts in the United States through a peer-to-peer recruitment of corporate leaders. At a kick-off ceremony at the White House with President Clinton in the summer of 1994, Alex Trotman, chairman of Ford Motor Company, said, "Our purpose today has been to discuss what we can do to further the aims of school-to-work programs in the United States with the greater objective of raising the competitiveness of the U.S. in an increasingly global marketplace."

But the council got off to a painfully slow start. It had only one full-time employee and required no financial commitment from its members. Member companies spent most of the first year trying to hammer out a mission and a game plan. By 1996 the council had expanded to only 58 member companies, and its original executive director had resigned. In April 1996, Patricia Stone, its new executive director and a former manager of corporate education programs at Bank of America, said the council would focus more on working at the state and regional levels with other employer organizations. In September 1996 the council unveiled its new employer-participation model to help illustrate the ways in which companies can become involved in school-to-work and jump-start its efforts.

By the mid-1990s, several other business-led initiatives also had picked up steam that focused on improving the performance of schools and the creation of school-to-work systems:

❖ The National Association of Manufacturers (NAM), which represents 14,000 firms and has 44 state-level associations, created a new nonprofit organization in 1996 to encourage its members to participate in school-to-work activities. Although manufacturing had rebounded, NAM worried that its workforce was not keeping pace with rapidly changing technologies and that young people were not entering the field. The association already had a history of participating in workforce development efforts. In 1995 it mounted a program with support from the Pew Charitable Trusts to tie networks of small supplier firms with local community colleges to help meet the training needs of the existing workforce. It also was collaborating with Johns Hopkins University, Hagerstown (Maryland) Junior College, and four other community colleges to devise an associate degree in high-performance manufacturing that would be recognized by employers nationwide. In the mid-1990s, it began considering how to link these initiatives with additional ways to address future workforce needs.

❀ With funding from the Commonwealth Fund, Jobs for the Future has organized a national health-employer network for school-to-work among 30 hospital executives committed to expanding school-to-work within the health-care industry. The network's participants are sharing information about quality programs, promoting the development of core competencies for health-care workers that are applicable nationwide, and recruiting new members. Jobs for the Future's goal is to institutionalize the network within an existing health-employer organization, such as the American Hospital Association.

❀ The National Alliance of Business, a nonprofit organization that focuses on the quality of the nation's workforce, also has mounted a recruitment effort focused on specific industries, including retail and hospitality, the financial-services sector, manufacturing, and health care. In partnership with Jobs for the Future, it has produced technical assistance guides, industry-specific resource materials, training workshops, and a business-to-business mentoring bank for companies about school-to-work systems.

❀ The U.S. Chamber of Commerce was discussing a pilot initiative to jump-start the involvement of local chambers in school-to-work systems. Already, a number of local chambers have developed business-led initiatives similar to those in Tulsa and Austin. These include the chambers in Appleton and Green Bay, Wisconsin; Fort Worth, Texas; and Louisville, Kentucky.

In 1992 the Green Bay Area Chamber of Commerce formed Partners in Education, representing 10 school districts, three post-secondary institutions, and local businesses in Brown County, Wisconsin. Its executive board is made up of half education and half business and community leaders. The vice-president of education for the chamber serves as its director, ensuring that the initiative has high visibility and access to the chamber's leadership. Three other full-time employees work on the effort. Each school district contributes $1 per student per year to help operate the consortium, which in 1996 had over 500 business and education volunteers working on various initiatives. Business provides about four fifths of the yearly budget.

Employers are involved in numerous ways. These include providing workplace experiences for teachers; job shadowing, company tours, and youth apprenticeships for students; and an annual career fair. One of the partnership's primary initiatives has been to create an "employability endorsement" for high school students. The certificate is issued to high school seniors who have demonstrated seven work-readiness characteristics identified as most desirable by the business community, such as the ability to work in teams, take initiative, and manage time efficiently. "That has been a tremendously helpful tool for businesses," says B. J. Cassidy, the education assistant to Dan Bollom, the chairman of the board of the Wisconsin Public Service Corporation, which helped form the partnership. Local businesses have agreed to ask students applying for jobs for their employability ratings as well as their high school transcripts and attendance record.

In Fort Worth, Texas, the school district and the Fort Worth Chamber of Commerce formed Project C3 (for Community, Corporations, and Classrooms) to help prepare students for the modern workplace. Beginning in 1991, some 300 companies analyzed the tasks and knowledge needed for 900 different jobs, information then used to revise classroom practices and standards. Area businesses provide company tours for middle school students (so they can see how academic skills are used on the job), summer internships for high school students, and teacher internships. Teachers also have worked with local employers to design instructional units for grades K–12 that allow students to learn rigorous academic content by working on real-world problems.

❀ In 1995 the American Gas Association and the Edison Electric Institute formed the Utility/Business Education Coalition. The nonprofit organization consists of utilities and other community-based organizations that are willing to work together to develop a skilled labor force and improve the schools. Steven Kussman, the executive director of the coalition, says, "Utility companies are bound to their local communities by the wires and pipelines that carry their products and services. They are, therefore, dependent on the quality of the economic resources—namely, the workforce—in their service area." In 1996 the coalition surveyed 300 gas and electric company CEOs. Nearly 100 of them reported concerns about the employability of high school graduates, and 90 percent reported that their business customers had expressed concerns about the availability of employable or skilled workers. About 90 percent of the respondents also reported having entry-level positions for high school graduates, although half reported having difficulty filling those positions. The coalition's goal is to create local partnerships of educators and employers in at least 100 sites nationwide over the next five years. Utility managers and corporate executives in these sites would assume leadership roles in shaping and promoting school-to-work initiatives as part of a broader school-reform agenda.

❀ In September 1996, the Business Roundtable, the National Alliance of Business, and the U.S. Chamber of Commerce called on their more than 218,000 employer-members to use high school transcripts in making hiring decisions and to consider a state's commitment to high academic standards when locating their businesses. "The time for feel-good education-spending programs is over," said Keith Poston, a spokesman for the National Alliance of Business. "We want our companies to see results for the money that they spend."

Employers have not stampeded toward the school-to-work movement. Finding incentives to generate substantial and sustained employer involvement remains a major challenge. Many of these new efforts are in their earliest stages. It is hard to tell how substantive they really are. But they have made considerable progress in a relatively short time. If they mark just the beginning of a much broader trend, school-to-work systems could undergo a healthy expansion.

CHAPTER 6

School-to-Work and School Reform

*F*or more than a decade our nation has been engaged in one of the most feverish periods of school reform in our history. The beginning of the reforms is usually dated to a 1983 federal report by the National Commission on Excellence in Education called *A Nation at Risk*—although many states had begun to make changes prior to that time. The report warned of a "rising tide of mediocrity" in the classroom. It called for stiffer high school graduation requirements, a tighter curriculum, a longer school day and year, higher standards for entrance into college, and higher salaries and better preparation for teachers.

By the end of the 1980s, virtually every state had made improvements in its education system to better prepare students for work and college. Forty-two states had raised high school graduation

187

requirements. Nearly every state had instituted a student-testing program. Three fourths of high schools reported stricter attendance standards.

These have been important changes and have made the performance of American students better than it was. American students today are taking more and tougher academic courses as a result. But their performance is still far from what it must be to meet the demands of the twenty-first century.

First, the good news. Student test scores have been rising gradually since the early 1970s, even before the release of the commission's report. Academic course taking among high school students is up, in part because of the standards imposed since *A Nation at Risk* was published. Since 1982 the proportion of high school graduates who have taken advanced algebra has nearly doubled, as has the proportion taking a sequence of biology, chemistry, and physics. Fifty-one percent of all high school graduates now take four years of English and three years each of mathematics, science, and social studies.

Research shows that students who take more academic courses learn more. In schools that expect all students to take a core curriculum, students achieve more. Increased course taking in mathematics and science may have contributed to the fact that students score higher on national tests in those subjects today than they did in 1982.

There is other good news as well. In the past two decades, the large gap in performance between white and African American students in the United States has narrowed, although it remains unacceptably large. The pattern is less clear and less consistent for Latino students.

On international assessments of basic literacy, our students on average score better than those from other large countries. Our eighth-graders score above average on international assessments in science but below average in mathematics, in part because they cover more material in less depth.

Now for the reality check. Students may be doing better, but in many subjects, that means their average proficiency has returned to about the same levels, or only slightly higher, than that of their counterparts in the early 1970s. Moreover, only a tiny fraction of students score at the highest levels on national assessments of performance in reading, mathematics, science, and writing. In 1992, for example, only half of twelfth-graders could consistently solve math problems using fractions, decimals, and percents, as well as elementary concepts in geometry, statistics, and algebra. Only 6 percent could consistently solve relatively complex problems involving geometric relationships, algebra, or functions. There also is some evidence that in the past four years, the achievement gap between black and non-Hispanic white students has begun to widen again and that achievement differences among social classes are becoming more pronounced.

Put bluntly, while achievement has improved, there is no cause for mass rejoicing. Our average students still are not performing well enough.

Moreover, many of our urban school systems are in crisis. According to a study by the Rand Corporation, half the students in big city school systems drop out before high school graduation, four times the national average. A national longitudinal study conducted by the U.S. Education Department found that in 1992 the proportion of top-achieving seniors from the lowest income group was smaller than in 1972.

The majority of Americans do not think our students are doing well enough either. Almost half of Americans do not believe that a high school diploma guarantees that a student has learned the basics, and more than 80 percent favor higher standards than are now required in mathematics, English, history, and science for students to graduate from high school.

There has been a lot of debate about how much these academic weaknesses can be ascribed to the schools, as opposed to changes in student demographics or in society. Students' test scores are strongly correlated with the size of their families and whether their parents are affluent or poor, college educated or not. The academic support that parents provide at home is strongly correlated with how much young people achieve.

In *Beyond the Classroom: Why School Reform Has Failed and What Parents Need to Do*, lead author Laurence Steinberg correctly points out that some of these problems are beyond the power of schools to ameliorate. He blames a teenage culture that discourages high academic achievement and an adult culture that either doesn't care or doesn't communicate its concern positively to young people. In a comprehensive national study of high school students, Steinberg and his colleagues found a pervasive lack of student engagement in academics. Roughly 40 percent of students surveyed said they were "just going through the motions" in school. More than one third said they do not do the homework they are given (which averaged only four hours a week). Fewer than one in five said their friends think it is important to get good grades, and 20 percent said they do not try as hard as they could because they are worried about what their friends might think.

More than half of the students surveyed said they could bring home grades of C or worse without their parents getting upset. Although most students thought it was important to graduate to be successful, they did not think doing well in school mattered. "No degree of school reform, no matter how carefully planned, will be successful in solving the achievement problem unless we first face and resolve the engagement problem," Steinberg writes.

School-to-work cannot eliminate the "engagement problem." But it is one of the few school reforms that can make some inroads by helping students see how what they are learning relates to life beyond school and by changing how content is taught.

Yet today, school-to-work is rarely thought of as a central part of the school-reform movement. In many places, it has been relegated to a reform of vocational education. The result could be the worst of both worlds. States could raise academic standards for

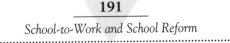
some students and consign others to a new and marginally improved version of job training.

As this chapter shows, school-to-work can help contribute to a broader reform of American high schools. Some of these efforts are based on reforming whole schools. Others are based on creating smaller schools within schools that are oriented around broad career themes. All have tried to connect core academics with their application in the outside world. The experience in Oregon has been particularly illuminating. Since the early 1990s the state has been committed to helping all students meet challenging academic standards, in part by extending the classroom into the workplace.

The Oregon Tale

Oregon's school-reform law, the Oregon Education Act of the 21st Century, grew directly out of an influential 1990 report, *America's Choice: High Skills or Low Wages!* , produced by a commission appointed by the National Center on Education and the Economy, a Washington, D.C., think tank led by Marc S. Tucker. The commission was cochaired by two former U.S. secretaries of labor and chaired by Ira C. Magaziner, a close friend and adviser of President and Mrs. Clinton.

Released during a period of heightened concern about the state of the U.S. economy, *America's Choice* got a lot of attention. It warned that the standard of living in the United States would decline unless Americans raised the skills of their workforce and improved the productivity of their companies. It noted that while foreign nations had different economies and cultures, they all shared a common approach to education and training: "They insist that virtually all of their students reach a high educational standard. We do not. They provide 'professionalized' education to non-college-bound students to prepare them for their trades and to ease their school-to-work transition. We do not."

The report advocated creating an Americanized version of the European systems, beginning with a radical restructuring of the American high school. All students would have to demonstrate that they had met a high standard of academic achievement during the first stage of their secondary school education. Those who did would earn something called a "certificate of initial mastery," typically at around age 16. During the upper stage of secondary school, students could either enter college directly, spend additional time preparing for the more competitive colleges and universities, or begin to pursue a professional and technical certificate, which most likely would require some postsecondary education.

At the time, Vera Katz was vice chairman of the House Education Committee in Oregon and a member of the National Center's board of directors. Katz saw an opportunity to apply the adage that "all politics is local." From her offices in Salem, she decided to put the commission's recommendations to the test. The bill that she sponsored in the Oregon legislature mirrored many of the recommendations in *America's Choice*. It passed in 1991 with little opposition and with the strong backing of both the governor and the state's business community.

It called for all students to earn a certificate of initial mastery in the core academic subjects by grade 10. After that, all students would pursue a "certificate of advanced mastery" (or CAM) in one of six career pathways for their last two years of high school. Within each pathway (in arts and communications, business and management, health services, human resources, industry and technology, and natural resources) students could earn either a college-preparatory endorsement or a professional-technical endorsement, or both.

Supporters of the new law hailed it as the end of tracking in the high schools. Because all students would have to meet a common academic standard to receive a certificate of initial mastery, all would have to demonstrate command of high-level academic content.

Opponents of the new law depicted it as tracking writ large. They claimed that because students at the age of 16 would have to select a career pathway and decide whether they were pursuing entry in a four-year college or not, their opportunities would be limited. They also worried that the law would encourage students to drop out of high school once they had earned the certificate of initial mastery.

The Oregon Education Association, the state's largest teachers union, came down hard against the new law. "Schools should not be forged as a service industry for business, nor should we be misdirected by the assumption that our economic ills are somehow the fault of the public schools," the union protested.

The majority of parents and students surveyed also opposed having to choose a career focus by the middle of high school, particularly if young people could not change their minds. However, they liked the idea of providing both college-bound and non-college-bound students with a sense of how their academic courses applied to the real world, and they thought high schools should provide students with some career preparation.

The David Douglas Experience

At least one high school in Oregon had already been contemplating some of the changes proposed in the new law. David Douglas High School, located in the David Douglas School District on the outskirts of Portland, typifies the demographics of Oregon as a whole. Situated in a neighborhood of small, single-family homes, its student body is primarily white and middle to lower-middle class.

The school, which serves about 1,850 students in grades 9–12, consists of two buildings: one for the academic departments, the other for the vocational and fine arts programs. It's a clean, orderly, comfortable school, the kind that sprouted up all over the country in the baby boom years of the 1950s and 1960s.

In the fall of 1989, just before Vera Katz started thinking about her experiment with educational policy making, Douglas officials began to wonder what had happened to their graduates. So they surveyed the previous year's seniors. It was an eye-opening experience. Approximately 17 percent of the 1989 graduates were enrolled in four-year colleges. Another 30 percent were in two-year colleges, many of them part time. A few were in the military. The rest—over 50 percent—were in the workplace. And they were not doing particularly well.

"They were working in jobs that they did not feel offered them opportunity for growth or for advancement," recalls Marybeth Stiner, the school-improvement coordinator. "They did not feel like they had the skills to take them somewhere else. Most of them liked the time they had spent at David Douglas, but they didn't feel that they were prepared to do what they ended up doing."

With the support of the principal, John Harrington, David Douglas's teachers, parents, and community members began to look at the alternatives. Eventually they decided that they could make students' course work more engaging and better prepare them for life after high school by focusing their last few years of study around a broad career theme. When the state passed the Oregon Education Act of the 21st Century and began looking for sites to develop certificates of advanced mastery, David Douglas signed up. It received an initial grant of $96,000 from the state.

In November 1993 the school district received an added boost when the Oregon Business Council selected it as a partner. The council, which represents 43 of the state's largest companies, had been a strong supporter of the education-reform act, and now it was anxious to prove that the law could work on the ground.

In the summer of 1994, teams of educators and businessmen began meeting on a regular basis to hammer out what a certificate of advanced mastery would look like in each of seven career fields. To provide teachers with time to meet and to develop new curriculum, the school board agreed on a special schedule for the 1994–95 school year: Twice a week, school opened ninety minutes late so that teachers could get together with each other or with their business partners and work.

The school already had at least one model to emulate. The previous year, two teachers at the school, Pam Ramsey and Kristy Eby, had launched a "law network" for 30 juniors and seniors who were interested in law-related careers. The two-period class integrated law, sociology, American literature, and communications. Every Tuesday a guest speaker from the community came in to talk about a particular aspect of the law. Students also went on job shadows; visited prisons, jails, courtrooms, and forensics laboratories; and undertook community-service projects. In class they engaged in mock trials and small-group work.

On the day I visited the class, small groups of students were deciding whether the First Amendment protections applied to a list of charged situations, such as publicly criticizing the President, making racist remarks, or campaigning through residential neighborhoods with a loudspeaker. When the groups were done debating the merits of each case, Ramsey polled the class and pressed students to justify their reasoning.

Some of the students I interviewed wanted to be lawyers; others, police officers, social workers, or juvenile psychologists. But all of them felt privileged to be in the special class and proud that they had chosen the class on the basis of their own interests. Katrina Zeissler, a 16-year-old junior, said, "This class is by far harder than all my other classes. They have higher standards. They expect you to do good work." Students were expected to revise every piece of work until they earned an A or a B. Substandard work was not accepted. Zeissler added that she liked the class better because "you're reading about stuff you want to do. You don't get bored. We're working until the bell rings. You come in here with your own opinions and stuff, and you get your opinions challenged." The class stressed critical thinking and communications skills, not narrow job training.

As in other school-to-work programs, the success stories were particularly notable. Koby Shelton, a big, blond 17-year-old junior, was leading a group in an animated discussion when I arrived. I assumed that he was a top student, vocal and self-assured. But he later told me, "Last year, I had almost straight F's." This year, he had a B-plus grade-point average. "I do my work for this class and it makes me want to do my work for other classes," he explained. "They're in here to educate us on what we want to do when we grow up. We go in our other classes, and we just sit there. I've learned more in this class in the last couple of months than in all my other years in school. I learned more about what I can do and what I can't do. What I want to do. You don't just hear it from the teachers. You hear it from the people actually out there on the job."

Much of the credit belonged to Kirby and Ramsey, who had developed the curriculum and the teaching methods for the course from scratch. "We started off with nothing," Ramsey told me. "We wanted to have them read something of high interest. To have speakers who made them think about issues. To work in groups and be able to critically evaluate materials. To get emotional enough to become engaged. I believe the purpose is to give them real-world skills. To educate them not only in regular content, but also about what's needed to survive, and not just in the workplace."

David Douglas wanted to generate the same enthusiasm and rigor in its other career clusters. All ninth- and tenth-graders must take a core of required courses in such subjects as English, mathematics, science, social studies, and technology. Beginning with the class of 1999, students must maintain a grade-point average of 2.0 or above and earn a certificate of initial mastery to graduate. To merit a certificate, they must complete the required courses with a grade of C or better, score in the average-to-proficient range on standardized tests, and collect a portfolio of scored work samples.

To decide what career area interests them, ninth- and tenth-graders also take a semester-long course called Personal Finance and Career Exploration. As part of the class, they go on company tours and job shadows organized by the business partners. Each pupil also has a faculty mentor, a teacher or administrator, to help ensure the student is making progress toward meeting the certificate of initial mastery requirements. Every teacher and administrator in the school is responsible for no more than 10 students, with whom they meet every six weeks.

In 1995–96 the school was piloting career-related courses in all seven career clusters. The work-site experiences in the courses ranged from internships to community-service projects to school-run enterprises. In the natural resources cluster, students were learning about the requirements of ecosystems and what it meant to be stewards of the natural environment. For their career-based experiences, they had remodeled a park near the public library and designed and built displays about the natural ecosystem they had created. In health services, juniors learned about anatomy and physiology and participated in a one-day job shadow. Seniors had three clinical rotations for a total of nine weeks in various health-care settings. Students also assisted school nurses with vision screening at a local elementary school and blood-pressure screening at the high school. Students in the business and management cluster helped run a school store and a branch of the Interstate Bank.

At first, Mimi Bushman, the director of education programs for the Oregon Business Council, personally recruited companies to participate, securing the commitment of about 20 companies in the Greater Portland area. But since then, Jeanne Yerkovich, the school's full-time school-to-work coordinator, has been responsible for maintaining contact with area businesses.

The quality of students' work-site experiences varies widely. On one company tour I attended to the U.S. Postal Service, ninth-graders heard a canned, uninspired presentation that made almost no reference to career opportunities beyond unskilled, entry-level positions. Yerkovich says this was one of 25 tours during the 1995–96 school year, most of which exposed students to a broader array of career opportunities in companies ranging from hotels, athletic clubs, and retailers to insurance firms and lumber companies.

The school also surveys tenth-graders prior to their job-shadowing experience, so that students can be matched with employees in their area of interest. Standard Insurance Company, for example, placed students with employees ranging from lawyers to accountants to computer network operators. In the industrial and engineering cluster, students participated in multiweek internships and prepared independent projects related to their work-site experiences. Special-needs students also participate in the ninth-grade career-exploration activities.

Overall parent and student responses to the changes at David Douglas have been positive. In a survey of David Douglas's community, 79 percent of parents favored having all high school students participate in off-campus work experiences so that they could explore their career interests. Jesse Ruede, a senior in the health sciences cluster, told me, "I have learned so much. I don't really apply myself. But this class, I've applied myself so much. I find myself coming to this class more than I do to my other classes just because I like it. This class is an elective, and so I chose it, and I chose to come. But my general education classes are pointless."

Some of the greatest challenges for David Douglas lie ahead. In 1995–96, students still enrolled in CAM courses as an elective, and only a small percentage of students did so (about 200 students out of 850 juniors and seniors). Only about a dozen of Douglas's 112 faculty members had volunteered to teach a CAM class. Beginning in 1997–98, all eleventh- and twelfth-graders will be required to take a CAM course in addition to their core academic subjects. That will significantly increase the number of teachers needed to teach such courses and the number of work-site experiences needed for students. "It's kind of scary," admitted Principal Harrington. "What it means is the classes that are riding on the backs of well-intentioned, energetic teachers will have to be supplemented by other teachers who are on the periphery right now."

In late 1996, educators were still hammering out what students would have to do to achieve a certificate of advanced mastery. For example, teachers had agreed that a required senior English paper now would be done on a career-related topic. Students would have to pick a subject related to their career pathway, write a paper, present it orally to a panel of teachers and community members, and write a reflection on it. Each student also would receive guidance from an adult mentor and be involved in community service as a part of this requirement.

The new David Douglas High School is still a work-in-progress. But educators there have shown that high academic standards and the concepts undergirding school-to-work are not mutually exclusive. Instead, the school is raising its standards and integrating real-world experiences for its students simultaneously.

Making It Work Elsewhere

The experiences at David Douglas suggested school-to-work could help engage students in large high schools filled with predominantly middle-class kids. But what about high schools with more problems?

Roosevelt High School, in a working-class neighborhood in north Portland, would be a test. In the early 1980s it had the highest absenteeism and dropout rates in Portland. Half of all ninth-graders never made it to graduation. A survey of the school's faculty in 1989 found that 85 percent felt they were not meeting the needs of the students.

In the early 1990s, while the Oregon Education Act of the 21st Century was making its way through the legislature, Roosevelt began implementing a series of career pathways for students, which it dubbed Roosevelt Renaissance 2000, in honor of the coming millennium. For a year, school opened an hour late once a week so that teachers could develop the pathways in collaboration with business and community members. It also encouraged teachers to participate in job shadows and internships at local companies.

Since 1992–93, all freshmen have been required to take an introductory course that orients them to the six career pathways through a series of hands-on projects. They also participate in at least one job shadow in a career area, and they learn basic study and organizational skills that will help them succeed in high school. Once a month, local businesspeople come in to meet with the freshmen and talk about such issues as communications and employability skills. The forums are organized by the Business Youth Exchange, an intermediary group associated with the local chamber of commerce.

As sophomores, all students enroll in a career-related course that introduces them to the basic terminology and concepts in their career field. They also participate in two more job shadows. The rest of their time is spent in academic subjects.

In many high schools that use career clusters, including both Roosevelt and David Douglas, students take their regular academic subjects outside the cluster. Roosevelt also has experimented with tying some academic courses to a student's career focus. For example, seniors in health services also take an English course that combines a study of literature with topics from the medical field. Students might write about the greatest medical advances of the twentieth century and read literature by A. J. Cronin, Somerset Maugham, and Sinclair Lewis.

In many cases, however, the pathway class is the only career-related class that students take. Both David Douglas and Roosevelt have been reluctant to group students together for too many classes on the basis of their career interests because of concerns that it would segregate young people or give the academic curriculum too extreme an occupational focus. At Roosevelt, for example, there are almost no females enrolled in the manufacturing technology and engineering pathway. Scheduling conflicts also have made it difficult to cluster academic and career-related classes.

In any case, explained Judy Holmboe, a social studies teacher who helped develop the freshman course, "This program is not about guaranteeing kids they will spend the rest of their lives in this career. This is about exciting kids through connections to careers. We really need to continue to encourage sixteen- and seventeen-year-olds to change their minds."

For some students at Roosevelt, Holmboe says, the career connection is the only thing that keeps them there. "If you don't connect high school education with the adult world, then the education doesn't mean enough. In some cultures, kids will go to school and do their classes just because you tell them to. They won't do that here. They want to know, 'What is this going to get me? Why is this more important than going to work and helping my family put food on the table?' And if we can't tell them that, then something is wrong."

Like David Douglas, Roosevelt has made a point of blending classroom academics with practical, real-world learning. As of October 1996, almost 550 students had participated in internships outside the classroom. Freshmen and sophomores had engaged in nearly 2,300 job-shadowing experiences. Almost 300 employers have opened up their doors to Roosevelt's young people.

"It's been pretty phenomenal in terms of the number of individual participants who have worked with us, either in job shadows or internships or both," says René Leger, who had been the business-partnership coordinator for Roosevelt since the initiative began. He estimates that more than 11,050 businesspeople have worked with the school since 1992, "and they keep coming back for more. The perceptions of each one of the stakeholders has been very, very positive," he notes. "The kids continue to rate their internship or job-shadowing experiences as one of the best—if not the best—activities of the year."

In 1995–96 the school surveyed its teachers to find out what they thought about the work-based experiences. About 94 percent agreed that work-based learning should be part of the curriculum for every Roosevelt student, and most thought that graduates were better prepared since the reforms began.

Semret Tesfaldet, a senior in the health-services pathway, has undergone the kind of experiences that the school is trying to produce. As a freshman, she did her first job shadow at a local bank. It didn't appeal to her, so she tried health care. Two job shadows in her sophomore year, one in the physical therapy department of a local hospital and another with a pediatric nurse, convinced her that she liked medicine, but she didn't like watching children undergo invasive procedures. "It was too sad. The kids were always crying," she explained.

In her junior year, she did two internships—one in a dental office, another in a pharmacy, where she worked behind the counter. The pharmacy hired her to work part time during the school year. But she decided that she was more interested in dentistry because she liked working with patients. As a senior, she was back at the dentist's office and was applying to college. Because she had selected the health-services pathway, she had taken both biology and chemistry, courses she said she would have skipped otherwise. In her senior year, she was taking anatomy and physiology.

Nora Beck, a registered nurse who teaches the health-services class, said, "The big thing I see students gaining is commitment. Our adolescents do not know how to commit to something and have goals for themselves. And I can tell you my seniors do. It really doesn't matter if they switch careers later on, but what they're being asked to do is commit to something."

Early results from Roosevelt suggest that the pathway focus actually may encourage students to take more, not less, academics. In 1995–96, Roosevelt had 32 students in its physics classes, compared to about a dozen in previous years, and enrollment in both algebra 2 and chemistry had increased. The dropout rate for freshmen also has declined, from 13 percent in the late 1980s to about 6.5 percent in the early 1990s. Test scores, however, have not improved.

One of the school's biggest challenges remains how to fit work-based learning for large numbers of students into the class schedule. Most students average only 12 to 20 hours out at the work site because of scheduling conflicts.

We Are Not Europe

In the rest of the state there has been less acceptance of the Oregon education-reform law. Part of the problem was that the act called for massive changes in education without putting any of the infrastructure in place. What must students know and be able to do to earn a certificate of initial mastery? What would happen to them if they did not earn the certificate? Would the certificate of advanced mastery replace the high school diploma? How much career-specific material would students be expected to learn in high school?

At the time the law was passed, there were no answers to any of these questions. Oregon funded design teams around the state to work on draft standards for both the certificates of initial and advanced mastery. But it took five years of intense work to write the standards, circulate them for review, and then revise them. By the fall of 1996, the standards for the certificate of advanced mastery still had not been adopted by the state board of education.

"When we first put this out, it was so poorly understood, and there was not a vision of how it would work," acknowledged Judy

Patterson, the assistant state superintendent of education. "So people assumed either you would learn the academics and be headed off to college, or we would shift you into some vocational area and that would be it."

By 1993, opposition to the new law had mounted, especially from the conservative right, which viewed the certificate of advanced mastery as a departure from traditional academics. "My greatest worry is that they have made big business the consumer of education," said Sen. Marilyn L. Shannon, a Republican. "It used to be that parents were the consumers of education on behalf of their children. Now they are trying to turn out compliant group workers instead of educated citizens."

Surveys showed that parents and students also were uneasy about the law. They particularly disliked the idea of having students choose a career focus by the middle of high school. MaryLee Block, the manager of the Good Samaritan Clinic at Saint John's Hospital, had worked with Roosevelt students. And she liked the idea that they were getting a real-world view of what working in a clinical setting was like. But as a parent with high school children of her own, she worried: "I think we're asking our kids to make decisions too soon. I don't personally like the pathway idea. I think that high school should be for the basics, not for specializing them the last two years of their education. Rather than having my daughter be away from school, I would like to encourage her to take more biology or chemistry or something in class."

The Oregon Education Association urged the state to delay implementing the certificates. Others argued that the cost of the reforms was too high in light of a 1990 measure that had limited local property taxes and shifted more of the burden for financing education onto the state. Rural communities complained that they lacked the resources to offer career pathways in multiple fields.

It was the business community, including the Oregon Business Council and Associated Oregon Industries, that helped save the law during the 1995 session. Key business leaders met with state lawmakers and told them in no uncertain terms that they wanted the act retained with only minor modifications. Gov. John Kitzhaber, a Democrat, also threatened to veto any measure that eliminated the certificates.

In the end, lawmakers voted to retain most of the original act, although they pushed back the timelines for its implementation. They stressed that to achieve the certificate of initial mastery, students would have to demonstrate competence in the core academic disciplines of math, science, history, geography, economics, and civics. The certificate of advanced mastery would be issued to students who met high academic standards beyond the level required for the CIM. There would be no separate endorsements for college-bound versus career-bound students. And students would be allowed to move easily among career areas. Districts also would continue to issue standard high school diplomas.

Only students who chose to do so would begin pursuing a more specific endorsement in a professional or technical field while still in high school. To receive the endorsement, they probably would have to complete some postsecondary education and training. But by 1996 the consequences of not achieving a certificate of initial mastery and the rewards for earning a certificate of advanced mastery were still unclear.

"School-to-work is a method of teaching," explained Norma Paulus, the state superintendent of education. "So it is not the school-to-work experience that we will assess, it is the result: What did the students learn in math? What did they learn in science? What did they learn in English as a result of this experience? Why do we want to do it? It makes learning more relevant."

Whether that is a message that Oregon parents, students, and teachers will embrace enthusiastically remains to be seen.

Meanwhile, however, the business community has come out four-square behind the reforms. In 1996 the Oregon Business Council decided to draw upon its experiences with the David Douglas School District to get far more businesses engaged in school-to-work around the state. It hired René Leger, from Roosevelt, to help with its efforts. The state organization representing chambers of commerce in 75 Oregon cities, Oregon Chamber Executives, also announced that it had formed a partnership with the Oregon Department of Education to provide high school students with more opportunities to apply their learning to careers. The chambers represent 28,000 active business members in the state.

Career Academies

Oregon demonstrates how school-to-work principles could provide a foundation for far-reaching changes, even in large comprehensive high schools like David Douglas. But the Oregon story also illustrates some of the difficulties that will accompany legislative changes on such a massive scale. In particular, parents and students will reject school-to-work if they perceive it as narrowing young people's options prematurely.

There is another approach to school reform based on career-related experiences. Instead of starting with large high schools, it starts small. Instead of mandating a career focus for all students, it makes it a matter of student choice. This approach has the potential to make a big difference in how high schools are structured and run in this country.

Throughout the country, small high schools are forming and attracting students through the promise of career-related learning. "Career academies" are usually smaller schools-within-schools organized around a broad career theme, such as health care or arts and communications. Each academy usually includes a team of teachers—one each in English, math, science, and the career area—who work together to design the curriculum. Students take all four subjects from these teachers, with whom they stay for several years. Usually they take the rest of their classes in the larger high school. Business partners in the career area related to the academy typically provide mentors, company tours, presentations about specific aspects of the industry, and summer internships. They also help design the curriculum through their role on advisory committees.

Career magnet high schools, such as those attended by one third of public high school students in New York City, are larger schools-within-schools or even whole schools. Examples include Aviation High School in Queens, La Guardia High School for the Arts, and the High School of Fashion Industries in Manhattan.

W. Norton Grubb, an education professor at the University of California at Berkeley, has studied these high schools extensively. He notes several potential advantages to career academies: Because a group of teachers works with the same students over several years, the opportunities for coordinating their courses and creating projects that cut across subjects are substantial. The activities of the business partners provide other sources of instruction and motivation for students besides those provided by teachers. Finally, he notes, because academies create smaller communities of both students and teachers, students are less likely to feel "lost" than students in conventional high schools, and their problems are more likely to be identified.

For Greg Panossian, the Finance Academy at John Muir High School in Pasadena, California, was a "way out of trouble." The dark-haired, hazel-eyed, 17-year-old senior explained, "When I was a freshman, I didn't care a lot about school. I thought I'd graduate, get out of here, get a job. There was no purpose. Except for sports, I wasn't much interested."

Yet by his senior year, Panossian was earning A's and B's, described himself as "really involved in school," and planned to be the first in his family to attend college. In 1996 he was in his first year at Pasadena City College. Panossian credits his turnaround to the individual attention and career focus gained from the Finance Academy. "The main difference is that you're going somewhere with the academy," he told me. "You have future goals. The teachers understand the students individually because they see them every day. It helps a lot. The school means something to you."

The first career academy opened in Philadelphia in 1969 as a dropout-prevention measure. State-funded career academies in California also focus primarily on students who have had a past record of underachievement, irregular attendance, low motivation, or poverty. But the model has since spread throughout the country to encompass students of all abilities and backgrounds.

"I think what makes the academies exciting is that they are at the crossroads between the school restructuring and the school-to-work movements," says Robert J. Ivry, the senior vice-president for the Manpower Demonstration Research Corporation (MDRC), which is conducting a study of career academies nationwide. "There's a big movement to break down impersonal, comprehensive high schools into something that's more supportive, and academies are one variation on that."

In 1996, MDRC estimated that there were more than 300 career academies operating across the country. Many academies are in California, which since 1984 has provided a limited amount of money to help districts start and operate them. There are also networks of state-supported academies in Florida and Illinois. The New York–based National Academy Foundation, described in chapter 3, provides the curricula and program designs for more than 200 academies nationwide in the fields of finance, travel and tourism, and public service.

The Pasadena Unified School District, where Greg attended school, is an urban school system in the foothills of the San Gabriel Mountains, just east of Los Angeles. Since 1990 it has looked to career academies as a way to restructure its high schools and better serve its students. Pasadena's seven academies enroll about 700 teenagers, or 15 percent of the high school population. The programs—in finance, health care, geospace, high technology, graphic arts, visual arts and design, and computers—are dispersed among the district's four comprehensive high schools.

You can locate the Graphic Arts Academy at Pasadena High School by the small, printed sign over its door. Once inside, you enter a large, open space equipped with computers, cameras, printing presses, cutting machines, and a darkroom. The Printing Industries Association of Southern California, the academy's business partner, donated all of the equipment. It since has helped sponsor a number of graphic arts academies in the state.

On the day I visited, the students were working on their book project, an assignment that illustrates how the academies blend academic and vocational instruction. At the beginning of the year, in their English class, the students read a series of vignettes about a young girl's life. Then they each wrote a 12-chapter book about their own lives. Now, they were producing the books in their graphic arts class, after learning about layout, desktop publishing, binding, and printing. They also had calculated the cost of a print run of 10,000.

The same philosophy of integrated learning extended throughout the other academies in the district. In the Geospace Academy, students read science fiction in their English class and devised equations to chart a plane's descent. In the Health Careers Academy, they used ratios to fill drug prescriptions and geometric angles to assess the range of motion in an elbow.

Research has found that nationwide, many academies have not placed much emphasis on integrating academic and occupational courses. What enables Pasadena to overcome this drawback is time. Teachers in the Pasadena academies share a common planning period, and they also have an extra preparation period to tutor students. Longer class periods and block schedules provide the flexibility needed to adjust teaching styles and organize field trips.

Although the academies emphasize career themes and interdisciplinary work, all of the students must meet the state's high school graduation requirements. Academy courses also meet the admissions requirements for the California State University and University of California systems. In Pasadena, students also complete 100 hours of community service, and many take courses at Pasadena City College while still in high school. The district also has developed ties with several four-year colleges in the area to allow students to transfer easily to baccalaureate programs in their fields.

Exposure to the workplace complements the infusion of work-related themes in the classroom. Jason Potter, a student in the Finance Academy, described his experience there as a "life class. . . . They teach you how to go out into the world, how to get a job, how to keep one," he explained. "I don't think in the high school you actually know what's going on out there. But when you're in this program, they put you out in the world so that you can see for yourself." After working as a paid intern one summer, Jason landed a part-time job as a bank teller while he was still in high school. In 1996 he was enrolled in a community college in Arizona.

Finding enough work sites and mentors for Pasadena students has been difficult, however. In 1994, only about 30 percent of teenagers in the Pasadena career academies had managed to find paid internships after their junior year. Although the school system guarantees youths an interview for a possible internship, it does not promise them an actual placement. In addition, summer internships can't provide the kind of sustained and structured learning that characterizes more intensive work-based approaches, such as youth apprenticeships. In general, work experience historically has been the least well developed component of career academies. Many have only small work-based learning programs, and employer contributions consist primarily of equipment or funding rather than staff time to work with students either as mentors or workplace supervisors.

One career academy that had fewer problems arranging work experiences for students was the Health Academy. There, juniors have an unpaid internship at Kaiser Permanente of Southern California during the school year, a paid internship over the summer, and on-the-job training at St. Luke's Medical Center or Huntington Memorial Hospital during their senior years. Academy teachers visit the work sites once a week. Most Health Academy graduates will be certified in at least one entry-level occupation, and many in two or more. "These students are somebody," Marla Keeth, the health-occupations instructor, said. "They're not just out of high school flipping hamburgers. They really have an occupation behind them."

On the day I visited Kaiser, junior Albert Shaw was purging old materials from training folders in one of the supply rooms. Albert went to Kaiser twice a week for several hours at a stretch. Like most students, he said the career focus was part of what attracted him to the academy, but he also liked the smaller class sizes and personal learning environment. "The teachers get to know everyone better," he told me. "They know you by your first name. When I was at Pasadena High School, the teachers didn't have time to really spend with you."

Students and teachers often refer to the academies as an extended family. The average California academy has only 108 students. Those in Pasadena have 90 to 115 participants. Teenagers enter as sophomores and remain through their senior years. Class sizes average 25 students, compared with 36 in Pasadena's comprehensive high schools. Each teacher also serves as an adviser for a small group of teenagers from the time they enter the program until graduation.

Mark Hall, a former teacher in the Graphic Arts Academy, said it's the specialized focus, combined with the smaller setting and innovative pedagogy, that is the key to the academy's success. "Whenever we start to look more like the traditional classroom," he observed, "attendance goes down, morale goes down, and test scores go down."

There is still some question about whether career academies—many of which were originally designed to serve low-achieving or at-risk students—can serve all young people equally well. In Pasadena, teachers report that extremely bright students take so many advanced courses outside the academies that it poses a scheduling problem. Similarly, academies may not be able to provide enough support for young people who have severe behavioral problems or are reading well below grade level.

But a study of 10 of the original academies in California found that academy students had better attendance, failed fewer courses, earned more credits, got better grades, and were more likely to graduate than their nonacademy peers (although their chances of attending college or finding employment were no higher). Information on graduates from the National Academy programs indicates that more than 90 percent enroll in postsecondary education. A follow-up study of about 200 Academy of Finance graduates from seven programs in New York City also found that the majority of those who continued in postsecondary education pursued majors in business or finance and planned on making a career in this field. Of those who continued working full or part time, about half were working in financial services or a related field.

The graduates of Philadelphia's career academies—which now number more than 20—also fare well. A follow-up survey conducted six months and eighteen months after graduation found 50 percent in college and 30 percent working in the private sector. Another 5 percent were in the military or in trade schools. Less than 3 percent of academy students drop out of school versus 30 percent for the district as a whole.

The success of career academies bears out much recent research about successful schools. A study by researchers at the Center on the Organization and Restructuring of Schools at the

University of Wisconsin found that students tended to achieve more in schools where teachers agree on a common mission, where students are encouraged to think deeply and to apply their learning to real-world problems, and where strong professional communities take collective responsibility for student learning. Such schools are often characterized by small teams of teachers and students who stay together for several years, the availability of common planning time for teachers, mixed-ability grouping in the core academic subjects, and enrollment based on choice. All of these features typically characterize good career academies.

In their study of 10 career academies nationwide, the Manpower Demonstration Research Corporation found that many teachers were originally drawn to the academies and stayed in them because of the chance to work together with colleagues. These teachers also reported a strong sense of isolation prior to joining the academy. "Many of these teachers felt that the career academy enabled them to be better teachers," the researchers wrote, "to focus on the personal, as well as the academic, needs of their students, and to try out new material in their classes." Compared to nonacademy teachers, these teachers were more satisfied with their school environment, their jobs, and their relationships with their colleagues. They reported a far higher degree of collaboration; greater influence over curriculum and instruction; a stronger emphasis on developing personal relationships with students; and a greater perception that they were part of a learning community in which they had the opportunity to learn new things, receive professional stimulation, and solve problems rather than just talk about them.

The idea of career academies and other small high schools organized around a broad theme could be expanded much more. In 1992 a report by the California state department of education, *Second to None*, suggested that all students could be better served if schools were organized into clusters around career or interdisciplinary "majors" in grades 11 and 12. Similarly, a report published in 1996 by the National Association of Secondary School Principals and the Carnegie Foundation for the Advancement of Teaching recommended that all high schools be broken into units of no more than 600 students so that teachers and students can know each other better. The report also recommended reorganizing high schools so that subjects are more closely linked and students can apply what they have learned to real-life problems and situations. At the same time, it stressed that high schools should be clear about the essentials that all students must demonstrate to graduate.

In a few places, whole high schools have divided into four or five separate academies. Encina High School in Sacramento County, California, is divided into five academies: a freshman academy, which includes all ninth-graders, and four academies for grades 10–12 in health care, graphic arts, business, and career exploration. The career exploration academy includes students who are interested in criminal justice and human development, or who are not yet ready to pick a career focus. Each academy has at least one integrated project per year that combines the career theme with the separate academic subjects. Academic teachers are required to go out into the workplace during the summer to learn about their academy's professional field. Students also have opportunities for workplace mentors, job shadowing, paid and unpaid internships and apprenticeships, and field trips to work sites.

At Patterson High School in Baltimore, Maryland, the school's 2,100 students attend one of five separate academies: one for ninth-graders, and four more in sports studies and wellness, arts and humanities, business and finance, and transportation and engineering technology for students in grades 10–12. Students take all their classes within their academies.

The career focus is not the only thing that makes these academies different, however. Researchers from Johns Hopkins University have helped teachers at the school incorporate other elements of successful schools. These include tougher rules on tardiness and absenteeism; longer class periods; team teaching; teacher-mentors who act as advisers to students and help guide their class choices; and a twilight academy in which students come to school in the evening to help adolescents who are disruptive or who have failed a class.

The researchers are tracking the school's progress. They surveyed the school's teachers in the spring of 1995 and again the following fall. The percentage of teachers who thought tardiness was a problem in grades 10–12 dropped precipitously, from 88.9 percent to 6.8 percent. The percentage who thought absenteeism in those grades was a problem fell from 97.8 percent to 19.0 percent. The percentage who thought class cutting was a problem plummeted from 82.2 percent to zero. Teachers perceived that these problems had been cut roughly in half among ninth-graders. In addition, they reported decreases in vandalism, drug use, verbal abuse of teachers, drug peddling, fights, and theft. In 1996 researchers were working to adapt the reform model to at least seven more schools in Baltimore, the District of Columbia, and California. James M. McPartland, a research scientist in education at Johns Hopkins, told *Education Week:* "We think what we have here could be a national model."

In 1997 the Oakland, California, school district decided to convert its large, comprehensive high schools into smaller, more focused academies.

An Upper Phase of High School

American parents and teenagers likely would reject the early and formal differentiation between job-bound and college-bound students that occurs in many European countries. But forcing all students to pursue the same general education through age 18 without any opportunities to pursue individual interests or specialization is also unwise. We need to make more productive use of the upper years of high school.

This problem has been acknowledged by some of our nation's most respected educational thinkers. John I. Goodlad, Theodore R. Sizer, and the late Ernest L. Boyer all have proposed a different arrangement for the last few years of high school.

In *A Place Called School*, Goodlad proposes pushing high school graduation back to age 16 and having all students take a core curriculum until then. A new "fourth phase of education" would combine work, study, and community service to help ease students' transition into careers, higher education, and adult responsibilities.

Ernest Boyer proposed in his book *High School* that the early years of high school focus on a common core of learning, but that the last two years be considered a "transition school." Half of the time in this school would be devoted to completing the common core. The other half would focus on a program of "elective clusters"—five or six courses that would permit students to pursue advanced study in selected academic subjects, explore career options, or both. "Here is where specialized upper-level academic courses and quality vocational offerings would appropriately fit," he argued. "We recommend that the transition years include independent study, time with mentors, early college study, or apprenticeship experience off the campus."

In *Horace's School*, Theodore Sizer proposes something called an "early college" for the last year or two of high school, leading to an "advanced secondary diploma." Students in the "early college" would take an individualized program of study that could include advanced academic coursework, courses in new areas like Japanese or an occupational field, structured apprenticeships, and substantial independent study. Students could take some of these classes at the high school and others at nearby four-year colleges, community colleges, and technical institutes. "The Early College serves as a bridge between school and college or work," Sizer writes. "Despite its title, it is not elitist: there is something of consequence for every adolescent here, whatever his or her academic interest or serious career goal may be."

It is interesting that despite these authors' remarkable consensus, very few of these ideas have gone anywhere. This suggests just how difficult it will be to change the structure of American high schools. In 1997, a study of early efforts to implement school-to-work in eight states found that only two—Oregon and Kentucky—had made school-to-work activities a central part of their broader education-reform agenda. Changes in the school curriculum—such as developing career majors or integrating academic and vocational instruction—also were a relatively low priority, thus far, compared with attempts to provide career development and workplace activities for students. Only 2 percent of high school seniors surveyed in the spring of 1996 in 39 local school-to-work activities, including career development, career majors, and workplace activities linked to a school grade or assignment.

Yet, as this chapter demonstrates, school-to-work can contribute to broader efforts to improve schools. It can help focus upper-secondary education, emphasize new teaching methods, create smaller schools organized around career or other themes, bring more adults into contact with high school students, and provide greater opportunities for career exploration and guidance. But the primary emphasis must remain on gaining competence in a core academic curriculum for everyone.

Somehow, we need to devise a high school reform agenda that acknowledges that education is inevitably a preparation for both work and citizenship, as well as an avenue for personal and intellectual development. The next two chapters discuss how schools can provide opportunities for both coherence and choice.

CHAPTER 7

Making It Happen

*T*he Allentown Campus of Pennsylvania State University is a nondescript, concrete-block building located in the middle of a suburban housing complex. As I pull into the parking lot
at 7:20 A.M., the high school students are easily recognizable. A
small group of teens is congregated in the upper parking lot around
an assortment of pickup trucks, souped-up cars, and motorbikes,
car stereos blaring. Most of their attention is focused on a 1968
cherry-red Camaro convertible with black racing strips on the
hood and fuzzy dice suspended from the rearview mirror. I later
learn that the car belongs to Eric Heiney, a handsome teenager
with dark hair and eyes who has devoted the past year to lovingly
rescuing it from the junk heap. All of his paychecks have been
poured into the car, which features a rebuilt six-cylinder engine
and a $1,900 paint job. "It rocks the valley," he boasts.

In its own quiet way, the Greater Lehigh Valley Youth Apprenticeship Program, one of about two dozen youth apprenticeship sites with some initial funding from the state, also is beginning to "rock the valley." The 48 students in the program here—and the 36 high school students at the nearby Allentown College of St. Francis de Sales—alternate weeks spent on campus taking high school courses with weeks at the work site. Their career interests range from early childhood education to health care to business to machining, Eric's interest. They have come here for a variety of reasons, from a specific career interest to a thorough distaste for their traditional high schools. The program strives to prepare all of them for careers and college by combining mastery of academic subjects with their application at the work site.

All five teachers in the Greater Lehigh Valley Youth Apprenticeship Program previously worked in industry. None of them had teaching as their first career. Sandra Grow, the mathematics and computer-technology coordinator, used to be an applications programmer for the Pennsylvania Power and Light Company. "You try to pull from real-life experiences," she says of her classes. When she teaches linear and nonlinear equations, students work on the brake and reaction times for cars or compute how much postage it would take to mail something of a certain weight. Much of the instruction revolves around projects that students undertake in teams.

Eric Heiney's mother, Louise Roth, is thrilled with the changes she's seen in her son since he began attending the program and working for Loikits Industrial Service in nearby Northhampton, Pennsylvania. "Eric was never planning on going to college," she says. "Academically, he had a big turnaround this year. He pulled off straight A's. Before he pulled C's and B's, a D here and there. And this year he was straight A's. He said it was because he took an interest in it, and they were working towards something he wanted to do.

"I want to say the work was more challenging this year, whereas before he was more bored by it," she adds. "It was a challenge to him. He had to prove he could do it. I think it was more the career link. He's going to be a machinist. He has a job. He's staying where he's working now." Eric explains the difference this way, "I'm running out of time," he says. "If I don't learn it this year, I'm never going to learn it."

In the spring of 1995, when I visited the program, it was only nine months old. Both the teachers and the students were riding high on a wave of adrenaline "Eighty percent of the educators out there never thought this school would open on September 12," said Kathleen Foster, the program director, a Philadelphia native with a deep, engaging laugh. "But what's even more important is when we open next September and the year after that."

As I traveled around the country visiting school-to-work sites in 1995 and 1996, I repeatedly found myself asking, How did these efforts get started and what helped sustain them?

In Pennsylvania, the initial impetus came from the state, which in 1991 launched one of the first youth apprenticeship programs in the nation. By 1992–93, several groups in the Lehigh Valley, ranging from the Ben Franklin Technology Center to Lehigh Valley 2000, also had begun discussions about how to improve education and training in their communities. Once dominated by family-owned farms, the four-county area relied increasingly on a mix of heavy and light industry and financial, health, and human services. In late 1992, the state brought together a focus group of local educators and business leaders to talk about the potential for youth apprenticeships. The existing effort was born out of a discussion over the lunch table.

It would be impossible for just this combination of circumstances—or just this program—to arise elsewhere. We cannot simply replicate programs from one place to another, anymore than we can import another country's education-and-training system.

But we can be smarter about creating the conditions that enable such systems to take root. And we can share best practices so that every educator and employer does not have to recreate effective strategies from scratch.

As Larry Rosenstock, the director of the Rindge School of Technical Arts in Cambridge, Massachusetts, put it, "If there's any lesson from Rindge, it's about improving the conditions in the petri dish. And if you improve the conditions in the petri dish, then a lot of people will arise—many of whom you would not have expected—who will be doing their best work."

At the risk of simplifying a complex issue, I present here some of the common features that stood out in my visits to workplaces and school systems across the United States.

Leadership

In every place that I visited there was at least one stalwart champion—and most often a group of individuals—who had decided to make closer collaboration between schools and businesses a priority. Someone had called people to the table.

Leadership usually is not confined to a single individual. At the Rindge School of Technical Arts, the leaders were Larry Rosenstock and a dedicated team of educators that included Rob Riordan, Adria Steinberg, and Maria Ferri. At Sinclair Community College in Ohio and Tri-County Technical College in South Carolina, the outspoken commitment of two college presidents, David Ponitz and Don Garrison, joined by the tech-prep coordinators Bonnie Barrett and Diana Walter and by such committed department chairmen as Tom Carlisle and Jim Wood made the difference. In Boston, leadership shown by the Boston Compact and the Private Industry Council, led by its executive director, Neil Sullivan, and the school-to-work coordinator, Lois Ann Porter, made school-to-work a reality.

"This won't happen without leadership," Sullivan told me, "because these are not natural formations in this country. In fact, in private, the two sectors [education and business] do not view each other favorably."

Depending on the circumstances, key players came from within the high schools, the colleges, or the business community. But somewhere, someone took the initiative and the responsibility to make things happen. Many of the partnerships transcended school district boundaries because companies operate regionally, but they all had strong community roots. Inevitably, each of the partnerships rested on local relationships and local trust.

At the state level, the leadership of governors and state superintendents of education often has been essential. Wisconsin's school-to-work initiative stems in large part from the perseverance of the former chief state school officer, Bert Grover, and Governor Tommy G. Thompson. In Maine, former governor John R. McKernan, Jr., made school-to-work one of the top priorities of his tenure. In particular, gubernatorial leadership makes it easier and more attractive for businesses to become involved and for those in the system to take risks. Congressional passage of the School-to-Work Opportunities Act in 1994 has served as a catalyst to spread school-to-work practices, encouraging every state to develop a school-to-work plan. But in the current anti–federal government political climate, the primary leadership will have to come from the state and local levels.

Leadership also must come from the business community. Without constant and consistent pressure from the business community to raise academic standards and to forge closer ties between schools and workplaces, education is all too likely to withdraw into itself. Businesses *are* a key customer of education, no matter what schools think of that concept. Businesspeople have every right to make their needs and desires known.

At the same time, education is not the top priority of business—business is. Nor are businesses the only customers of the schools. School-to-work must reflect business priorities and will fail miserably without business participation. But it is unrealistic to expect businesses to lead the charge alone.

Seed Money

School-to-work initiatives cannot get started without an initial infusion of flexible seed money. In every site I visited, these funds were over and above the schools' routine costs of doing business. One study estimates that the cost of establishing a youth-apprenticeship program can be 30 percent to 50 percent higher than the average per student cost in a high school. These estimates include initial expenses, such as curriculum development and staff training, as well as ongoing funds to coordinate the program. In New Castle County, Delaware, a one-cent property tax increase provided $200,000 a year for professional development and $400,000 a year for technology purchases over a five-year period, as well as monies for facility improvements. The state of Maine contributed $3 million to Maine Career Advantage during its first five years. In Austin the mayor and the city council committed approximately $200,000 a year to help launch a school-to-work system. Almost every site that I visited had benefited from at least one federal grant, and often from more than one, under either the School-to-Work Opportunities Act or other programs. Although funding provided under the School-to-Work Opportunities Act was modest—$245 million in fiscal 1995 and even less in fiscal 1996—it clearly made a tremendous difference in getting programs off the ground.

Foundations also have played a key role in getting school-to-work initiatives started in this country, particularly given the limited amount of government support. The DeWitt Wallace–Reader's Digest Fund, the Pew Charitable Trusts, and the Ford, Lilly, Charles Stewart Mott, and Alfred P. Sloan foundations all were early contributors to the school-to-work movement. The Autodesk Foundation in California also has worked with K–12 schools across the United States to expand the use of project-based learning, which helps young people apply their academics to the real world.

These start-up funds served a number of essential functions. They paid for individuals who could act as coordinators and intermediaries between school systems and businesses. They supported curriculum development and professional development for teachers and work-site mentors. They bought equipment and materials. They bought time. There is a particularly strong need for well-researched, validated curriculum and instructional models that could help change what occurs in classrooms on a daily basis.

While these start-up funds could be substantial—more than $700,000 in the case of Rindge for program development and dissemination—it is not clear how much it will take above existing school and business budgets to sustain and operate school-to-work systems in the long run. In part, the answer will depend on whether schools and businesses are willing to reallocate existing resources to fit a new set of priorities.

Few sites that I visited had reached a point where they clearly would survive if these extra start-up funds disappeared. One exception was a commitment by the Boston School Committee to fund school-to-work coordinators in some of its high schools in 1995. All school systems are going to have to make similar innovative arrangements if school-to-work programs are to have a future.

A Supportive Government Framework

Educators and employers are the pivotal partners in a school-to-work system, but for such initiatives to succeed, government must provide the glue. In California and Florida, state funding and technical assistance for career academies have greatly expanded the number of such programs statewide. In Ohio, collaboration between higher education and high schools is greatly enhanced because the state board of regents and the state department of education share responsibility for tech-prep programs. Wisconsin and Oregon are working to develop competency-based admissions standards for higher education that would enable high schools to break away from traditional course transcripts and lockstep instruction. Wisconsin has developed skill standards for its youth apprenticeship and cooperative education programs to ensure that students across the state learn the same core skills within an industry. Maryland has created an incentive pool to encourage trade associations, labor unions, and consortia of employers to develop skill standards, work-based learning programs, and training for work-site supervisors.

The states that appear to be making the most progress in developing a school-to-work system also have a comprehensive vision for how school-to-work fits into their overall education-reform efforts. They have made clear linkages between school-to-work and their broader economic and workforce-development initiatives. In Massachusetts, for example, school-to-work initiatives are being developed in industries that the state has identified as critical growth areas, such as financial services, biotechnology, and marine sciences. Locally, school-to-work is being coordinated with other workforce-development efforts through new regional employment boards.

At the national level, a new National Skill Standards Board is working with employers, educators, labor, and other stakeholders to create voluntary standards for what workers should know and be able to do in broad clusters of occupations.

Bridge Builders

In many of the sites that I visited, intermediary organizations such as a local chamber of commerce or a community-based organization acted as go-betweens and interpreters for the various partners. In some cases, these were brand-new organizations, such as the Capital Area Training Foundation in Austin or the Northern Tier Industry Education Consortium in Pennsylvania. In other cases, these were preexisting groups that had taken on new roles. Often, they were some of the strongest entities within the community.

Intermediary groups have played an equally important role at the national level, by sharing information on best practices, conducting research, bringing the players together, providing technical assistance and training, and serving as a rallying voice for change. The National Academy Foundation, the National Alliance of Business, the National Center on Education and the Economy, Schools & Main, and High Schools That Work, among others, all have helped put school-to-work on the map. Jobs for the Future, based in Boston, has probably done more than any other national entity to set the agenda for school-to-work and to push for systems of high quality.

In her book *World Class: Thriving Locally in a Global Economy*, Rosabeth Moss Kanter talks about the importance of creating the infrastructure for collaboration: "The infrastructure for collaboration consists of the pathways by which people and organizations come together to exchange ideas, solve problems, or form partnerships. It helps people move across the barriers of localism, parochialism, or provincialism that divide them. It is the means by which people and organizations can come together across sectors to recognize, value, and leverage their area's assets for mutual gain. It might take concrete form as civic leadership groups, public-private partnerships, industry councils, or other institution-spanning bodies. It is broader but less formal and more fluid than government and, in some cases, much more important in getting things done."

School-to-work simply cannot survive without this kind of an infrastructure, since it inevitably requires a deep and ongoing collaboration among educators, employers, employees, government, and community-based groups that do not have a strong history of cooperation.

Almost invariably, individuals who could maneuver among these different cultures defined new roles for themselves. Each of the houses within Fenway Middle College High School had a "coordinator," a faculty member with a reduced teaching load whose job was to recruit businesses and help develop internships for students. "It's a lot of time. It's very labor-intensive," said Pam Mape, the coordinator for Crossroads House. "You have to say, as a school, is our development of these work sites just as important as the education that we're basing here, and are we willing to reduce the teacher's workload to do it?"

Many of the people in these bridge-building capacities came from business—people such as René Leger at Roosevelt High School in Portland, Oregon; Jeanne Yerkovich at David Douglas High School, also in Portland; and Tom Bryan at the Boston Private Industry Council. Others were educators who were willing to take risks and step outside traditional boundaries. Whatever their background, these successful intermediaries were comfortable in both worlds. "You have to have a broker who talks both languages and can bring them together," explained Leger. "The way I look at me and the folks that work with me, we're a transition team that helps make this happen."

Many of the larger employers—such as Children's Hospital and NYNEX in Boston, Autodesk in California, Advanced Micro Devices in Austin, and St. Christopher's Hospital in Philadelphia—have assigned individuals to coordinate their company's school-to-work efforts almost full time. The Fred Meyer Corporation in Portland, Oregon, has established a school-to-work committee within the company. In both schools and businesses, people must be formally assigned to coordinate young people's work-based learning and to coach, supervise, and mentor young people in the workplace.

Several intermediary organizations, such as the Northern Tier Industry Education Consortium and the Capital Area Training Foundation, made good use of retired businesspeople or educators who were well respected in the community and who were willing to work for little pay, in part as a community service. Others have made use of part-time executives on loan from businesses.

But in too many places, teachers and company employees are expected to shoulder these new responsibilities without any recognition or reward—and without any reduction of their previous workloads. This is not a viable option in the long run. Most educators—especially good ones—are already overwhelmed with responsibilities. They cannot take on school-to-work activities in addition to their other tasks. The same could be said for most work-site supervisors and mentors.

Equal Partnerships

Many people have advocated that school-to-work should be "business led." Without business in the driver's seat, the argument goes, the resulting efforts are unlikely to meet the needs of employers or to generate a sense of business ownership.

But true partnerships require both sides to come together from positions of equal strength. In places where these initiatives seem to work best, both business and education have something to contribute, they operate from a position of trust, and there is a clear division of labor and responsibilities. Dennis Loftus, the superintendent of the New Castle County Vocational-Technical School District, said, "To me, it's not a true partnership unless both sides bring respect to the table."

Where business barged in and tried to set the agenda and the schools participated on a begrudging basis, problems inevitably arose. The same was true where schools developed a program and then approached companies with a fait accompli. For example, one of the high schools that I visited in Austin was having trouble finding work-site placements for its students because it had no business partner.

Because school people vastly outnumber businesspeople in most school-to-work partnerships, the tendency is for educators to take over. They have a hard time letting go of the notion that they are solely responsible for the education of the young. "[School-to-career] can easily disappear into education, which is a massive public infrastructure," said Neil Sullivan, the executive director of the Boston Private Industry Council. "When that imbalance appears, the private sector pulls back. This has got to be a fifty-fifty proposition."

Involving Parents, Students, and Workers

Schools and businesses cannot be the only partners. Almost entirely absent from many existing school-to-work efforts are the voices of students and parents.

This is a huge mistake, and it has encouraged the misunderstandings that have opened school-to-work to attacks from the conservative right. As Robert Glover, a research scientist in economics at the Center for Human Resources at the University of Texas at Austin, told me, "You need to have some sort of countervailing force to business interests because they are not always consistent with the general interest."

Businesses naturally want to attract the most qualified and motivated young people. Educators, meanwhile, want to make high-quality learning opportunities available to as many students as possible. Small employers, in particular, may want to equip students with skills that are of immediate use in the workplace, while educators tend to favor the acquisition of broad knowledge and skills that provide a foundation for the future. Young people may benefit most by gaining a mixture of specific and broad-based knowledge and skills.

Glover summarizes the role of parents and students this way: "Employer interests cannot dominate all aspects of the school-to-careers system without some community checks on their behavior. Indeed, youth and their parents may have the largest stake in preparing students for good jobs within a labor market.

"At the same time," he continues, "a school-to-career partnership without engaged employers is doomed to failure. The use of such terminology as 'employer led' or 'school led' may be at best misleading and at worst simply inflammatory. Each group has valid and important roles to play."

The experiences in Austin, Boston, and other places suggest that special outreach efforts are needed to gain significant industry involvement, and that businesses will stop coming if they are too heavily outnumbered. Glover notes that labor unions and existing workers also need to be part of the process. Although firms have been very sensitive about upsetting their incumbent workforce, he notes, they have not necessarily sought their employees' input in designing school-to-work initiatives.

Time

Creating partnerships between education and industry takes time. Employers and educators in Boston have been at work on the Boston Compact for nearly 15 years. European countries commonly set a 10- to 20-year agenda for their education-and-training policies and then refine them as they go. Most of the sites that I visited are part of school-to-work efforts that began in the early 1990s, so this book is a preliminary assessment of the initiatives.

The wise use of time can be a crucial element in other ways. Most of the efforts described in this book provided substantial time for teachers to plan new curricula and programs, to engage in professional development, and to meet with employers. Rindge, for example, scheduled daily meeting time for CityWorks faculty to reflect and collaborate, even though it meant closing the vocational shops for a period. The three vocational-technical high schools in New Castle County, Delaware, revamped their entire schedule to create a common planning time for teachers. The school board agreed to start and end the school day earlier so that teachers could meet for forty minutes at the end of each day. Fenway Middle College High School has made common planning time for teachers an integral part of its structure from the beginning. Both Roosevelt and David Douglas high schools in Oregon rearranged their schedules for an entire year—allowing students to come to school late—so that teachers would have time to plan. But schools have been less successful at providing teachers with time to spend in workplaces so that they can make direct connections between workplace-based knowledge and their classroom subjects.

Many high schools also have rearranged their schedules to give students time for in-depth study and for workplace experiences. Block schedules that move away from the traditional 50-minute class period give students and teachers time for hands-on learning, interdisciplinary classes, and the in-depth exploration of topics. Innovative schedules also can provide some of the flexibility needed for students to leave campus for job shadows and work-site placements without missing school course work.

Allowing for a greater integration of school-based and work-based learning will require even more creative thinking about how to structure students' time in high schools. Solutions might range from one morning or afternoon a week dedicated to off-campus activities to the use of short intersessions focused on off-site learning to summer and after-school internships. At Fenway Middle College High School, juniors and seniors participate in a full-time internship for six weeks after Christmas vacation, rather than attending classes. Every Wednesday afternoon, students at the High School of Economics and Finance in New York City participate in seminars, field trips, and workshops conducted by the school's business partners. The Pennsylvania youth apprenticeship programs schedule classes on alternate days or weeks, so that students can spend full days out at the work site.

We commonly tend to think of learning as occurring only when a teacher is standing up and lecturing in front of the classroom. But it could be that both teachers and students are spending too much time in classrooms and not enough time learning in other ways.

Getting Started

Even though it takes time to create a school-to-work system, many people told me it was important to have something that participants could accomplish in the short term. Employers will simply stop coming if all that happens is talk.

Some sites probably did not spend enough time on planning, and launched school-to-work programs with far less care than they would pay to a new product line. But in most cases, jumping in after six months to a year and then continuing to refine and reflect upon the partnership along the way appeared to work. In fact, you could argue that these kinds of efforts are so new that this is the only way to proceed. Many of the bugs simply cannot be worked out or even contemplated in advance, and some of the most thoughtful practitioners viewed their efforts as continuous works-in-progress.

Setting Benchmarks

A few school-to-work systems have begun to set benchmarks to measure their progress and to hold the different partners accountable, if not for results, then at least for doing what they had pledged to do on a reasonable schedule. One example was New Castle County, Delaware, which provided schools with a wealth of survey and performance data that they could use to improve their programs and be more responsive to their customers, including businesses, students, teachers, and parents. As the school district develops closer relationships with its business partners, it will be interesting to see whether similar benchmarks are developed to hold employers to their end of the bargain.

That is exactly what the Boston Regional Employment Board is trying to do by developing short-term and long-term benchmarks for both schools and companies. Some of the benchmarks concern student attendance and performance; others concern the number of work placements provided for students and the number of high schools with career majors. Similarly, in 1989 Oregon created the Oregon Progress Board, a statewide planning board chaired by the governor and charged with developing indicators that would monitor the quality of life and economic development in the state.

Individual programs also have developed quality-control mechanisms such as written contracts and individual learning plans among students, parents, educators, and workplace mentors that clarify the responsibilities on all sides. Particularly when programs are first starting out, these kinds of written arrangements help establish the ground rules.

Benchmarks force participants to clarify the goals for their school-to-work systems. Is the purpose to get students into jobs or into higher education? To provide students with career exploration or specific occupational competencies? What percentage of graduates must pursue employment related to their training in order for companies to justify their investments?

Jobs for the Future's Benchmark Communities Initiative is working with five sites—Boston; Milwaukee; Philadelphia; Jefferson County, Kentucky; and North Clackamas, Oregon—that have agreed to hold themselves accountable as they create a comprehensive school-to-career system. Each of these communities has pledged to put in place within five years more than 20 mutually agreed upon elements that would characterize a high-quality system, although the precise design will vary by community. Moreover, there are specific benchmarks set for the percentage of young people and employers that will be participating in high-quality school-to-career experiences at the end of the five years. Jobs for the Future will evaluate and report on the progress of these benchmark communities through a combination of site visits; employer, teacher, and student surveys; and analysis of student performance.

Choice

At the time that I visited them, none of the school-to-work initiatives were mandatory for students, teachers, or employers. Even the career clusters at David Douglas High School were still optional. They were all programs of choice.

Choice programs in schools typically have greater flexibility and autonomy than are found in traditional comprehensive high schools. Rindge, for example, is a school-within-a-school. So are the career academies in Pasadena, California. Fenway is a pilot school within the Boston Public Schools, which means it has more leeway to control its own budget, scheduling, curriculum, and staffing.

Choice also has important implications for students. Because students select these programs themselves, they are more likely to commit to the learning that occurs there. They are more likely to feel special and to identify strongly with the group, and they have a greater incentive to meet expectations.

Given the prominence of choice in existing school-to-work efforts, there is the potential for individual school-to-work programs to skim off the best students. I have heard this concern raised particularly in urban areas with high concentrations of minority and disadvantaged young people. But in general, this does not appear to be happening. Though individual programs do have some admissions standards, they are typically modest. At the same time, few programs are focused on the most academically or behaviorally troubled students, who could benefit most from alternative approaches to instruction. It also is important to note that admissions criteria differ from program to program, with some more stringent than others.

I saw more evidence of gender differentiation among programs. As you might expect, girls tended to cluster in health care and business programs; boys tended to dominate—almost to the point of exclusion—in many industrial and engineering programs. This seemed to stem less from discrimination on the part of the initiatives, many of which were actively trying to recruit both sexes, than from stereotypes within society at large. A few places, such as Procter & Gamble, had managed to surmount these preconceptions and recruit nearly as many young women as young men.

A school-to-work *system* that can serve large numbers of young people in a country as diverse as ours inevitably will encompass a lot of variations. There is no one recipe for how to proceed. Across the United States, hundreds of school-to-work efforts are now in place. They are demonstrating that school-to-work can serve a wide variety of young people, engage them in learning, and serve employers' interests. We can continue to pile up such program models indefinitely. The greater challenge is to create a system that links these individual programs into some sort of coherent whole.

CHAPTER 8

What Needs to Be Done

I started this book to explore whether there is an effective way for educators and employers to collaborate in preparing the next generation for work and adulthood. My point is not that businesses should take over the education of the young. They shouldn't. Nor should schools sacrifice the preparation of a thinking democratic citizenship on the altar of work. But a climate of mutual exclusion and distrust is detrimental to both and is increasingly unrealistic in an information-based society.

Over the course of a year, I visited apprenticeship programs where students spend half their time on the job and career academies where students spend most of their time in the classroom. I visited programs that serve a dozen students and programs that serve 400. Most of these programs are only a few years old. If they were children, they would barely have learned to walk. Not surprisingly, data on their performance are limited. But there is a growing accumulation of qualitative and anecdotal evidence about their potential. What does it tell us?

❀ School-to-work can motivate young people to learn. Many young people report that they are more interested in and more challenged by these programs than by traditional academic course work. In particular, they note that working in teams, solving real-world problems, engaging in hands-on activities, and planning and completing projects are more enjoyable and help them learn more. For once, they can see the relevance of and real-world connection to what they are learning. "It gives you a different idea of school, when you're out there," explains Matt Ciprich, an apprentice at Ingersoll Rand in Pennsylvania. "You have to take pride in your work. At school, you can say, 'Who cares?' Out there, what you do could be live-or-die for the company. And if you don't care about it, then that's serious. You understand that instead of just being [in school] and listening to everybody talk all day long, you have to take some of this stuff in. If you're going to be an engineer, if you don't know some of the formulas or you can't read some of the drawings, where will you be?

"I'm just astounded at everything that I've done," he adds. "I mean, I worked at a level that I didn't think I could."

❀ School-to-work can encourage young people to pursue further education and training. In sites ranging from ProTech in Boston to the Education for Employment Consortium in Kalamazoo, Michigan, high percentages of young people are choosing to pursue postsecondary education because they understand the connection between learning and a good job.

❀ School-to-work can engage young people in career planning and make them more optimistic about the future. As one young person explained, "It gives you a fresh start. You know what direction you want to go in. It just gives you a real good outlook on what you want to do, and what you expect for yourself." In New York City, students in career magnet high schools engage in what the education researcher Robert L. Crain and his colleagues at Columbia University's Teachers College call "parallel career planning." They prepare simultaneously for both higher education and employment. Their research has found that graduates of career magnet high schools were more likely to have declared a college major and earned more college credits when they went to college than their peers from traditional high schools with no career focus. On average, they also were employed more months after graduation.

❖ School-to-work can satisfy employers, many of whom are surprised by what young people can accomplish when given the opportunity. The growth in employer participation, while not overwhelming, has been slow and steady.

All of these results have been achieved by young people who are often invisible within the current educational system. Students who too often are written off as average have been made to feel special, capable, and directed.

The extent to which school-to-work can raise academic achievement is less clear. Some studies have found that students in school-to-work programs at least maintained their grade-point average, class rank, and attendance. Others report that these students perform better than nonprogram participants. In my own travels, I found a loose fit between learning that occurred at the workplace and in schools. Programs also varied in their stress on academic learning and performance. Sometimes the intellectual content of work-based learning was not obvious. In other cases, students' course taking and how content was taught within high schools had barely altered. In a few instances, school and work-based learning competed for young people's attention. Unless *learning* is placed front and center as the goal of school-to-work initiatives, they could too easily dissolve into watered-down work experiences for some students.

Many school-to-work initiatives either provide very limited work-based learning to large numbers of students or intensive work-based learning to only a handful of young people. Providing high-quality school-to-career experiences for many students remains a serious challenge. There is every indication that youth apprenticeships will continue to grow in the United States, but at a painfully slow rate. As Robert Egloff, the apprenticeship consultant from Zurich, Switzerland, pointed out (chapter 5), apprenticeships are most likely to succeed in industries with a deep concern for quality, a desperate need for qualified workers, and enough prosperity to invest in the future. This combination clearly applies to America's rebounding manufacturing sector, which I believe is ripe for a greater use of apprenticeships. In general, however, I think education and training will remain more school-bound in the United States than they are in European countries.

American businesses today have very little experience in designing work-based education. They are not generally involved in school-to-work efforts. To build a new infrastructure in this country that brings together educators and employers will require patience, perseverance, and a long-term view.

At the same time, I'd take issue with some well-known economists and pundits who have already given up on school-to-work. I have been in enough communities where businesses are engaged to believe that it is doable, and I have been struck repeatedly by the level and sincerity of their involvement.

Basic School-to-Work Principles

So what would I propose? As interest in school-to-work grows, quality must be maintained for these efforts to be worth doing. What follows are a set of principles or components that I believe should undergird good school-to-work systems and high-quality education for adolescents in general.

Primacy of Learning

The central goal of school-to-work systems should be to help students achieve more academically. All students should engage in intellectually challenging work and should graduate on the basis of what they know and can do. Not every student will reach the same heights in mathematics or science or English or history. But as Arthur Powell and his colleagues suggested more than a decade ago, all students should be expected to move in the same direction. "Many of the most serious 'life skills' that high schools can teach—speaking cogently, writing clearly, reading with understanding, listening with empathy, having facility with numbers, solving problems— are not the exclusive domain of one subject," Powell and his colleagues wrote. "They need constant reinforcement in many subjects throughout high school."

Students should be able to demonstrate a command of these skills, as well as of challenging content, before they graduate. Because students today graduate on the basis of an accumulation of credit hours and course titles rather than performance, the high school diploma has become blatantly meaningless for many students, parents, and employers. We need to reexamine the rigor of the courses that students take and what they can do when they're finished, not just the hours spent in class.

But until we agree about what students should know and be able to do at the end of high school and how they should demonstrate it, I am reluctant to say that any student needs less than three years of math or science. Students cannot possibly learn what they are not taught. The Southern Regional Education Board noted in a recent report, "Simply requiring all students to complete 13 or more courses in the core subject areas will not guarantee that test scores will go up dramatically, that the number of students placed in remedial courses in college will be reduced substantially, or that employers will be satisfied with the skills and knowledge that high school graduates bring to entry-level jobs.

What we do know is that *not* requiring challenging courses results in mediocre test scores, high percentages of students entering college in remedial courses, and high school graduates who are unprepared for the workplace."

This has important implications for any school-to-work system. It means that all students must master a common core of upgraded academic content. Even students who choose to pursue technical specialties, through apprenticeships or other avenues, should receive a solid dose of academics. In Germany, apprentices spend one or two days a week in public technical schools, where they study such topics as mathematics, German, and religion.

At the same time, I see no reason why the traditional sequence of academic courses or the traditional segregation of academic disciplines should be sacrosanct. Most students need probability and statistics more than they need calculus. Similarly, students interested in technical fields would be well advised to take physics. Yet traditionally, only the elite few make it through the obstacle course of the earth sciences, biology, and chemistry ever to reach a physics class. Leon M. Lederman, a Nobel Prize–winning physicist, has proposed reversing the traditional sequence so that all students take physics in their freshman year, followed by chemistry and then biology. Though most high schools remain wedded to the traditional sequence, any change in curriculum or scheduling should consider the importance of physics in many technical careers.

In the field of mathematics, some of the most exciting new curricula combine real-life applications with a more integrated approach to mathematical content. One example is the Interactive Math Program now used at Fenway Middle College High School, which was developed by high school and college teachers at the University of California at Berkeley and San Francisco State University. In general, integrated curricula offer possibilities that are impossible to create otherwise. Some of the most demanding and engaging classes that I observed, for example, the Law Network at David Douglas High School, integrated traditional academic subjects, such as English and social studies, around a common real-world theme.

If we were more successful at spelling out what students should know and be able to do at the *end* of high school, schools would have greater freedom to create these more innovative and interdisciplinary courses. In fact, states who move their graduation requirements away from discipline-based Carnegie Units, a system for standardizing the high school curriculum developed in 1905, and toward other measures of performance probably will have the most success in making room for a school-to-work system.

Having clear expectations of what a high school diploma stands for does not mean that all students will achieve at the same level. There should be room to recognize outstanding and advanced performance. But it does mean that performance below a certain level would not qualify a student to graduate. Right now, the level for most high school competency tests is set at the eighth or ninth grade. As the Southern Regional Education Board notes, this reflects what students should know before they enter high school, not when they leave it.

Relevance of Knowledge

We need to focus more on changing students' day-to-day learning experiences in school so that they are of high quality. All students should have the opportunity to learn by doing, to complete projects, and to apply their knowledge to problems beyond school. Not everything in education needs to be immediately useful or practical. Applied learning or career-focused instruction can be taken too far. There is nothing worse than asking students to write a memo to Macbeth. But we can't expect all young people to be motivated by abstract ideas and principles. At some point, students will ask, "When am I going to need this?"

To the extent possible, the lines between school and non-school must become blurred so that young people as early as elementary school can see how knowledge is used on a daily basis. This means including more real-world problems and projects in the curriculum. It means more community-based learning opportunities that enable young people to view their community and themselves as resources. The sites involved in Jobs for the Future's Benchmark Communities Initiative have pledged that at the end of five years all high school students would take at least two courses in academic subjects, such as English and mathematics, in which they learn by designing and applying solutions to real-world problems.

Anything can be taken to extremes. Community- or work-based learning does *not* mean converting every elementary school classroom into a simulated supermarket or bank. The goal is not to produce minicapitalists or pint-sized consumers. It is to produce students who can do something with the knowledge that they have.

For this to happen, we first need to acknowledge that schools and academic learning are too isolated from the rest of the world. We need to give teachers some tools and some strategies for integrating real-life applications and hands-on learning into their classrooms, including the chance for internships in the work site and the time to work together to plan. We need to bring community people into the classroom to judge projects and participate in classroom discussions. And we need to get students out into the community.

Work-based learning represents the ultimate marriage of theory and practice. But not every student will have the time or inclination to participate in an apprenticeship or even a summer internship. Projects and simulations will have to fill some of that gap. I was particularly impressed by schools—such as Hodgson Vocational-Technical High School, David Douglas High School, and Fenway Middle College High School—that require students to complete a senior project combining a research paper and a product, such as a scale model of a house, a plan for where to locate a pharmacy in the community, or a brochure on managed health care. Too many seniors are floating through their final year in high school in a combination of elective classes and study hall. A senior project that requires students to make use of what they have learned and encourages them to focus on a passionate interest of their choosing can both demonstrate mastery and serve as a useful preparation for work and college. In Denmark, all students in vocational programs in upper-secondary education are given a week to complete a major written assignment on a topic of their choosing, during which they do not receive instruction. The paper is corrected and assessed by the teacher and by one external examiner.

Work Ethics

Schools need to emphasize and demand basic work ethics and good citizenship from students. Work ethics such as dependability, persistence, honesty, and initiative are best taught—and modeled—in real workplaces where their importance is self-evident. But they should also be the concern of schools. This does not mean offering a separate class on employability skills, as some high schools have done. Rather, it means expecting students to attend class, to show up on time, to do their homework, to honor their commitments, to listen respectfully to the opinions of others and to raise questions, to solve conflicts through nonviolent means, and to revise their work until it meets quality criteria.

These are also the characteristics of good citizenship, and they should be emphasized in the teaching of all subjects. These traits cannot be taught unless parents and the larger community support schools that impose real consequences for tardiness or nonattendance and maintain real standards for student work.

When companies hire students without regard to their high school attendance or performance, they unfortunately send the message that such traits do not really matter. Teaching such basic elements of character requires schools to teach values and they needn't be ashamed of it.

The comment I heard most often from students was that at school any effort was "good enough," but that at work quality counted. Students didn't think twice about showing up late for class—or not coming at all—but they knew that if they showed up late for work, they'd be fired. And if they didn't know, they soon found out. The expectations were simply higher. When students talked about schools or classes that stood out from the everyday fare—such as the Greater Lehigh Valley Youth Apprenticeship Program or the Academy of Travel and Tourism at Miami Springs High School—typically what they commented upon was that teachers expected and pushed them to achieve and that the general school climate supported hard work. Students were not given the option of choosing not to learn.

Exploring Career Options

All students should have opportunities for career exploration and a broad perspective on career options. Career exploration differs from the traditional sequence of vocational classes that train young people for a specific job. It involves visits to the workplace, combined with writing and reflection, such as the job-shadowing activities that I observed at Roosevelt High School or the work-site seminars at Rindge. It involves participation by businessmen and other community leaders in and out of classrooms. Where possible, it involves internships and work-related projects.

Sending students to the library to do research reports on two possible careers simply is not adequate. All students should be required to do a more thorough level of career exploration or internship as a prerequisite for graduation from high school.

In Denmark, educational and vocational guidance is a compulsory topic from the age of 12 or 13. The aim is to make students aware of their own capabilities and options after leaving school. The topic is not given a separate place in the curriculum but is mainly incorporated into a weekly discussion period with the student's primary classroom teacher. In Denmark, Germany, and Scotland, all students spend several days to several weeks in the workplace, beginning in their preteen years, so that they can actually experience different careers and occupations. Such exposure should begin in middle school and increase in intensity and focus in high school.

At the same time, we need to be aware of the difference between career exploration and career preparation. Apprenticeships and other programs with clear, competency-based standards provide students with real, marketable skills and a credential when they graduate. They strengthen the ties between students and potential employers. Students who graduate from a career pathway with only one or two courses in a career-related field and no prior contact with employers do not necessarily have better prospects for employment than any other high school graduate (although they may benefit from seeing how academics are applied outside the classroom).

Planning Education and Careers

All students should have individual career and education plans. Research suggests that students who have a plan that focuses and guides their course taking in high school are more likely to take classes necessary to succeed in college and in careers. Decisions about students' future educational and career plans should rest unequivocally in the hands of young people and their parents. But all students should have a purposeful course of study that goes beyond the formality of signing up for classes. It should reflect a student's abilities, interests, and future goals. It should be reviewed and adjusted regularly. It should be taken seriously, not simply be a pro forma activity.

The researchers Gary Orfield and Faith Paul note that the point of an individual career and education plan is not to track students, but rather to give parents and students more information so that they can make sound decisions about the future. One of the criteria for a good school-to-work system is that students should be able to change their minds. In some cases, this may require some additional course work, but the flexibility to switch directions and the pathways that are open to students should remain clear.

For students and parents to make such decisions, they need better information about career options and their requirements and personal advising on an ongoing basis. This simply is not possible with our existing system of career guidance and counseling, in which counselors are responsible for anywhere from 250 to 500 students. Instead, all teachers should assume responsibility for advising a small group of students throughout their years in high school, and time should be carved out of the school schedule to do this. At David Douglas High School, every teacher is responsible for a small group of incoming freshmen. At Howard High School of Technology, every teacher is responsible for working with a group of young people on their career plans and portfolio.

Advisers also could be drawn from outside the school, for example, business and community mentors and work-site supervisors. Adults such as those in Career Beginnings can provide students with additional support and guidance about colleges and careers.

Feedback Between Teachers and Employers

All students would benefit from the ongoing exchange of information between employers and educators. Teachers, parents, and students all need access to better information about colleges and careers than is commonly available. They need to know what the job openings are in their region and the forecasts for additional job growth. Employers need better data about the quality of schools and the meaning of high school transcripts. Community-based career centers and computer and on-line services provide one source of information. This is an area that needs much more work. Most state labor-market data currently are not useful or intelligible to students or educators to help them make better decisions. The exchange of better information also could reduce the recruitment, screening, and hiring costs for employers.

Community of Peers and Mentors

Every student should have the chance to be part of a small, supportive learning community and to develop close relationships with adults. Participants in career academies report that one of the biggest differences is the chance for students and teachers to know each other personally. That goal should be extended to all students. Our big comprehensive high schools are simply too big. They need to be broken up.

This might mean the creation of more schools-within-schools, charter schools, magnet schools, and other schools of choice—as is already happening in high schools around the country. In large urban areas, the result would be greater opportunity to choose among career magnet high schools or numerous career and theme-oriented academies.

At this point, it is not possible to mandate that all high schools be broken into small units, but smaller learning communities can be created in less dramatic ways. For example, such a learning community could develop around a multiyear course in which a group of students and teachers remained together over a period of time and got to know each other well.

Adult coaches and mentors from the workplace also provide an important source of support, information, and guidance for students. The apprentices whom I interviewed frequently commented on the help they had received from mentors at the workplace, and mentors often commented on the close working relationships they had developed with young people.

Facilitate Transition

The last year or two in high school should be explicitly transitional and focus on helping students make the transitions to the next phase. As students reach the end of their high school careers, there should be room for them to focus on what interests them most. Those who want to head directly for work, or who have clear career goals, might choose to participate in apprenticeships that begin in their junior or senior year. Others might take two to four vocational courses at a community college or a technical institution. They might complete a sequence of electives that provide advanced study in a broad career field. Some students might want to pursue a combination of high school and community-college course work. Others might want to take a concentration of advanced-placement courses or courses on college campuses. Many states already have options that allow high school juniors and seniors to take courses at public colleges and universities for credit.

A student who is interested in computer technology might want to combine an internship in a local software company during the summer with a college course in computer-assisted design during the school year. Such diversity is fine, as long as students have met or continue to accumulate the knowledge and skills needed to graduate with a meaningful high school diploma.

Many of these options cannot be offered by high schools alone. Instead, high schools will have to work with community colleges, four-year institutions, vocational-technical schools, and businesses to prepare transitional experiences. In essence, high school education should be far more universal in the early years and far more individualized in the later years. As I noted in chapter 6, the three major reports on high schools during the 1980s—by John I. Goodlad, Ernest L. Boyer, and Theodore R. Sizer—all recognized the need for an explicitly transitional upper end to the high school experience.

Encourage Ongoing Learning

All students should be prepared to pursue further education and training beyond high school. As I hope this book has made clear, a high school education is no longer the key to job stability or success. Today, close to half of all young people ages 25 to 34 still have not gone beyond high school. To expect them all to earn a bachelor's degree is ludicrous, but to expect the vast majority of young people to pursue at least some postsecondary education and training is essential. High schools need to develop clear and explicit connections with postsecondary institutions, on the one hand, and businesses, on the other, so that students can climb clear ladders to success.

Roles of Partners in School-to-Work

Where school-to-work efforts appear to be thriving, they have done so through strategic networking and partnerships, in which the responsibilities of each party are clearly spelled out. What are some of the things that each of the partners can do to make school-to-work happen?

Role of Businesses

❧ Communicate clearly to students, parents, and educators the skills and knowledge required in the workplace, now and in the future. These include the broad employability skills described by SCANS (see chapter 3), the core academic requirements, and the occupational skill standards being developed at the state and national levels.

❧ Hire young people in part on the basis of their academic performance in high school. At the 1996 National Education Summit in Palisades, New York, business leaders pledged that within a year they would implement hiring practices that required applicants to demonstrate academic achievement through school-based records such as academic transcripts, diplomas, and portfolios.

According to the advisory board of the National Center on the Educational Quality of the Workforce, companies that use school grades to help screen employees have lower turnover and are more likely to rate their workers as fully proficient in their jobs. Employers in the service industry who check grades before hiring young workers have a more productive workforce.

❧ Refuse to employ high school students for more than 20 hours a week during the school year. Make school attendance and a minimum grade-point average conditions for continued employment, even offering tutoring for those who need it. Research suggests that students who work excessive hours perform less well in school. In contrast, employers who take an interest in how young workers are doing in school send a clear message that attendance and performance count—throughout life. I have run across a number of apprentices who worked long hours in part-time jobs *in addition* to their apprenticeships. Employers should discourage such practices.

❀ Open their doors to teachers and students for work-based learning experiences. Companies like the Boeing Company and BellSouth provide summer internships and employment for teachers as well as students, so that educators can begin to make the connection between academics and the changing workplace.

❀ Change personnel policies to recognize and reward the staff time that it takes to supervise, coach, teach, and mentor students and to work with schools.

❀ Document the costs and benefits of participating in school-to-work, rather than treating it solely as a charitable contribution.

Role of High Schools

❀ Clarify what they expect young people to know and be able to do to earn a high school diploma. In particular, schools need to go beyond traditional high school transcripts and the accumulation of course credits to develop high school diplomas with meaning.

❀ Refuse to track young people into rigid "college-bound" and "non-college-bound" or "vocational" and "academic" categories. Demand that all young people complete a rigorous academic curriculum and learn how to apply their knowledge.

❀ Eliminate narrow job-training programs, those geared to low-wage, low-skill occupations, and those that do not reflect labor-market needs.

❀ Change how content is taught to emphasize more project-based learning, interdisciplinary studies, hands-on laboratories and activities, and opportunities for students to apply their knowledge.

❀ Provide incentives for teachers and administrators to spend time in workplaces and bring those experiences back into the classroom.

❀ Rethink the use of time, providing opportunities for teachers to plan and collaborate and for students to engage in substantive activities in and outside the school building.

Role of Institutions of Higher Education

❀ Develop performance-based admissions standards in addition to, or in place of, more traditional entrance requirements. Specify the knowledge and skills that young people should have *before* they begin postsecondary education.

❀ Raise college admissions standards so that young people have an incentive to work harder and achieve more in high school.

❀ Pursue arrangements that enable capable young people to take college courses for credit while still in high school—on college campuses, in high school, or via computer and long-distance learning.

❀ Find ways to recognize, encourage, and accommodate work-based learning among college applicants and students and encourage college faculty to pursue integrated, hands-on pedagogy. Kalamazoo College in Michigan, for example, has a 35-year-old internship program that provides the majority of students with academic credit for work-based experiences.

❁ Provide funds, time, and incentives at the college level for faculty to work with high schools and with area businesses to develop school-to-work systems and to work with each other to integrate curricula.

Role of State and Local Governments

❁ Provide ongoing funding for connecting activities, curriculum development, and staff training, as well as special grants to get innovations started.

❁ Set rigorous standards for what students should know and be able to do to graduate that do not force high schools to use Carnegie Units and credit hours.

❁ Work with employers, educators, and employee organizations to develop voluntary skill standards for broad groups of occupations or industries.

❁ Rationalize funding streams and the regional boundaries for education and workforce-development programs so that schools, colleges, businesses, and government agencies can mesh programs and services to the benefit of young people.

❁ Revise child-labor laws, workmen's compensation policies, and insurance laws that discourage work-based learning.

❁ Use the bully pulpit to make school-to-work an ongoing part of the school-reform agenda.

Role of Parents

❧ Take responsibility for limiting the number of hours children work during the school year.

❧ Insist that all high school students have an individualized plan to help them choose their courses and think through career and college decisions.

❧ Advocate to ensure that a child is taking the courses necessary to succeed in work and college.

❧ Support internships, job shadowing, work-based projects, and other experiences that help children see the relevance of their schoolwork and focus their choices as they decide whether to go to college or start work immediately.

❧ Encourage children to pursue education and training beyond high school. Be willing to entertain other routes to success besides a bachelor's degree for children who do not wish to enter undergraduate education immediately, or who have not demonstrated that they are capable of performing college-level work.

❧ Open up their own businesses to students and teachers and volunteer to become mentors and work-site supervisors for young people.

High schools and companies have been isolated from each other for a very long time. Their cultures are very different. To change their relationship will require new graduation requirements, new arrangements of time and schedules, new curricula and pedagogy for teachers, and new thinking about what constitutes valid business costs and investments. These changes will not be easy, but all are important. If we do not take the first few steps, school-to-work will become another marginal reform and in the end nothing will change.

There are barriers and obstacles on all sides. Many employers are disillusioned about school reform. Many educators are weary from the constant battering of the public schools. Many teachers and parents view school-to-work as a dilution of the "basics" or a new-and-improved version of vocational education. They don't see it as a different way to teach worthwhile content.

Moreover, improving the skills of the future workforce will not necessarily lead to the availability of more high-wage, high-skill jobs, just as preparing more young people for college will not help if they do not have the financial means to attend. It goes without saying that the ideas in this book are only one part of a much broader public policy debate on economic priorities.

In spite of these factors, I believe that the forces drawing employers and educators—and work and learning—closer together are irresistible. "Corporations can't ignore education forever," says Nancy Shiels of Children's Hospital in Boston. "Students are the people who, one way or another, will end up on our doorstep to fill our jobs. Since government hasn't been adequately preparing students for real jobs in the rapidly changing workforce, I think it only makes good business sense for the business community to step in. Companies are already paying for training programs to give employees the basic skills they should have learned in high school. So why not invest their resources sooner, where it's really going to count?"

Notes

Preface

Page vii. *"The skills that students need"*: Consortium on Productivity in the Schools, 1995, *Using What We Have*, p. 9.

Chapter 1—The Need for a New Alliance

Page 1. *When asked whether our nation's public schools*: National Alliance of Business and Scholastic, 1995, "Education in the U.S."

Page 2. *Because businesspeople have so little faith*: National Center on the Educational Quality of the Workforce, 1995, "First Findings from the EQW National Employer Survey," p. 14.

Page 2. *Nor do they reward young people*: Bishop, 1995, *Expertise and Excellence*, p. 23.

Page 2. *Companies with good jobs*: For a discussion of the problem, see Osterman, 1991, "Is There a Problem with the Youth Labor Market . . . ?" and Zemsky, 1994, "What Employers Want."

Page 2. *Educators, meanwhile, often view business*: See Farkas and Friedman, 1995, "Westchester School-to-Work Initiative."

Page 2. *"Across the country, whether surrounded"*: Steinberg et al., 1996, *Beyond the Classroom*, p. 13.

Page 3. *"Education is becoming the fault line"*: U.S. Labor Secretary Robert Reich, speech delivered in Washington, D.C., May 24, 1996, at the New American High School conference. For discussions about changes in American business practices and the upskilling of the American workforce, see Carnevale, 1991, *America and the New Economy*; Drucker, 1993, *Post-Capitalist Society*; Berryman and Bailey, 1992, *Double Helix of Education and the Economy*; Marshall and Tucker, 1992, *Thinking for a Living*.

Page 3. *"Today's vehicles"*: Interview with Stephen Ash, Sinclair Community College, Dayton, Ohio, March 1996.

Page 6. *Employers who train teenagers:* National Center on the Educational Quality of the Workforce, 1995, "Other Shoe: Education's Contribution to the Productivity of Establishments," p. 5, and Lynn and Wills, 1994, *School Lessons, Work Lessons.*

Page 6. *"Business absolutely needs"*: Interview with Mimi Bushman, Portland, Oregon, November 1995.

Page 6. *"I had absolutely no idea"*: Interview with Erika Pyne, Bronson Methodist Hospital, Kalamazoo, Michigan, December 1995.

Page 7. *"It's very economical for us"*: Interview with Robert Doud, director of public affairs, Bronson Methodist Hospital, January 1995.

Page 7. *Such apprenticeships (called "externships" in Kalamazoo)*: Federal Ministry of Education and Science, 1994, "Vocational Training in Germany."

Page 8. *Coordination with school-based learning is often weak:* Bailey and Merritt, 1993, *School-to-Work Transition and Youth Apprenticeship,* pp. 19, 36.

Page 8. *First established in Philadelphia about 1970:* Kemple and Rock, 1996, *First Report on the Career Academies.*

Page 10. *Charlie Coppola:* Interview with Charlie Coppola, Procter & Gamble Paper Plant, Mehoopany, Pennsylvania, May 1995. Employment figures for the plant come from Joseph DiMarco, director of communications.

Page 11. *In 1988, a report:* The William T. Grant Commission on Work, Family, and Citizenship, 1988, *The Forgotten Half.*

Page 11. *In 1990, America's Choice:* Commission on the Skills of the American Workforce, 1990, *America's Choice: High Skills or Low Wages!*

Page 11. *By the early 1990s, no fewer than 20 reports:* U.S. Congress, Office of Technology Assessment, 1995, *Learning to Work.*

Page 12. *Americans who traveled abroad noted:* See Bottoms, 1996, "Lessons from Europe for Improving School-to-Work Programs," p. 1.

Page 13. *"I think the single most important lesson"*: Interview with Anne Heald, Bethesda, Maryland, June 1996.

Page 13. *Studies of large, comprehensive high schools:* Goodlad, 1983, *A Place*

Called School; Sizer, 1983, *Horace's Compromise;* Boyer, 1983, *High School;* Powell, Farrar, and Cohen, 1985, *Shopping Mall High School.*

Page 14. *Two thirds of high school students:* Johnson, Farkas, and Bers, *Getting By,* 1997.

Page 14. *"Her name was Joelle":* John Tobin, as quoted in Vogl, "Schools: Should Business Set Their Agenda?" June 1995, p. 22.

Page 14. *A separate body of cognitive research:* For a summation of cognitive research on learning see Resnick, 1987, *Education and Learning to Think;* Berryman and Bailey, 1992, *Double Helix;* Sue E. Berryman, 1994, "Apprenticeship as a Paradigm of Learning," in *Education Through Occupations in American High Schools,* ed. W. Norton Grubb, pp. 192–205; and Raizen, 1989, *Reforming Education for Work.*

Page 16. *By the fall of 1996:* U.S. Department of Education and U.S. Department of Labor, 1996, "Implementation of the School-to-Work Opportunities Act of 1994," p. 16. "Education, Labor Award $58.9 Million to Get School-to-Work Going," November 21, 1996, press release, School-to-Work Office.

Page 16. *Between the ages of 18 and 27:* Stern et al., 1995, *School-to-Work: Research on Programs in the United States,* p. 1.

Page 16. *In 1994 the unemployment rate:* U.S. Department of Education, 1996, *Condition of Education 1996,* p. 106.

Page 17. *The unemployment rate for black:* Ibid., p. 106.

Page 17. *High school dropouts, she writes:* Schorr and Schorr, 1988, *Within Our Reach,* p. 8.

Page 17. *"Our common stake":* Ibid., p. xix.

Page 18. *Studies suggest that the vast majority:* See Bailey and Merritt, 1997, *School-to-Work for the College Bound.*

Page 18. *"It's not like I'm thinking a lot here":* Interview with Christina Betances, Herndon, Virginia, August 1995.

Page 18. *Today most high school students:* Csikszentmihalyi, ed., 1996, *Youth and Work in America,* p. 3. Information in the following paragraph also stems from this study.

Page 19. *In a recent survey of high school seniors:* Gray and Herr, 1995, *Other Ways to Win,* p. 5.

Page 19. *The percentage of young people:* U.S. Department of Education, 1996, *Condition of Education 1996,* p. 52.

Page 19. *But the dirty little secret:* American Council on Education, 1994, *Twelfth Annual Status Report;* U.S. Department of Education, 1994, *Digest of Education Statistics 1994,* Table 11, "Highest Level of Education Attained by Persons Age 18 and Over."

Page 19. *A 1992 Labor Department study:* Eck, 1993, "Job-Related Education and Training," pp. 21–38.

Page 20. *According to U.S. News & World Report:* Elfin, 1996, "High Cost of Higher Education," p. 93.

Page 22. *"In addition to basic skills":* Policy statement adopted at the National Education Summit, Palisades, New York, March 27, 1996.

Page 24. *In 1996 the Clinton administration estimated:* U.S. Department of Education and U.S. Department of Labor, 1996, "Implementation of the School-to-Work Opportunities Act of 1994," p. 26.

Page 25. *We know from the research to date:* For a summary of the research that has been done, see Jobs for the Future, 1995, *Promising Practices;* U.S. Congress, Office of Technology Assessment, 1995, *Learning to Work,* p. 41; Pauly et al., 1995, *Home-grown Lessons;* Stern et al., 1995, *School-to-Work;* Stern, Raby, and Dayton, 1992, *Career Academies.*

Page 25. *The most extreme critics:* See Hearne, 1995, *Paychecks and Power.*

Page 26. *The majority of high school students:* Stern et al., 1995, *School-to-Work.*

Chapter 2—The Missing Elements in Education

Page 29. *"I chose the laborer":* This and other quotes from Rindge are based on a site visit to the Rindge School of Technical Arts in Cambridge, Massachusetts, November 1995.

Page 30. *In their 1985 book:* Powell, Farrar, and Cohen, 1985, *Shopping Mall High School.*

Page 30. *How can students get excited:* For a good study of how passive students are in school, see Schneider, Csikszentmihalyi, and Knauth, 1995, "Academic Challenge, Motivation, and Self-Esteem," pp.183–184.

Page 32. *It was the first public vocational high school:* Rosenstock and Steinberg, 1995, "Beyond the Shop," p. 41.

Page 33. *He took the job at Rindge:* Rosenstock left Rindge in 1997 to direct the New Urban High School project a nationwide reform initiative to provide high academic standards and career skills for all students.

Page 34. *All ninth-graders take a class:* For a description of CityWorks see ibid., pp. 41–57.

Page 36. *"I didn't like school":* Quotes and descriptions of Alfreda's experiences are based on an interview with her in November 1995 and on her presentation at a Jobs for the Future conference in Boston in July 1995.

Page 37. *"I'm not big into the academics":* Interview with Christopher Scott-Martin, Cambridge, Massachusetts, November 1995.

Page 37. *The attendance rate at Rindge is higher:* Ferdinand, 1994. Attendance and postsecondary education statistics from an interview with Larry Rosenstock, November 1995. It is unclear whether the higher postsecondary-education attendance rate is attributable to the program or to some self-selection characteristic among the students who choose to participate in the internships.

Page 38. *When Rindge opened in 1888:* U.S. Department of Education, 1982, *Digest of Education Statistics,* Table 35, p. 44.

Page 38. *The University of Michigan historian:* See Cohen, 1985, "Origins," pp. 233–308. This is one of the best, most concise descriptions of the evolution of mass public education in the United States.

Page 39. *On one side of the argument was the Committee of Ten:* See Ravitch, 1995, *National Standards in American Education,* pp. 36–39.

Page 39. *In 1906, a report by the Massachusetts Commission:* Excerpt from "Report: Massachusetts Commission on Industrial and Technical Education," reprinted in Lazerson and Grubb, 1974, *American Education and Vocationalism,* pp. 69–80.

Page 39. *The National Association of Manufacturers:* Excerpt from National Association of Manufacturers, "Reports of the Committee on Industrial Education," reprinted in Lazerson and Grubb, 1974, *American Education and Vocationalism,* pp. 88–100.

Page 40. *Dewey advocated rewriting the curriculum:* John Dewey, "An Undemocratic Proposal," in Lazerson and Grubb, 1974, *American Education and Vocationalism*, pp. 143–147. For an excellent discussion of Dewey's philosophy of education and his opposition to narrow industrial training, see chapters 4 and 6 in Westbrook, 1991, *John Dewey and American Democracy*.

Page 40. *"The problem of the educator":* Dewey, 1916, *Democracy and Education*, pp. 196–197.

Page 41. *By the 1930s:* Cohen, 1985, "Origins," pp. 246, 250.

Page 41. *Today, these tracks have become more muddled:* See Stevenson et al., 1994, "Sequences of Opportunities for Learning," pp. 184–198.

Page 41. *Students in the more-advanced classes:* See Oakes, 1985, *Keeping Track*, as well as the descriptions in Powell, Farrar, and Cohen, 1985, *Shopping Mall High School*.

Page 42. *Throughout the twentieth century:* E. Gareth Hoachlander, "Industry-Based Education: A New Approach for School-to-Work Transition," in U.S. Department of Education, 1994, *School-to-Work*, pp. 91–92; Committee for Economic Development, *Investing in Our Children*, pp. 30–35.

Page 42. *And the more vocational classes students take:* U.S. Department of Education, 1995, *Vocational Course-Taking and Achievement*, p. 20.

Page 42. *Vocational students who secure a job:* But fewer than half of vocational graduates find employment in the occupation for which they trained: Boesel et al., 1994, *National Assessment of Vocational Education*, pp. 141–143.

Page 42. *One study of the high school class:* Crawford, Johnson, and Summers, 1995, "Climbing the Ladder of Success," p. 47.

Page 42. *"The most serious problem":* Grubb, 1994, "Occupation as a Context for Instruction," p. 29.

Page 43. *It cautioned that this trend:* Boesel et al., 1994, *National Assessment of Vocational Education*, p. 28.

Page 43. *The general studies curriculum:* Green et al., 1995, *National Education Longitudinal Study of 1988*, p. iii.

Page 44. *"It was really a bleak period":* Interview with Dennis Loftus, December 1995, during site visit to New Castle County Vocational-Technical School

District. Information on the district based on interviews and observations during that visit.

Page 46. *Demand for these skills has percolated:* See Ancess and Darling-Hammond, 1994, *The Senior Project,* especially pp. 19–21.

Page 47. *Since the initiative began:* Southern Regional Education Board, 1995, "Integrating Vocational and Academic Studies," p. 22.

Page 48. *Customer satisfaction, as measured by:* Stearrett, 1994, "New Castle County Vocational-Technical School District: Customer Satisfaction."

Page 48. *In writing, the school system's students:* Stearrett, 1995, "New Castle County Vocational-Technical School District: Analysis," pp. 2, 4.

Page 48. *Individual students at the three schools:* Ibid., p. 6.

Page 48. *In 1994–95, more than half:* Stearrett, 1995, "New Castle County Vocational-Technical School District: Performance Indicators."

Page 48. *In the 1980s, SREB:* Southern Regional Education Board, 1981, *Need for Quality.*

Page 49. *"Students who reach these goals":* Bottoms and Mikos, 1994, "Seven Most-Improved 'High Schools That Work' Sites," p. 3.

Page 49. *In just three years:* Ibid., p. 3.

Page 49. *When Clifford Adelman:* Adelman, 1994, *Lessons of a Generation,* p. 32.

Page 49. *Similarly, in a study:* Orfield and Paul, 1994, *High Hopes, Long Odds,* pp. 4–5.

Page 49. *"The purpose of a plan":* Ibid., pp. 11–12.

Page 50. *Indeed, some studies suggest:* Murname and Levy, 1996, *Teaching the New Basic Skills,* pp. 37–46.

Page 50. *They also have altered how content is taught:* For a description of pedagogical and other changes at these sites, see Bottoms and Mikos, "Seven Most-Improved 'High Schools That Work' Sites."

Page 51. *But recent research suggests:* For a summation of cognitive research on learning see Resnick, 1987, *Education and Learning to Think;* Berryman and Bailey, 1992, *Double Helix;* Berryman, 1994, "Apprenticeship as a Paradigm of Learning," in Grubb, 1994, *Education Through Occupations,* pp. 192–205; and Raizen, 1989, *Reforming Education for Work.*

Page 51. *In contrast, most of today's high school students:* Schneider, Csikszentmihalyi, and Knauth, 1995, "Academic Challenge, Motivation, and Self-Esteem," pp. 183–184.

Page 51. *Paul Barton, a researcher:* Barton, 1990, *From School to Work*, p. 18.

Page 52. *"Basically, what we learn":* Interview with Roxanne Lloyd, Wilmington, Delaware, December 1995.

Page 52. *"you have to keep notes":* Interview with Christine Klingler, Wilmington, Delaware, December 1995.

Page 52. *One study of 16 school-to-work programs:* Pauly, Kopp, and Haimson, 1995, *Home-Grown Lessons*, pp. 150–152.

Page 52. *Another study of students:* Schneider, Csikszentmihalyi, and Knauth, 1995, "Academic Challenge, Motivation, and Self-Esteem," p. 187.

Page 53. *In the early 1990s:* Orfield and Paul, 1994, *High Hopes, Long Odds*.

Page 54. *Another study found:* Crawford, Johnson, and Summers, "Climbing the Ladder of Success," p. 46.

Page 55. *"It makes me feel good":* Interview with Kiya Crippen, Wilmington, Delaware, December 1995.

Page 55. *"I think it's real good":* Interview with Micah Goldston, Wilmington, Delaware, December 1995.

Page 56. *The Fenway Middle College High School:* The description of the Fenway Middle College High School is based on a site visit in December 1995; materials distributed by Fenway; and Technical Development Corporation, 1993, "An Evaluation."

Page 57. *In 1994, Fenway became one of three schools nationwide:* The description of Working to Learn is based on draft curriculum materials provided by Technical Education Research Center in December 1995 and on interviews with Working to Learn developers Margaret Vickers, Riley Hart, and Amy Weinberg in December 1995.

Page 58. *On the blustery December day:* Observations at Children's Hospital and interviews with Children's Hospital employees based on a site visit in December 1995.

Page 59. *"We graduate our kids":* From brochure prepared for the New American High School Conference, U.S. Department of Education and the National

Center for Research in Vocational Education, Washington, D.C., May 1996.

Page 59. *In a three-year evaluation:* Technical Development Corporation, 1993, "An Evaluation."

Page 59. *"What really happened":* Interview with Larry Myatt, Boston, Massachusetts, December 1995.

Page 60. *"Developmentally, this is a period":* Interview with Stephen Hamilton, Cornell University, October 1995.

Page 61. *At least 40 students:* Phone interview with Nancy Shiels, coordinator of the Children's Hospital–Allied Health/Fenway Collaborative Program, January 1996.

Page 61. *Jacqueline Concepcion, now 24:* Phone interview with Jacqueline Concepcion, December 1995.

Page 61. *"The training that we used to do":* Presentation by Hermann Schmidt, president, Federal Institute for Vocational Training, Bonn, Germany, October 1995.

Page 61. *Switzerland has expanded its school-based training:* Hamilton, 1994, "Employment Prospects as Motivation for School Achievement," p. 274. For information on Sweden, see p. 277.

Page 62. *In France, graduates of vocational programs:* Stern, Bailey, and Merritt, 1996, "School-to-Work Policy Insights," pp. 15–16, 37.

Page 62. *In 1994, Denmark's minister of education:* Jens Pehrson, general inspector of education, Danish Ministry of Education, Department of Vocational Education and Training, personal communication, October 1995.

Page 63. *A new state curriculum:* Discussion with Karl Waidelich, principal, Königin-Olga-Stift-Gymnasium, Stuttgart, Germany, October 1995.

Page 63. *In 1994, Scotland launched:* Scottish Office Education Department, 1994, *Higher Still.*

Page 63. *Even Japanese schools:* Stern, Bailey, and Merritt, 1996, "School-to-Work Policy Insights from Recent International Developments," pp. 14–15.

Page 64. *This is particularly true:* Little, 1992, *Two Worlds.*

Chapter 3—How Does Business Benefit?

Page 69. *Today, many companies get involved:* See U.S. Congress, Office of Technology Assessment, 1995, *Learning to Work,* p. 84.

Page 69. *One study:* National Center on the Educational Quality of the Workforce, 1995, *Other Shoe,* p. 5.

Page 69. *"Over and over again":* U.S. Congress, Office of Technology Assessment, 1995, *Learning to Work,* p. 42.

Page 70. *"If we can learn how to create":* Hamilton and Hamilton, 1996, "Quality-Based Learning: Principles from Apprenticeships," p. 7.

Page 71. *German companies spend the equivalent:* Federal Ministry of Education and Science, 1994, *Vocational Training in Germany,* p.12.

Page 71. *an average of $12,000 in gross:* von Bardeleben, Beicht, and Feher, 1996, "Study of the Costs and Benefits of Vocational Training in Germany," p. 12.

Page 71. *"German companies believe that schools":* Presentation by Wolfgang Breitmeier at the Mercedes-Benz technical training center in Stuttgart, Germany, October 1995.

Page 72. *Young people in the Dual System:* Good summations of the German Dual System are contained in two documents published by the Federal Ministry of Education and Science, 1994, *Vocational Training in Germany,* and 1992, *Vocational Training in the Dual System;* and a document published by the Federal Institute for Vocational Training, 1993, *Training Ordinances.*

Page 72. *Wage differences are one reason:* Dietmar Harhoff and Thomas J. Kane, "Financing Apprenticeship Training: Evidence from Germany" in *School-to-Work: What Does Research Say About It?,* U.S. Department of Education, 1994, p. 37. Their article provides one of the best explanations for why German companies participate in the Dual System.

Page 72. *They typically earn:* Harhoff and Kane, 1994, "Financing Apprenticeship Training," p. 34.

Page 72. *"Why train?":* Horst Locher, interview, Multifirm Training Center in Electrical Engineering in Stuttgart, October 1995.

Page 73. *This combination:* Osterman, 1995, "Involving Employers in School-to-Work Programs," p. 81.

Page 73. *Although only 20 percent of German companies:* Harhoff and Kane, 1994, "Financing Apprenticeship Training," p. 5.

Page 74. *Employers in Germany complained to me:* Based on discussions with German officials and businessmen in Bonn and Stuttgart, October 1995.

Page 74. *In 1996, German unemployment hit:* B. Powell, 1996, "Sick at Heart?," p. 18.

Page 74. *In 1995, Chancellor Helmut Kohl:* Presentation by Hermann Schmidt, president, Federal Institute for Vocational Training, Bonn, Germany, October 1995.

Page 74. *In 1993, half of all:* Margaret Vickers, "Employer Participation in School-to-Work Programs: The Changing Situation in Europe," in Bailey, 1995, *Learning to Work*, p. 32.

Page 76. *"We had thirty or so technicians a year":* Interview with Gary R. Garman, manager of training and professional development, Siemens Stromberg-Carlson, July 1995.

Page 76. *So Siemens decided to adapt:* The outlines of the Siemens program are described in press releases and fact sheets from Siemens Stromberg-Carlson and the Siemens Corporation.

Page 77. *For Ryan Bouley:* Descriptions of Ryan's experiences are based on a site visit to the Lake Mary training facility in May 1995 and on an interview with Ryan Bouley and a phone interview with his father, Dennis Bouley, that same month.

Page 78. *"One thing I noticed":* Interview with Chris Pierce at the Lake Mary training facility, May 1995.

Page 78. *Dmetra Campbell, a senior:* Interviews with Dmetra Campbell and Charity Watson, Lake Mary training facility, May 1995.

Page 80. *The cost of the different apprenticeship models:* Information provided by John Tobin, director of vocational training, Siemens Corporation, March 1996.

Page 80. *"It's not altruistic":* Interview with John Tobin, July 1995.

Page 80. *One young woman:* Example provided by Chris Pierce, Lake Mary facility, May 1995.

Page 80. *In 1995, for example, the Raleigh facility:* Phone interview with Barry Blystone, February 1996.

Page 81. *"Apprenticeship is contagious":* Ibid.

Page 82. *"Almost everybody here":* Ibid.

Page 82. *In under six months:* Smith, 1995, *Rethinking America,* p. 177.

Page 83. *"This is just an awesome program":* Interview with Paul Gouvian, Serigraph Company, West Bend, Wisconsin, September 1995.

Page 83. *"Here, it's more one-on-one":* Interview with Jeff Kannenberg, Serigraph Company, West Bend, Wisconsin, September 1995.

Page 84. *"Everyone was all over him":* Interview with John Torinus, Serigraph Company, West Bend, Wisconsin, September 1995.

Page 85. *"There aren't people on the street":* Interview with Bill Wollin, Serigraph Company, West Bend, Wisconsin, September 1995.

Page 85. *A two-year evaluation of five sites:* Orr, 1994, *Wisconsin Youth Apprenticeship Program in Printing,* and Orr, 1996, *Wisconsin Youth Apprenticeship Program in Printing: Evaluation.*

Page 86. *"The reaction we got":* Phone conversation with Margaret Terry Orr, Institute on Education and the Economy, Teachers College, Columbia University, June 1996. Information in this paragraph is based on her evaluation of the program under a contract with Jobs for the Future and the state of Wisconsin.

Page 86. *Of the first 11 apprentices to graduate:* Smith, 1995, *Rethinking America,* p. 183.

Page 86. *"Someday, twelve or fifteen years from now":* Interview with John Torinus, Serigraph Company, West Bend, Wisconsin, September 1995.

Page 87. *By 1996, Wisconsin had standards:* Information provided by Vicki J. Poole, executive director, Governor's Office for Workforce Excellence, State of Wisconsin, June 1996.

Page 87. *"We've got the German system":* Interview with Wisconsin's Governor Tommy G. Thompson, Milwaukee, Wisconsin, April 1996.

Page 87. *"High rates of job turnover":* Bishop, 1996, "Vocational Education and At-Risk Youth in the United States," p. 7.

Page 88. *In Wisconsin, for example, about 15 percent:* Telephone interview with Jack Hayes, president, Printing Industries of Wisconsin, Spring 1996.

Page 88. *"If you get most of the local employers":* Telephone interview with John Tobin, June 1996.

Page 89. *Of the first 38 students to graduate:* Osterman, "Involving Employers in School-to-Work Programs," p. 79.

Page 89. *In Kalamazoo, Michigan, about 90 percent:* Information provided by Kalamazoo Valley Education for Employment Consortium, December 1995.

Page 89. *During their second year after high school:* Percentages are based on 36 participants in the first two cohorts, the classes of 1993 and 1994. Personal communication from Mary Agnes Hamilton, November 8, 1996.

Page 90. *Then Peter Butler:* Interview with Peter Butler, Mehoopany, Pennsylvania, May 1995.

Page 91. *Pennsylvania had already taken the plunge:* This description of the early years of the Pennsylvania Youth Apprenticeship Program is based on Richard Kazis, 1991, *Pennsylvania Youth Apprenticeship Program.*

Page 92. *By 1996, 40 companies:* Communication from Peter Butler, Procter & Gamble, Fall 1996.

Page 92. *"We wanted to make sure":* Interview with Beth Lunger, site trainer, Procter & Gamble Paper Plant, Mehoopany, Pennsylvania, May 1995.

Page 93. *"I can't wait for Thursday":* Interview with Joseph LaRue, Procter & Gamble Paper Plant, Mehoopany, Pennsylvania, May 1995.

Page 93. *"He was a good student":* Phone interview with Arnold LaRue, May 1995.

Page 94. *"For me, it's hard to put into words":* Interview with Charlie Coppola, Procter & Gamble Paper Plant, Mehoopany, Pennsylvania, May 1995.

Page 95. *"I've learned a lot":* Interview with Jackie Dymond, Procter & Gamble Paper Plant, Mehoopany, Pennsylvania, May 1995.

Page 96. *The commission's report:* Secretary's Commission on Achieving Necessary Skills, 1991, *What Work Requires of School.*

Page 96. *Peter Cappelli, the codirector:* Cappelli, 1992, *Is the "Skills Gap" Really About Attitudes?;* and Cappelli and Iannozzi, *Rethinking the Skills Gap.*

Page 97. *Service jobs now account for 77:* Committee for Economic Development, 1996, *American Workers and Economic Change,* p. 24.

Page 98. *"In the Academy"*: Interview with Elvis Vasquez, Coral Gables, Florida, August 1995.

Page 100. *"We want people educated in this industry"*: Interview with Gina Hartmann, director of marketing for Latin America, the Caribbean, and Spain, Division of Tourism, Florida Department of Commerce, Coral Gables, Florida, August 1995.

Page 100. *According to the foundation*: Academy for Educational Development, 1990, "Employment and Educational Experiences of Academy of Finance Graduates"; National Academy Foundation, 1991, "Proposal to the National Diffusion Network"; National Academy Foundation, 1994, "Academy of Travel & Tourism"; National Academy Foundation, 1995, "General Statistical Overview."

Page 101. *In 1994, for example, Kalamazoo*: Kalamazoo County, 1995, *Education for Employment*.

Page 101. *Similarly, the Cornell*: Apprenticeship evaluation record notebooks provided by the Cornell Youth Apprenticeship Program, October 1995.

Page 101. *"Graduates of the dual system"*: James C. Witte and Arne L. Kalleberg, "Determinants and Consequences of Fit Between Vocational Education and Employment in Germany," in U.S. Department of Education, 1994, *School-to-Work*, pp. 3–32.

Page 102. *One study*: Silverberg, 1997, *Experiences and Lessons of the School-to-Work Youth Apprenticeship Demonstration*, p.4.

Page 102. *"I just wanted to try it"*: Interview with Jeff Alderson, Lyman High School, Longwood, Florida, May 1995.

Page 103. *"I wasn't good with the hands-on stuff"*: Interview with Natalie Martin, Lyman High School, Longwood, Florida, May 1995.

Page 103. *Of the 100 apprentices*: Information provided by Mary Agnes Hamilton, October 29, 1996.

Page 103. *"We have records"*: Hamilton and Hamilton, 1996, "Quality-Based Learning," p. 55.

Page 104. *This was the case with an appliance-repair*: Emanuel and Rossi, 1995, "Linking the Classroom and Work-Based Learning."

Page 105. *The Sears Corporation*: Ibid.

Page 105. *In Pennsylvania the number of students:* Information provided by Pennsylvania Department of Education, Office of School-to-Work Opportunity, February 1996.

Page 105. *Rob McIlzaine, the director:* Telephone interview with Rob McIlzaine, February 1996.

Page 105. *In Philadelphia:* Telephone interview with Nicholas Coviello, project coordinator for the manufacturing school-to-work program in the Philadelphia Public Schools, February 1996.

Page 106. *A study by Mathematica Policy Research:* Hershey and Silverberg, 1993, "Employer Involvement in School-to-Work Transition Programs."

Page 108. *They recommend that participating companies:* Hamilton and Hamilton, 1996, "Quality-Based Learning: Principles from Apprenticeships."

Page 108. *Another study:* Goldberger, Kazis, and O'Flanagan, 1994, *Learning Through Work.*

Page 109. *The American Federation:* American Federation of Teachers, 1997, *Reaching the Next Step,* pp. 20–24.

Page 109. *"Because there are only":* U.S. Congress, Office of Technology Assessment, 1995, *Learning to Work,* p. 6.

Page 110. *In 1993 the McDonald's Corporation:* Packer et al., 1996, *School-to-Work,* pp. 163–169.

Page 110. *In 1995 the General Motors Corporation:* General Motors Corporation, 1995, "GM Youth Educational Systems."

Page 110. *"Now, when an automotive student":* Finn, 1995, "GM to Set Up Mechanic Program at Va. School."

Page 111. *Since 1990 the Boeing Company:* Based on descriptions in Packer et al., 1996, *School-to-Work,* pp. 208–213; and Center for Occupational Research and Development Inc., 1995, *Making Students Work-Ready,* pp. 10–11.

Page 111. *A state survey:* Pepin et al., 1996, "State School-to-Work System Development–1996."

Page 112. *Today, most American companies are not:* National Center on the Educational Quality of the Workforce, Advisory Board, 1995, "On Connecting School and Work," p. 5.

Chapter 4—The Link with Higher Education

Page 113. *First, the education requirements for employment:* See Levy and Murnane, 1992, "U.S. Earnings Levels and Earnings Inequality"; Committee for Economic Development, 1996, *American Workers and Economic Change;* and Johnson and Packer, 1987, *Workforce 2000.*

Page 113. *In 1994, male college graduates:* Decker, 1996, "Education and Worker Productivity," p. 6.

Page 114. *In a 1992 survey:* U.S. Department of Education, 1993, *Statistics in Brief,* p. 3.

Page 114. *Today, a record 62 percent:* U.S. Department of Education, 1996, *Condition of Education 1996,* p. 52.

Page 114. *Postsecondary institutions have a better track record:* Boesel et al., 1994, *National Assessment of Vocational Education,* p. 157.

Page 114. *"Realizing the educational value":* Elfin, 1996, "High Cost of Higher Education," p. 93.

Page 115. *Similarly, an article:* Johnson, 1996, "In the Changed Landscape of Recruiting, Academic and Corporate Worlds Merge."

Page 115. *Each year, medical schools:* U.S. Department of Commerce, 1995, *American Almanac, 1995–96, Statistical Abstract of the United States,* Table 302.

Page 115. *U.S. law schools:* U.S. Department of Commerce, 1995, *American Almanac, 1995–96,* Table 302.

Page 115. *In contrast, only about 6 percent:* U.S. Department of Education, *Statistics in Brief,* November 1993.

Page 115. *Since 1950, the number:* Richman, 1994, "New Worker Elite," p. 57.

Page 115. *The Bureau of Labor Statistics:* Gray and Herr, 1995, *Other Ways to Win,* p. 105.

Page 116. *About one third of college freshmen:* Astin et al., 1993, *American Freshman National Norms for Fall 1993.*

Page 116. *The average college graduate now takes:* U.S. Department of Education, 1996, *Condition of Education 1996,* pp. 60–61.

Page 116. *Changing schools or majors:* Thomas M. Smith, "Minorities in Higher Education," in U.S. Department of Education, 1996, *Condition of Education 1996,* p. 24.

Page 116. *Only about half:* American Council on Education, 1994, *Twelfth Annual Status Report on Minorities in Higher Education.*

Page 116. *In a longitudinal study:* Adelman, 1994, *Lessons of a Generation,* p. 161.

Page 116. *Other analyses suggest:* Grubb, 1995, *Return to Education and Training in the Sub-Baccalaureate Labor Market.*

Page 117. *"Students who drop out":* Traub, *City on a Hill,* p. 346.

Page 117. *In 1994, only 25 percent of males age 25 or older:* U.S. Department of Commerce, 1995, *American Almanac, 1995–96,* Table 239.

Page 118. *The majority already provide:* Dilcher, *Learning That Works,* p. 7.

Page 118. *Their number has nearly doubled since 1947:* American Association of Community and Junior Colleges, 1988, *Building Communities,* p. vii.

Page 118. *They now serve about 5.5 million:* American Association of Community Colleges, 1996, *Pocket Profile of Community Colleges,* pp. 1, 2.

Page 118. *Their attrition rates:* U.S. Department of Education, 1996, *Condition of Education 1996,* pp. 56–59.

Page 119. *As the Cornell University economics professor:* Bishop, 1995, *Expertise and Excellence,* p. 62.

Page 120. *The Maine Times:* Beem, 1994, "Essence of Reform."

Page 120. *By 1996 the initiative:* Personal communication from Jean Mattimore, executive director, Maine Center for Career Development, May 1996.

Page 120. *"I really believe":* Interview with John Fitzsimmons, Augusta, Maine, 1994.

Page 121. *Maine Career Advantage is designed:* The description of Maine Career Advantage is based on a site visit in 1994 and materials distributed by the Maine Center for Career Development.

Page 121. *"What we're doing is opening up":* Interview with Maine's then governor, John R. McKernan, Jr., Augusta, 1994.

Page 122. *In 1994, Maine officials estimated:* Olson, 1994, "Technically Speaking," p. 16.

Page 123. *Since 1994, the state has contributed:* Communication from Jean Mattimore, executive director, Maine Center for Career Development, May 1996.

Page 123. *"I had reservations"*: Phone interview with Diane Wescott, 1994.

Page 123. *"I wasn't a very hardworking student"*: Phone interview with Matt Burr, 1994.

Page 123. *Of the eight interns*: Communication from Jean Mattimore, executive director, Maine Center for Career Development, May 1996.

Page 124. *"Sometimes it seems as if every other person"*: Rimer, 1996, "A Hometown Feels Less like Home."

Page 124. *In the mid-1970s, the National Cash Register Company*: Ibid.

Page 125. *"We have in this community"*: Personal interview with David Ponitz, Sinclair Community College, Dayton, Ohio, March 1996.

Page 125. *By 1996 the program had enrolled*: Application, American Association of Community Colleges Tech Prep Awards, 1996.

Page 126. *Parnell recommended*: Parnell, 1985, *Neglected Majority*.

Page 126. *One of the primary features*: These examples are from the Oakland Health Academy in Oakland, California, the work-based curriculum developed by the Learning Research and Development Center at the University of Pittsburgh for the Pennsylvania Youth Apprenticeship Program, and the Principles of Technology curriculum developed by the Center for Occupational Research and Development in Waco, Texas.

Page 127. *Today, there are more than 1,058*: Phone interview with Marsha Silverberg, Mathematica Policy Research, October 1996.

Page 127. *But tech prep in many communities*: See Silverberg and Hershey, 1995, *Emergence of Tech-Prep at the State and Local Levels*, and Bragg, Layton, and Hammons, 1994, *Tech Prep Implementation in the United States*.

Page 128. *"It's a lot more interesting"*: Personal interview with Brett Cottle, Greene County Career Center, Xenia, Ohio, March 1996.

Page 129. *"It's an incredible relationship"*: Personal interview with Bill Holden, Greene County Career Center, Xenia, Ohio, March 1996.

Page 129. *So far, this is a tiny fraction*: Information provided by Wendy Johnson, Miami Valley Tech Prep Consortium, March 1996.

Page 129. *"I'm expecting that within the next two or three years"*: Personal interview with Tom Carlisle, Sinclair Community College, Dayton, Ohio, March 1996.

Page 130. *About 80 percent of all Sinclair freshmen:* Information provided by Wendy Johnson, Miami Valley Tech Prep Consortium, March 1996.

Page 130. *In 1995, 86 percent:* Application, American Association of Community Colleges Tech Prep Awards, 1996.

Page 130. *Of the 17 students who enrolled:* Information provided by Tom Carlisle, Sinclair Community College, Dayton, Ohio.

Page 130. *Studies have found that in most tech-prep consortia:* See Grubb et al., 1996, "Community College Innovations in Workforce Preparation," and Hershey, Silverberg, and Owens, 1995, *Diverse Forms of Tech-Prep.*

Page 131. *In 1974, an automotive technician:* Personal interview with Stephen Ash, Sinclair Community College, Dayton, Ohio, March 1996.

Page 132. *"The reason [this college] was created":* Personal interview with Don Garrison, Tri-County Technical College, Pendleton, South Carolina, March 1996.

Page 134. *"We are a service organization":* Personal interview with Diana Walter, Tri-County Technical College, Pendleton, South Carolina, March 1996.

Page 134. *"Tri-County has been instrumental in guiding":* Personal interview with Wayne Frady, Tri-County Technical College, Pendleton, South Carolina, March 1996.

Page 135. *"I was mainly interested in":* Personal interview with Dale Campbell, Tri-County Technical College, Pendleton, South Carolina, March 1996.

Page 137. *"This approach addresses our need":* Walter and Turlington, 1994, "Tech Prep: A Practitioner's Perspective," p. 58.

Page 137. *By 1993–94 more than 5,700 students:* Packer and Pines, 1996, *School-to-Work,* p. 198.

Page 137. *A June 1995 evaluation:* Bucci and Lee, 1995, "PACE Model Tech Prep Education Project."

Page 138. *But most articulation agreements:* This paragraph is based on the discussion of drawbacks to articulation agreements in Hershey, Silverberg, and Owens, 1995, *Diverse Forms of Tech-Prep,* and Pauly, Kopp, and Haimson, 1995, *Home-Grown Lessons,* pp. 209–210.

Page 139. *Fourth, the flexibility of community colleges:* Kazis, 1991, "The Future of Two-Year Colleges in Improving the School-to-Work Transition," pp. 69–80.

Page 140. *In the 1980s, School & Main:* Bailis and Rose, 1996, "Evaluation of the National Higher Ground Initiative." The document describes the Higher Ground model as well as an evaluation of its effectiveness.

Page 141. *About one third of high school graduates:* U.S. Department of Education, 1996, *Condition of Education 1996,* p. 52.

Page 143. *Another effort:* Based on description in Packer and Pines, 1996, *School-to-Work,* pp. 122–131.

Page 144. *Between 1985 and 1994:* Stern and Wagner, in press, "School-to-Work Policies in Industrialized Countries as Responses to Push and Pull," p. 12.

Page 144. *At a Mercedes-Benz plant:* Site visit in October 1995, sponsored by the Center for Learning and Competitiveness and the German Marshall Fund of the United States.

Page 145. *Great Britain recently has created:* Stern, Bailey, and Merritt, "School-to-Work Policy Insights from Recent International Developments," pp. 18, 25–26.

Page 145. *In 1990 Denmark:* Ibid., pp. 28–30.

Page 145. *"Yesterday, we told young people":* Jorgen Brodman, vice-chairman of the board, Copenhagen Technical College, Copenhagen, Denmark, October 1995.

Page 146. *It is true that most new jobs created:* Committee for Economic Development, *American Workers and Economic Change,* 1996, pp. 24–25. Winifred I. Warnat, "Tech Prep Education: A U.S. Innovation Linking High Schools and Community Colleges," in American Association of Community Colleges, 1994, *Tech Prep Associate Degree Challenge,* p. 33.

Page 146. *John H. Bishop, an economics professor:* Bishop, "Is the Market for College Graduates Headed for a Bust?," p. 2.

Page 146. *Managerial, professional, technical, and high-level sales:* Bishop, 1995, *Expertise and Excellence,* p. 35.

Page 146. *According to the Bureau of Labor Statistics:* Winifred I. Warnat, "Tech Prep Education: A U.S. Innovation Linking High Schools and Community Colleges," in American Association of Community Colleges, 1994, *Tech Prep Associate Degree Challenge,* p. 33.

Page 146. *According to the U.S. Department of Education:* Decker, 1996, "Education and Worker Productivity," p. 7.

Page 147. *"These results demonstrate"*: Murnane and Levy, 1996, *Teaching the New Basic Skills*, p. 44.

Page 147. *Many economists believe*: Bound and Johnson, 1995, "What are the Causes of Rising Wage Inequality in the United States?" p. 13. See also Juhn and Murphy, 1995, "Inequality in Labor Market Outcomes," p. 31.

Page 147. *People who use a computer at work*: Committee for Economic Development, 1996, *American Workers and Economic Change*, p. 37.

Page 147. *In the future, says Rosabeth Moss Kanter*: Kanter, *World Class*, p. 157.

Page 148. *"The fact is that effective education"*: Sizer, 1994, "School to Work."

Chapter 5—The New Frontier: Regional School-to-Work Strategies

Page 150. *In Germany, only 20 percent of companies*: Harhoff and Kane, 1994, "Financing Apprenticeship Training," p. 5.

Page 150. *In all the European systems*: Interview with Anne Heald, executive director, Center for Learning and Competitiveness, University of Maryland, June 1996.

Page 150. *There is a huge gap*: See Whiting and Sayer, 1995, "School-to-Work or School-to-What?"

Page 150. *There are over 20,000 trades*: McNeil, 1993, "Role of Industry Associations in School-to-Work Transition," p. 1.

Page 150. *But education and training*: Ibid., p. 2.

Page 152. *Known as "Craftsmanship 2000"*: The description of Craftsmanship 2000 and Career Partners Inc. is based on a site visit to Tulsa in April 1996, interviews with the program's founders, and material prepared by the Metropolitan Tulsa Chamber of Commerce.

Page 153. *"I really didn't have anything going for me"*: Interview with Ben Boren, Tulsa Technology Center, Tulsa, Oklahoma, April 1996.

Page 154. *By 1996, Craftsmanship 2000 had reduced*: Figures provided by Steve Gilbert, executive director of Career Partners Inc, April 1996.

Page 154. *"We're saying to business"*: Interview with Wayne Rowley, Tulsa, Oklahoma, April 1996.

Page 155. *In total, these programs served:* Figures provided by Steve Gilbert, executive director of Career Partners Inc., April 1996.

Page 155. *"What the chamber did":* Interview with Jenny Auger Maw, Tulsa, Oklahoma, April 1996.

Page 155. *"Hilti probably":* Interview with Karl-Heinz Gaertner, Hilti Corporation, Tulsa, Oklahoma, April 1996.

Page 157. *"It's not just about pilot programs anymore":* Benning, 1994, "U.S. Grants $1.2 Million for School, Work Effort Now, 400 Students in City to Benefit."

Page 157. *"In 1982 the business community":* Presentation by William Spring, meeting of Jobs for the Future Benchmark Communities, Boston, Massachusetts, July 1995.

Page 158. *Students in ProTech:* Descriptions of ProTech are based on a site visit to Boston in December 1995; materials prepared by ProTech and the Boston Private Industry Council; and an evaluation of the program by Kopp, Goldberger, and Morales, 1994, *Evolution of a Youth Apprenticeship Model.*

Page 158. *In 1996 the combined cost:* Information provided by Lois Ann Porter, former director of work-based learning for the Boston Private Industry Council, December 1995.

Page 158. *In 1995 one report estimated:* Osterman, 1995, "Involving Employers in School-to-Work Programs," p. 78.

Page 159. *An initial evaluation:* Goldberger, 1993, *Creating an American-Style Youth Apprenticeship Program.*

Page 159. *A second evaluation:* Kopp, Goldberger, and Morales, 1994, *Evolution of a Youth Apprenticeship Model.*

Page 160. *By the 1995–96 school year:* Figures provided by Lois Ann Porter, Boston Private Industry Council, December 1995.

Page 162. *"There's no one cut-and-dried reason":* Interview with Lois Ann Porter, Boston, December 1995.

Page 162. *"I'll probably make":* Interview with Tom Bryan, Boston, December 1995.

Page 163. *Some of the needed changes:* Based on a visit to Madison Park Technical Vocational High School in Boston in December 1995, and an interview with the lead teachers for the craft and technical academy.

Page 163. *"It was a great opportunity for me"*: Interview with Kwesi King at NYNEX headquarters, Boston, December 1995, and his mentor, Steve Campbell.

Page 164. *"It was not a situation"*: Presentation by Joan Rahavy at the Jobs for the Future Conference, Long Beach, California, July 1996.

Page 164. *"Here was an opportunity"*: Presentation by Edward B. Carle at the Jobs for the Future Conference, Long Beach, California, July 1996.

Page 164. *"There is no shortage of people"*: Telephone interview with Karen James Sykes, June 1996.

Page 165. *Boston's goal:* Based on interviews with Lois Ann Porter and Neil Sullivan, executive director of the Boston Regional Employment Board, December 1995.

Page 166. *Like Boston:* The historical information on the development of the Austin Capital Area Training Foundation is based on a draft paper written by Glover, 1996, "Engaging Industry in Building School-to-Career Opportunities." It is one of the best case studies written to date on the experiences of creating an employer-led school-to-work movement.

Page 167. *In 1995 its unemployment rate:* Ibid., p. 4.

Page 168. *The foundation was working with:* Ibid., p. 23.

Page 168. *By the early 1990s there were more than 800:* Ibid., p. 4.

Page 169. *"That had never been done"*: Interview with Kathrin Brewer, former program manager for computer-systems integration, Advanced Micro Devices, during a site visit to the company in April 1996.

Page 170. *"I would call the foundation"*: Interview with Allyson Peerman, director of community affairs, Advanced Micro Devices, April 1996.

Page 170. *The program had some growing pains:* Interview with a group of AMD mentors, April 1996.

Page 171. *"The banks were very impressed"*: Interview with Robert Egloff, Austin, Texas, April 1996.

Page 172. *The foundation funded:* Glover, 1996, "Engaging Industry in Building School-to-Career Opportunities." Also status reports to the U.S. Departments of Education and Labor, School-to-Work Opportunities Office, 1996.

Page 173. *The importance of such third-party players:* Silverberg, 1997, *Experiences and Lessons of the School-to-Work/Youth Apprenticeship Demonstration,* pp. 6, 171.

Page 175. *In 1996, Massachusetts:* Based on a conversation with Neil Sullivan, executive director, Boston Regional Employment Board, December 1995, and a summary of the legislation.

Page 175. *Austin has found:* Glover, 1996, "Engaging Industry in Building School-to-Career Opportunities," p. 36.

Page 176. *In 1996 the National Employer Leadership Council:* National Employer Leadership Council, 1996, "Connecting Learning & Earning."

Page 177. *Employer incentives also:* Silverberg, 1997, *Experiences and Lessons of the School-to-Work/Youth Apprenticeship Demonstration,* p. 6.

Page 177. *The company's human-resources staff:* BellSouth, 1995, "BellSouth Connections," p. 4.

Page 178. *"I think the largest barrier":* Phone interview with Lee Doyle, Summer 1996.

Page 179. *In contrast, the United States:* Wills, 1993, "Overview of Education and Industry Skill Standards in the United States."

Page 179. *Most have relied upon:* Bailey and Merritt, 1995, "Making Sense of Industry-Based Skills Standards."

Page 180. *Studies also suggest:* Stasz et al., 1996, *Workplace Skills in Practice,* p. xiii.

Page 180. *In 1991, Sweden developed:* Schaeffer et al., 1994, *Education for Employment in the New Economy.*

Page 180. *Some case studies suggest:* Villeneuve and Grubb, 1995, "Indigenous School-to-Work Programs."

Page 181. *"Companies don't see state lines":* Phone interview with Patricia Stone, executive director, National Employer Leadership Council, May 1996.

Page 181. *"Our purpose today":* Press conference outside the White House, Summer 1994.

Page 182. *By 1996 the council:* Phone interview with Patricia Stone, May 1996.

Page 182. *The National Association of Manufacturers:* Based on information provided by Phyllis Eisen, National Association of Manufacturers, June 1996.

Page 183. *With funding from the Commonwealth Fund:* Phone interview with

Kenneth Joseph, vice-president, Benchmark Communities Initiative, Jobs for the Future, April 1996.

Page 183. *The National Alliance of Business:* Interview with Peter Joyce, director of school-to-work programs, National Alliance of Business, Fall 1995; and materials provided by National Alliance of Business.

Page 183. *In 1992 the Green Bay Area:* Phone interview and written communication from B. J. Cassidy, assistant (education) to the president, Wisconsin Public Service Corporation, October 1996.

Page 184. *In Fort Worth, Texas:* Fort Worth Independent School District, 1991, "Fort Worth: Project C3: Community, Corporations, Classrooms." Business Roundtable, 1996, "A Business Leader's Guide to Setting Academic Standards," p. 21.

Page 185. *In 1995 the American Gas Association:* Presentation by Steven Kussman at the Jobs for the Future Conference in Long Beach, California, 1996.

Page 185. *In September 1996:* Business Roundtable, U.S. Chamber of Commerce, and National Alliance of Business, 1996, "A Common Agenda for Improving American Education."

Page 185. *"The time for feel-good":* Lawton, 1996, "Three Business Groups Advocate Common Reform Agenda," p. 10.

Chapter 6—School-to-Work and School Reform

Page 187. *The report warned of a "rising tide of mediocrity":* National Commission on Excellence in Education, 1983, A Nation at Risk, p. 5.

Page 187. *By the end of the 1980s: Education Week,*1993, *From Risk to Renewal,* p. xiii.

Page 188. *Student test scores have been rising:* Campbell et al., 1996, *Report in Brief.*

Page 188. *Since 1982 the proportion:* Green et al., 1995, *Trends Among High School Seniors, 1972–1992,* p. 22.

Page 188. *Fifty-one percent of all high school graduates:* U.S. Department of Education, 1996, *Condition of Education 1996,* p. 98.

Page 188. *Research shows that students who take more academic:* Newmann and Wehlage, 1995, *Successful School Restructuring,* p. 37.

Page 188. *Increased course taking in mathematics and science:* U.S. Department of Education, 1996, *Condition of Education 1996,* p. 98; Sommerfeld, 1995, "Upper-Level Math, Science Enrollment Is Up, Study Says," p. 10; and Sommerfeld, 1996, "Math, Science Test Scores Up, NSF Reports," p. 6.

Page 188. *In the past two decades, the large gap in performance:* U.S. Department of Education, 1996, *Condition of Education 1996,* p. 70; Green et al., 1995, *Trends Among High School Seniors, 1972–1992,* pp. 25–27; and Campbell et al., 1996, *Report in Brief.*

Page 188. *The pattern is less clear and less consistent:* U.S. Department of Education, 1996, *Condition of Education 1996,* p. 70; Campbell et al., 1996, *Report in Brief.*

Page 188. *On international assessments of basic literacy:* U.S. Department of Education, 1996, *Condition of Education 1996,* p. 82.

Page 188. *Our eighth-graders score:* U.S. Department of Education, 1996, *Pursuing Excellence.*

Page 189. *"but in many subjects, that means:* Mullis et al., 1994, *NAEP 1992: Trends in Academic Progress;* see also Ravitch, 1995, *National Standards in American Education,* p. 75, and Campbell et al., 1996, *Report in Brief.*

Page 189. *In 1992, for example, only half of twelfth-graders:* Mullis et al., 1993, *NAEP 1992: Mathematics Report Card for the Nation and the States,* p. 4.

Page 189. *Only 6 percent:* Ibid., p. 4.

Page 189. *According to a study by the Rand Corporation:* Hill, 1992, "Urban Education," p. 127.

Page 189. *A national longitudinal study:* Green et al., 1995, *Trends Among High School Seniors, 1972–1992,* p. iv.

Page 189. *Almost half of Americans:* Johnson et al., 1995, *Assignment Incomplete,* p. 19.

Page 190. *In Beyond the Classroom:* Steinberg et al., 1996, *Beyond the Classroom.*

Page 190. *"No degree of school reform":* Ibid., p. 61.

Page 191. *"They insist that virtually all":* Commission on the Skills of the American Workforce, 1990, *America's Choice,* p. 4.

Page 193. *"Schools should not be forged":* Oregon Education Association, *1992 Oregon Education Association Representative Assembly Report,* p. 1.

Page 193. *The majority of parents and students surveyed:* Conkling, Fiskum & McCormick Inc., 1994, Summary of Statewide Opinion Research Survey.

Page 194. *Approximately 17 percent of the 1989 graduates:* Information provided by Marybeth Stiner, school-improvement coordinator, David Douglas High School, during site visit, November 1995.

Page 194. *"They were working in jobs":* Interview with Marybeth Stiner at David Douglas High School, Portland, Oregon, November 1995.

Page 194. *In the summer of 1994:* Descriptions of the David Douglas High School school-to-work initiative and its history are based on a site visit to Portland, Oregon, in November 1995 and on an interview with Mimi Bushman, the director of education programs for the Oregon Business Council.

Page 195. *"This class is by far harder":* Interview with Katrina Zeissler, David Douglas High School, November 1995.

Page 196. *"Last year, I had almost straight F's":* Interview with Koby Shelton, David Douglas High School, November 1995.

Page 196. *"We started off with nothing":* Interview with Pam Ramsey, David Douglas High School, November 1995.

Page 198. *"I have learned so much":* Interview with Jesse Ruede, David Douglas High School, November 1995.

Page 198. *In 1995–96, students still enrolled in CAM courses:* Statistics were provided by John Harrington, principal, and Marybeth Stiner, David Douglas High School, November 1995.

Page 199. *"It's kind of scary":* Interview with John Harrington, principal, David Douglas High School, November 1995.

Page 199. *In the early 1980s:* Descriptions of Roosevelt High School's school-to-work initiative are based on a site visit to Portland, Oregon, in November 1995 and the description in Pauly et al., 1995, *Home-Grown Lessons.*

Page 201. *"This program is not about guaranteeing":* Interview with Judy Holmboe, Roosevelt High School, November 1995.

Page 201. *As of October 1996:* Telephone interview with René Leger, October 1996.

Page 201. *"It's been pretty phenomenal":* Telephone interview with René Leger, October 1996.

Page 202. *Semret Tesfaldet, a senior:* Based on an interview with Semret Tesfaldet, Roosevelt High School, November 1995.

Page 202. *"The big thing I see":* Interview with Nora Beck, Roosevelt High School, November 1995.

Page 203. *"When we first put this out":* Telephone interview with Judy Patterson, Oregon assistant state superintendent of education, May 1996.

Page 204. *"My greatest worry is":* Quoted in Sommerfeld, 1995, "Pioneering Reform Act Under Attack in Oregon," pp. 13, 19.

Page 204. *"I think we're asking our kids":* Interview with Mary Lee Block at the Good Samaritan Clinic, Portland, Oregon, November 1995.

Page 205. *"School-to-work is a method of teaching":* Interview with Norma Paulus, Oregon state superintendent of education, April 1996.

Page 205. *In 1996 the Oregon Business Council:* Information from telephone interview with Duncan Wyse, president, Oregon Business Council, October 1996, and from the council's brochure (1997), "Oregon Worksite 21: Expanding School-to-Work Opportunities for a 21st Century Workforce: A Program to Promote and Assist Employer Involvement in School-to-Work."

Page 207. *W. Norton Grubb, an education professor:* Grubb, 1996, "New Vocationalism," pp. 535–546.

Page 207. *"When I was a freshman":* Interview with Greg Panossian, Pasadena, California, January 1994.

Page 208. *"I think what makes the academies exciting":* Telephone interview with Robert Ivry, Winter 1994.

Page 208. *In 1996, MDRC estimated:* Kemple and Rock, 1996, *First Report on the Career Academies Demonstration and Evaluation.*

Page 209. *Research has found that nationwide, many academies:* Ibid.

Page 210. *"They teach you how to go out into the world":* Interview with Jason Potter, Pasadena, California, January 1994.

Page 210. *In 1994, only about 30 percent of teenagers:* Information provided by Alma Dillard, coordinator of academy programs, Pasadena Unified School District, January 1994.

Page 210. *In general, work experience historically has been the least well developed:* Kemple and Rock, 1996, *First Report on the Career Academies Demonstration and Evaluation.*

Page 211. *"These students are somebody":* Interview with Marla Keeth, Pasadena, California, January 1994.

Page 211. *"The teachers get to know everyone":* Interview with Albert Shaw, Pasadena, California, January 1994.

Page 211. *The average California academy:* Dayton, 1995, *California Partnership Academies 1993–94.*

Page 211. *"Whenever we start to look":* Interview with Mark Hall, Pasadena, California, January 1994.

Page 212. *But a study of 10 of the original academies:* Stern, Raby, and Dayton, 1992, *Career Academies,* pp. 56–71.

Page 212. *Information on graduates:* National Academy Foundation, *General Statistical Overview,* 1996.

Page 212. *A follow-up study of about 200:* Academy for Educational Development, 1990, *Employment and Educational Experiences of Academy of Finance Graduates.*

Page 212. *A follow-up survey conducted six months:* Packer et al., 1996, *School-to-Work,* p. 110.

Page 212. *A study by researchers at the Center on the Organization and Restructuring of Schools:* Newmann and Wehlage, 1995, *Successful School Restructuring.*

Page 213. *In their study of 10 career academies nationwide:* Kemple and Rock, 1996, *First Report on the Career Academies Demonstration and Evaluation.*

Page 213. *"Many of these teachers":* Ibid., p. xx.

Page 213. *In 1992 a report by the California state department of education:* California High School Task Force, 1992, *Second to None.*

Page 213. *Similarly, a report published in 1996 by the National Association:* Commission on the Restructuring of the American High School, 1996, *Breaking Ranks.*

Page 214. *Encina High School in Sacramento County:* U.S. Department of Education and the National Center for Research in Vocational Education, 1996, "New American High School," conference materials and presentation.

Page 214. *At Patterson High School in Baltimore:* Viadero, "Environmental Studies," pp. 35–38.

Page 215. *"We think what we have":* Ibid., p. 38.

Page 216. *In A Place Called School:* Goodlad, 1984, *A Place Called School.*

Page 216. *"Here is where specialized":* Boyer, 1983, *High School,* pp. 128, 130.

Page 216. *"The Early College serves":* Sizer, 1992, *Horace's School,* p. 159.

Page 217. *In 1997, a study:* Hershey, April 1992, *Partners in Progress,* p. xviii.

Chapter 7—Making It Happen

Page 220. *In its own quiet way:* The description of the Greater Lehigh Valley Youth Apprenticeship Program is based on a site visit in May 1995, interviews with program officials, and written materials.

Page 220. *"Eric was never planning":* Telephone interview with Louise Roth, May 1995.

Page 221. *"I'm running out of time":* Interview with Eric Heiney, Allentown, Pennsylvania, May 1995.

Page 221. *"Eighty percent of the educators":* Interview with Kathleen Foster, Allentown, Pennsylvania, May 1995.

Page 222. *"If there's any lesson":* Interview with Larry Rosenstock, Cambridge, Massachusetts, November 1995.

Page 223. *"This won't happen without leadership":* Interview with Neil Sullivan, Boston, Massachusetts, December 1995.

Page 224. *One study estimates:* Silverberg, 1997, *Experiences and Lessons of the School-to-Work/Youth Apprenticeship Demonstration,* pp. 10, 181.

Page 227. *"The infrastructure for collaboration":* Kanter, 1995, *World Class,* p. 363.

Page 228. *"It's a lot of time":* Interview with Pam Mape, Boston, Massachusetts, November 1995.

Page 228. *"You have to have a broker":* Interview with René Leger, Portland, Oregon, November 1995.

Page 229. *"To me, it's not a true partnership":* Interview with Dennis Loftus, Wilmington, Delaware, December 1995.

Page 230. *"[School-to-career] can easily disappear"*: Interview with Neil Sullivan, Boston, Massachusetts, December 1995.

Page 230. *"You need to have"*: Interview with Robert Glover, Austin, Texas, April 1996.

Page 230. *"Employer interests"*: Glover, 1996, "Engaging Industry in Building School-to-Career Opportunities," pp. 43–44.

Page 231. *Although firms have been:* Ibid., p. 43.

Page 232. *Every Wednesday afternoon:* Presentation by Susan de Armas at New American High School conference, May 22–24, 1996, Washington, D.C.

Page 234. *Jobs for the Future's Benchmark Communities Initiative:* Jobs for the Future, 1996, *Jobs for the Future: Benchmark Communities Initiative, Five-Year Goals*; personal communication from Hilary Pennington, president, Jobs for the Future, August 1996.

Chapter 8—What Needs to Be Done

Page 238. *School-to-work can motivate:* For a summary of the research that has been done, see Jobs for the Future, 1995, *Promising Practices*; U.S. Congress, Office of Technology Assessment, 1995, *Learning to Work*, p. 41; Pauly et al., 1995, *Home-Grown Lessons*; and Silverberg, 1997, *Experiences and Lessons of the School-to-Work/Youth Apprenticeship Demonstration.*

Page 238. *"It gives you a different idea of school"*: Interview with Matt Ciprich, Tunhannock High School, Tunhannock, Pennsylvania, May 1995.

Page 238. *School-to-work can encourage:* Jobs for the Future, 1995, *Promising Practices.*

Page 239. *In New York City:* Heebner et al., 1992, "Career Magnets."

Page 239. *Their research has found:* Bailey and Merritt, 1997, *School-to-Work for the College Bound*, p. 24.

Page 239. *School-to-work can satisfy:* Jobs for the Future, 1995, *Promising Practices*; U.S. Congress, Office of Technology Assessment, 1995, *Learning to Work*, p. 41; Pauly et al., 1995, *Home-Grown Lessons*; and Morgan, 1996, "What Employers Want."

Page 241. *"Many of the most serious 'life skills'"*: Powell, Farrar, and Cohen, 1985, *Shopping Mall High School*, p. 320.

Page 241. *"Simply requiring all students"*: Southern Regional Education Board, 1996, *High School Graduation Standard*, p. 8.

Page 244. *The sites involved in Jobs for the Future's*: Jobs for the Future, 1996, *Jobs for the Future: Benchmark Communities Initiative, Five-Year Goals*; personal communication from Hilary Pennington, president, Jobs for the Future, August 1996.

Page 247. *Research suggests that students who have a plan*: Orfield and Paul, 1994, *High Hopes, Long Odds*.

Page 251. *Today, close to half*: U.S. Bureau of the Census, 1995, *American Almanac*, Table 240.

Page 252. *According to the advisory board*: National Center on the Educational Quality of the Workforce, Advisory Board, 1995, "On Connecting School and Work," p. 7.

Page 252. *Research suggests*: Stern et al., 1995, *School to Work*; Greenberger and Steinberg, 1986, *When Teenagers Work*.

Page 254. *Kalamazoo College*: Whitelaw, 1996, "Weighing Security and Success," pp. 115–116.

Page 257. *"Corporations can't ignore education"*: Interview with Nancy Shiels, Boston, Massachusetts, December 1995.

Bibliography

Academy for Educational Development. October 1995. *Cross-Site Analysis. Learning from Experience: A Cross-Case Comparison of School-to-Work Transition Reform Initiatives*. New York: Academy for Educational Development.

———. 1990. *Employment and Educational Experiences of Academy of Finance Graduates*. Prepared for National Academy Foundation. New York: Academy for Educational Development.

Adelman, Clifford. 1994. *Lessons of a Generation: Education and Work in the Lives of the High School Class of 1972*. San Francisco: Jossey-Bass Publishers.

Agee, Janice Lowen. 1992. *Second to None: A Vision of the New California High School*. Sacramento: California State Department of Education.

American Association of Community and Junior Colleges. 1988. *Building Communities: A Vision for a New Century*. Washington, D.C.: American Association of Community and Junior Colleges.

American Association of Community Colleges. 1996. *Pocket Profile of Community Colleges: Trends & Statistics, 1995–1996*. Washington, D.C.: American Association of Community Colleges.

———. 1994. *The Tech Prep Associate Degree Challenge*. A Report of the Tech Prep Roundtable. AACC Special Reports no. 6. Washington, D.C.: American Association of Community Colleges.

American Council on Education. 1994. *Twelfth Annual Status Report on Minorities in Higher Education*. Washington, D.C.: American Council on Education.

American Federation of Teachers. 1997. *Reaching the Next Step: How School to Career Can Help Students Reach High Academic Standards and Prepare for Good Jobs*. Washington, D.C.: American Federation of Teachers.

American Youth Policy Forum and Jobs for the Future. January 23, 1995. *Promising Practices: A Study of Ten School-to-Career Programs*. Boston: Jobs for the Future.

291

Ancess, Jacqueline, and Linda Darling-Hammond. September 1994. *The Senior Project: Authentic Assessment at Hodgson Vocational/Technical High School.* New York: National Center for Restructuring Education, Schools, and Teaching, Teachers College, Columbia University.

Applebome, Peter. February 20, 1995. "Employers Wary of School System." *New York Times*, p. 1.

Astin, Alexander, et al. 1993. *The American Freshman National Norms for Fall 1993.* Los Angeles: Higher Education Research Institute, University of California, Los Angeles.

Bailey, Thomas R. 1993. "Can Youth Apprenticeship Thrive in the United States?" *Educational Researcher* 22 (no. 3), pp. 4–10.

Bailey, Thomas R., ed. 1995. *Learning to Work: Employer Involvement in School-to-Work Programs.* Washington, D.C.: The Brookings Institution.

Bailey, Thomas R., and Donna Merritt. 1993. *The School-to-Work Transition and Youth Apprenticeship: Lessons from the U.S. Experience.* New York: Manpower Demonstration Research Corporation.

———. June 1995. *Making Sense of Industry-Based Skills Standards.* New York: Institute on Education and the Economy, Teachers College, Columbia University.

———. February 1997. *School-to-Work for the College Bound.* Berkeley, California: National Center for Research in Vocational Education.

Bailis, Lawrence Neil, and Brad Rose, with assistance from Dennis Learner. 1996. *Evaluation of the National Higher Ground Initiative: Executive Summary.* Boston: School & Main, New England Medical Center.

Bardeleben, Richard von, Ursula Beicht, and Kalman Feher. 1996. *Study of the Costs and Benefits of Vocational Training in Germany.* Translated by the Center for Learning and Competitiveness. College Park, Md.: Center for Learning and Competitiveness, University of Maryland.

Barton, Paul E. 1989. *Earning and Learning: The Academic Achievement of High-School Juniors with Jobs. The Nation's Report Card.* Report no. 17-WL-01. Princeton, N.J.: National Assessment of Educational Progress (ERIC Document Reproduction Service no. ED 309 179).

———. 1990. *From School to Work.* Policy Information Report (ERIC Document Reproduction Service no. ED 320 947). Princeton, N.J.: Educational Testing Service, Policy Information Center.

Beem, Edgar Allen. February 4, 1994. "The Essence of Reform." *Maine Times,* cover story.

BellSouth Corporation. June 1995. *BellSouth Connections: School-to-Work.* Atlanta: BellSouth Corporation.

Benning, Victoria. August 12, 1994. "U.S. Grants $1.2 Million for School, Work Effort Now, 400 Students in City to Benefit." *Boston Globe.* Metro Section, p. 31.

Berryman, Sue E., and Thomas R. Bailey. 1992. *The Double Helix of Education and the Economy.* New York: Institute on Education and the Economy, Teachers College, Columbia University.

Bishop, John. April 28, 1995. *Expertise and Excellence.* Cornell University Working Paper no. 95-13. Ithaca, N.Y.: Center on the Educational Quality of the Workforce and Cornell's Program on Youth and Work and Center for Advanced Human Resource Studies, New York State School of Industrial and Labor Relations, Cornell University.

————. Spring 1992. *Is a Skills Shortage Coming?* ILR Reprint no. 670. Ithaca, N.Y.: ILR Press, New York State School of Industrial and Labor Relations, Cornell University.

————. November 1995, draft. "Is the Market for College Graduates Headed for a Bust? Demand and Supply Responses to Rising College Wage Premiums." Ithaca, N.Y.: Cornell University.

————. 1989. "Occupational Training in High School: When Does It Pay Off?" *Economics of Education Review* 8 (no. 1), pp. 1–15.

————. 1994. *The Payoff to Schooling and Learning in the United States.* Ithaca, N.Y.: School of Industrial and Labor Relations, Cornell University.

————. Fall 1995. "The Power of External Standards." *American Educator* 19 (no. 3), pp. 10–43.

————. 1996. "Vocational Education and At-Risk Youth in the United States." Working Paper 95-19. Ithaca, N.Y.: Center for Advanced Human Resource Studies, Cornell University.

————. 1989. "Why the Apathy in American High Schools?" *Educational Researcher* 18 (no. 1), pp. 6–10.

Boesel, David, and Laurel McFarland. 1994. *National Assessment of Vocational Education: Final Report to Congress.* Washington, D.C.: U.S. Department of Education, Office of Research.

Boesel, David, Lisa Hudson, Sharon Deich, and Charles Masten. June 30, 1994. *National Assessment of Vocational Education: Final Report to Congress, Volume II.* Washington, D.C.: U.S. Department of Education, Office of Research.

Bottoms, Gene. March 1996. *Lessons from Europe for Improving School-to-Work Programs.* International Forum on Learning and Competitiveness. College Park, Md.: Center for Learning and Competitiveness, University of Maryland.

Bottoms, Gene, and Pat Mikos. 1995. *Seven Most-Improved 'High Schools That Work' Sites Raise Achievement in Reading, Mathematics, and Science.* Atlanta: Southern Regional Education Board.

Bottoms, Gene, et al. 1992. *Making High Schools Work.* Atlanta: Southern Regional Education Board.

Bound, John, and George Johnson. January 1995. "What Are the Causes of Rising Wage Inequality in the United States?" *Economic Policy Review* 1 (no. 1), pp. 9–17.

Boyer, Ernest L. 1983. *High School: A Report on Secondary Education in America.* New York: Harper & Row.

Bragg, Debra D., James D. Layton, and Frank T. Hammons. September 1994. *Tech Prep Implementation in the United States: Promising Trends and Lingering Challenges.* Berkeley, Calif.: National Center for Research in Vocational Education, University of California, Berkeley.

Bucci, Paul, and John B. Lee. June 1995. *PACE Model Tech Prep Education Project: Evaluation Report.* Prepared for the Partnership for Academic and Career Education. Washington, D.C.: Academy for Educational Development.

Business Roundtable. June 1996. *A Business Leader's Guide to Setting Academic Standards.* Washington, D.C.: Business Roundtable.

Business Roundtable, U.S. Chamber of Commerce, and National Alliance of Business. September 1996. *A Common Agenda for Improving American Education.* Washington, D.C.: Business Roundtable, U.S. Chamber of Commerce, and National Alliance of Business.

California High School Task Force. 1992. *Second to None: A Vision of the New California High School.* Sacramento: California Department of Education.

Campbell, Jay R., et al. October 1996. *Report in Brief: NAEP 1994 Trends in Academic Progress.* Washington, D.C.: National Center for Education Statistics, U.S. Department of Education.

Cappelli, Peter. 1992. *Is the "Skills Gap" Really About Attitudes?* EQW working paper. Philadelphia: National Center on the Educational Quality of the Workforce, University of Pennsylvania.

Cappelli, Peter, and Maria Iannozzi. 1995. *Rethinking the Skills Gap: Is It Craft or Character?* EQW Issue no. 9. Philadelphia: National Center on the Educational Quality of the Workforce, University of Pennsylvania.

Carnevale, Anthony P. 1991. *America and the New Economy.* Alexandria, Va.: American Society for Training and Development.

Center for Occupational Research and Development Inc. 1995. *Making Students Work-Ready: Is Your Business Involved?* Waco, Tex.: National Tech Prep Network.

Claus, J. 1990. "Opportunity or Inequality in Vocational Education: A Qualitative Investigation." *Curriculum Inquiry* 20 (no. 1), pp. 7–39.

Cohen, David. "Origins." In *The Shopping-Mall High School: Winners and Losers in the Educational Marketplace.* Ed. Arthur G. Powell, Eleanor Farrar, and David K. Cohen. 1985. Boston: Houghton Mifflin.

Commission on the Restructuring of the American High School. 1996. *Breaking Ranks: Changing an American Institution.* Reston, Va.: National Association of Secondary School Principals.

Commission on the Skills of the American Workforce. 1990. *America's Choice: High Skills or Low Wages!* Rochester, N.Y.: National Center on Education and the Economy.

Commission on Work, Family, and Citizenship. 1988. *The Forgotten Half: Pathways to Success for America's Youth and Young Families.* Washington, D.C.: W. T. Grant Foundation.

Committee for Economic Development. 1996. *American Workers and Economic Change.* New York: Committee for Economic Development.

———. 1991. *An Assessment of American Education: Views of Employers, Higher Educators, the Public, Recent Students, and Their Parents.* New York: Louis Harris Associates.

———. 1985. *Investing in Our Children: Business and the Public Schools.* New York: Committee for Economic Development.

Conkling, Fiskum & McCormick Inc. 1994. Summary of Statewide Opinion Research Survey of 744 Public, 325 Parents, 300 Business Owners, 194 Superintendents/Principals, 299 Teachers, and 401 Students. Portland,Ore.:

Conkling, Fiskum & McCormick. Personal communication and papers provided by Patricia Farrell.

Consortium on Productivity in the Schools. October 1995. *Using What We Have to Get the Schools We Need: A Productivity Focus for American Education.* New York: Consortium on Productivity in the Schools, Institute on Education and the Economy, Teachers College, Columbia University.

Corson, Wendy, and Marsha Silverberg. June 1994. *The School-to-Work/Youth Apprenticeship Demonstration: Preliminary Findings.* A report submitted to the U.S. Department of Labor. Princeton, N.J.: Mathematica Policy Research, Inc.

Council of Chief State School Officers and American Youth Policy Forum. 1994. *Building a System to Connect School and Employment.* Washington, D.C.: American Youth Policy Forum.

Crawford, David, Amy Johnson, and Anita Summers. January–February 1995. "Climbing the Ladder of Success: Post–High School Performance in the Labor Market." *Change* 27 (no. 1), pp. 45–48.

Csikszentmihalyi, Mihaly, ed. June 1996. *Youth and Work in America: A Summary of Results from the First Years of the Sloan Study of Youth and Social Development.* Chicago: University of Chicago Press.

Dayton, Charles. Spring 1995. *California Partnership Academies 1993-1994: Evaluation Report.* Prepared by Foothill Associates for the California Department of Education. Nevada City, Calif.: Foothill Associates.

Decker, Paul. "Education and Worker Productivity." In U.S. Department of Education, *The Condition of Education 1996.* National Center for Education Statistics publication NCES 96-304. Washington, D.C.: U.S. Government Printing Office.

Dewey, John. 1916. *Democracy and Education: An Introduction to the Philosophy of Education.* New York: Macmillan.

Dilcher, Ann Katherine. 1993. *Learning That Works: The Provision of Workplace Education by Community Colleges.* Washington, D.C.: American Association of Community Colleges.

Drucker, Peter F. November 1994. "The Age of Social Transformation." *Atlantic Monthly,* pp. 53–80.

———. 1993. *Post-Capitalist Society.* New York: HarperCollins.

Eck, Alan. October 1993. "Job-Related Education and Training: Their Impact on Earnings." *Monthly Labor Review* 116 (no. 10) (Washington, D.C.: U.S. Department of Labor), pp. 21–38.

The Economist. October 1993. "Put Germany Back to Work," p. 81; December 25, 1993, "The Richer, the Slower," p. 92; November. 5, 1994, "The Nordic Countries: Heading South," pp. 3–18.

Education Week. 1993. *From Risk to Renewal: Charting a Course for Reform.* Washington, D.C.: Editorial Projects in Education.

Elfin, Mel. September 16, 1996. "The High Cost of Higher Education." *U.S. News & World Report.* "America's Best Colleges: 1997 Annual Guide," pp. 91–101.

Emanuel, David A., Jr., and Kristi Rossi. December 1995. *Linking the Classroom and Work-Based Learning: A Case Study in Appliance Repair.* Prepared for the National Alliance of Business. Berkeley, Calif.: MPR Associates.

Farkas, Steve, and Will Friedman. 1995. *The Westchester School-to-Work Initiative: Prospects and Challenges.* New York: Public Agenda.

Federal Institute for Vocational Training. 1993. *Training Ordinances and the Procedure for Producing Them.* Bonn, Germany: Federal Institute for Vocational Training.

Federal Ministry of Education and Science. 1994. *Vocational Training in Germany.* Bonn, Germany: Federal Ministry of Education and Science.

———. May 1992. *Vocational Training in the Dual System in the Federal Republic of Germany: An Investment in the Future.* Bonn, Germany: Federal Ministry of Education and Science.

Ferdinand, Pamela. December 18, 1994. "At Rindge, 1 in 3 Fail at Least 1 Course." *Boston Globe,* City Weekly Section, p. 1.

Finegold, David. 1993. "Making Apprenticeships Work." RAND Issue Paper no. 1. Santa Monica, Calif.: RAND.

Finn, Peter. October 27, 1995. "GM to Set Up Mechanic Program at Va. School." *Washington Post,* p. B4.

Fort Worth Independent School District. 1991. "Fort Worth—Project C3: Community, Corporations, Classrooms." Fort Worth, Tex.: Fort Worth Independent School District.

General Motors Corporation. September 1995. "GM Youth Educational Systems: An Automotive School-to-Work Initiative." Detroit: General Motors Corporation.

Glover, Robert. April 1996. "Engaging Industry in Building School-to-Career Opportunities: Lessons to Date from the Experience in Austin, Texas." Prepared for the National Center for the Workplace. Austin, Tex.: General Motors Corporation.

Goldberger, Susan. 1993. *Creating an American-Style Youth Apprenticeship Program: The Formative Evaluation of Project ProTech*. Boston: Jobs for the Future.

Goldberger, Susan, and Richard Kazis. July 1995, prepublication draft. "Rethinking the School-to-Work Agenda for American High Schools." Boston: Jobs for the Future.

———. August 1995, prepublication draft. "Revitalizing High Schools: What the School-to-Career Movement Can Contribute." Boston: Jobs for the Future.

Goldberger, Susan, Richard Kazis, and Mary Kathleen O'Flanagan. January 1994. *Learning Through Work: Designing and Implementing Quality Worksite Learning for High School Students*. Prepared by Jobs for the Future for the Manpower Demonstration Research Corporation. New York: Manpower Demonstration Research Corporation.

Goodlad, John I. 1984. *A Place Called School: Prospects for the Future*. New York: McGraw-Hill.

Gray, Kenneth C., and Edwin L. Herr. 1995. *Other Ways to Win: Creating Alternatives for High School Graduates*. Thousand Oaks, Calif.: Corwin Press Inc.

Green, Patricia J., et al. June 1995. *National Education Longitudinal Study of 1988: Trends Among High School Seniors, 1972–1992*. NCES 95-380. U.S. Department of Education, Office of Educational Research and Improvement. Washington, D.C.: U.S. Government Printing Office.

Greenberger, Ellen, and Laurence D. Steinberg. 1986. *When Teenagers Work: The Psychological and Social Costs of Adolescent Employment*. New York: Basic Books.

Grubb, W. Norton. April 1996. "The 'New Vocationalism': What It Is, What It Could Be." *Phi Delta Kappan*, pp. 535–546.

———. November 1994, draft. "Occupation as a Context for Instruction." Berkeley, Calif.: National Center for Research in Vocational Education, University of California, Berkeley.

———. 1992. "Postsecondary Vocational Education and the Sub-Baccalaureate Labor Market: New Evidence on Economic Returns." *Economics of Education Review* 113, pp. 225–248.

————. May 1995. "Reconstructing Urban Schools with Work-Centered Education." *Education and Urban Society.*

————. May 1995. *The Return to Education and Training in the Sub-Baccalaureate Labor Market: Evidence From the Survey of Income and Program Participation, 1984–1990.* Berkeley, Calif.: National Center for Research in Vocational Education, University of California, Berkeley.

————. August 3, 1994. "True Reform or Tired Retread? Seven Questions to Ask About School-to-Work Programs." *Education Week.*

————. Spring 1993. "The Varied Economic Returns to Postsecondary Education. New Evidence from the Class of 1972." *Journal of Human Resources* 282, pp. 364–382.

Grubb, W. Norton, ed. 1994. *Education Through Occupations in American High Schools. Volume 1. Approaches to Integrating Academic and Vocational Education.* New York: Teachers College Press, Columbia University.

————. 1995. *Education Through Occupations in American High Schools. Volume 2. The Challenges of Implementing Curriculum Integration.* New York: Teachers College Press, Columbia University.

Grubb, W. Norton, and R. Wilson. 1992. "Trends in Wage and Salary Inequality, 1967–88." *Monthly Labor Review* 115 (no. 6), pp. 23–39.

Grubb, W. Norton, Noreena Badway, Denise Bell, and Eileen Kraskouska. January 1996, draft. "Community College Innovations in Workforce Preparation: Curriculum Integration and Tech Prep." Berkeley, Calif.: National Center for Research in Vocational Education, University of California, Berkeley.

Hamilton, Stephen F. 1990. *Apprenticeship for Adulthood: Preparing Youth for the Future.* New York: Free Press.

————. Spring 1992. "Apprenticeships for American Youth?" *TransAtlantic Perspectives* (published by the German Marshall Fund of the United States, Washington, D.C.).

————. 1994. "Employment Prospects as Motivation for School Achievement: Links and Gaps Between School and Work in Seven Countries." In *Adolescence in Context: The Interplay of Family, School, Peers, and Work in Adjustment.* Ed. Rainer K. Silbereisen and Eberhard Todt. New York: Springer-Verlag.

Hamilton, Stephen F., and Mary Agnes Hamilton. 1994. *Opening Career Paths for Youth: What Needs to Be Done? Who Can Do It?* Ithaca, N.Y.: Cornell

Youth and Work Program, Cornell University; American Youth Policy Forum; Jobs for the Future.

————. 1996, draft report. "Quality-Based Learning: Principles from Apprenticeships." Ithaca, N.Y.: Cornell Youth and Work Program, Cornell University.

Hamilton, Stephen F., and Klaus Hurrelmann. Winter 1994. "The School-to-Career Transition in Germany and the United States." *Teachers College Record.*

Hamilton, Stephen F., and Wolfgang Lempert. In press. "The Impact of Apprenticeship on Youth: A Prospective Analysis." *Journal of Research on Adolescence.*

Harhoff, Dietmar, and Thomas J. Kane. 1994. "Financing Apprenticeship Training: Evidence from Germany." In U.S. Department of Education, *School-to-Work: What Does Research Say About It?* Washington, D.C.: Office of Research, Office of Educational Research and Improvement, U.S. Department of Education.

Hearne, Donna. 1995. *Paychecks and Power: The OBE Road to Educational Reform and the Federal Paymaster.* St. Louis, Mo.: Constitutional Coalition.

Heebner, Amy, et al. August 1992. *Career Magnets: Interviews with Students and Staff.* Berkeley, Calif.: National Center for Research in Vocational Education, University of California, Berkeley.

Hernandez-Gantes, Victor M., and L. Allen Phelps. 1995. *Developing Career and Academic Aspirations: Opening New and Different Doors for Students in School-to-Work Programs.* Madison: Center on Education and Work, University of Wisconsin.

Hershey, Alan M., et al. April 1997. *Partners in Progress: Early Steps in Creating School-to-Work Systems.* Report submitted to the U.S. Department of Education. Princeton, N.J.: Mathematica Policy Research, Inc.

Hershey, Alan M., and Marsha K. Silverberg. October 29, 1993. "Employer Involvement in School-to-Work Transition Programs: What Can We Really Expect." Paper presented at the Association for Public Policy and Management Conference, Washington, D.C.

Hershey, Alan M., Marsha Silverberg, and Tom Owens. 1995. *Diverse Forms of Tech-Prep: Implementation Approaches in 10 Local Consortia.* Report submitted to the U.S. Department of Education. Princeton, N.J.: Mathematica Policy Research, Inc.

Hill, Paul. 1992. "Urban Education." In *Urban America: Policy Choices for America and the Nation*. Ed. James Steinberg et al. Santa Monica, Calif.: RAND.

Hill, Paul, G. Foster, and T. Gendler. 1990. *High Schools with Character*. Santa Monica, Calif.: RAND.

Hollenbeck, Kevin. May 1994. *The Workplace Know-How Skills Needed to be Productive. Executive Summary*. Kalamazoo, Mich.: Kalamazoo County Education for Employment Outcomes Task Force, Kalamazoo County Education for Employment Consortium.

Hull, Dan, and Dale Parnell. 1991. *Tech Prep Associate Degree: A Win/Win Experience*. Waco, Tex.: Center for Occupational Research and Development.

Jobs for the Future. 1996. *Jobs for the Future: Benchmark Communities Initiative, Five-Year Goals*. Boston: Jobs for the Future.

———. 1993. *McDonald's Youth Apprenticeship Program: Briefing Report*. Boston: Jobs for the Future.

———. August 1995, prepublication draft. "Promising Practices: A Study of Ten School-to-Career Programs." Boston: Jobs for the Future.

———. 1995. *School-to-Work and Youth Development: Identifying Common Ground: An Agenda for Action*. Boston: Jobs for the Future and the Academy for Educational Development.

Johnson, Jean, et al. 1995. *Assignment Incomplete: The Unfinished Business of Education Reform*. New York: Public Agenda.

Johnson, Kirk. December 4, 1996. "In the Changed Landscape of Recruiting, Academic and Corporate Worlds Merge." *The New York Times*, Education section.

Johnson, William B., and Arnold H. Packer. 1987. *Workforce 2000: Work and Workers for the 21st Century*. Indianapolis: Hudson Institute.

Juhn, Chinhui, and Kevin M. Murphy. January 1995. "Inequality in Labor Market Outcomes: Contrasting the 1980s and Earlier Decades." *Economic Policy Review* 1 (no. 1), pp. 26–34.

Kalamazoo County. May 1994. *Education for Employment: The Workplace Know-How Skills Needed to Be Productive*. Kalamazoo, Mich.: Kalamazoo County Outcomes Task Force.

Kanter, Rosabeth Moss. 1995. *World Class: Thriving Locally in the Global Economy*. New York: Simon & Schuster.

Kantor, H. Summer. 1994. "Managing the Transition from School to Work: The False Promises of Youth Apprenticeship." *Teachers College Record* 95 (no. 4), pp. 442–461.

Kazis, Richard. 1991. *Pennsylvania Youth Apprenticeship Program: An Historical Account from Its Origins to September 1991.* Boston: Jobs for the Future.

Kemple, James J., and JoAnn Rock. 1996. *First Report on the Career Academies Demonstration and Evaluation.* New York: Manpower Demonstration Research Corporation.

Kirsch, Irwin S., Ann Jungeblut, Lynn Jenkins, and Andrew Kolstad. 1993. *Adult Literacy in America: A First Look at the Results of the National Adult Literacy Survey.* Washington, D.C.: Office of Educational Research and Improvement, U.S. Department of Education.

Kopp, Hilary, Susan Goldberger, and Dionisia Morales. March 1994. *The Evolution of a Youth-Apprenticeship Model: A Second-Year Evaluation of Boston's ProTech.* Boston: Jobs for the Future.

Lawton, Millicent. October 2, 1996. "Three Business Groups Advocate Common Reform Agenda." *Education Week*, p. 10.

Lazerson, Marvin, and W. Norton Grubb, eds. (with an introduction and notes). 1974. *American Education and Vocationalism: A Documentary History, 1870–1970.* New York: Teachers College Press, Columbia University.

Levy, Frank, and Richard J. Murnane. 1992. "U.S. Earnings Levels and Earnings Inequality: A Review of Recent Trends and Proposed Explanations." *Journal of Economic Literature* 30 (no. 3), pp. 1333–1382.

Little, Judith Warren. November 1992. *Two Worlds: Vocational and Academic Teachers in Comprehensive High Schools.* Berkeley, Calif.: National Center for Research in Vocational Education, University of California, Berkeley.

———. May 1995. "What Teachers Learn in High School: Professional Development and the Redesign of Vocational Education." *Education and Urban Society* 27 (no. 3), pp. 274–293.

Little, Judith Warren, and S. Threatt. 1992. *Work on the Margins: The Experience of Vocational Teachers in Comprehensive High Schools.* Berkeley, Calif.: National Center for Research in Vocational Education, University of California, Berkeley.

Lynn, Irene, and Joan Wills. 1994. *School Lessons: Work Lessons.* Washington, D.C.: Institute for Educational Leadership.

Marshall, Ray, and Marc Tucker. 1992. *Thinking for a Living: Education and the Wealth of Nations*. New York: Basic Books.

McKernan, John R., Jr., with Jobs for America's Graduates, Inc. and Jobs for the Future. 1994. *Making the Grade: How a New Youth Apprenticeship System Can Change Our Schools and Save American Jobs*. New York: Little, Brown.

McNeil, Patricia W. 1993. *The Role of Industry Associations in School-to-Work Transition*. New York: Manpower Demonstration Research Corporation.

Morgan, Stephen. 1996. *What Employers Want: Youth Labor Markets and School-to-Work Transition Programs*. EQW Issues no. 6. Philadelphia: National Center on the Educational Quality of the Workforce, University of Pennsylvania.

Mullis, Ina V. S., et al. July 1994. *NAEP 1992 Trends in Academic Progress*. Prepared by the Educational Testing Service for the National Center for Education Statistics, Office of Educational Research and Improvement, U.S. Department of Education. Report no. 23-TR01. Washington, D.C.: National Center for Education Statistics, U.S. Department of Education.

————. April 1993. *NAEP 1992: Mathematics Report Card for the Nation and the States*. Prepared by the Educational Testing Service for the National Center for Education Statistics, Office of Educational Research and Improvement, U.S. Department of Education. Washington, D.C.: National Center for Education Statistics, U.S. Department of Education.

Murnane, Richard J., and Frank Levy. 1996. *Teaching the New Basic Skills: Principles for Educating Children to Thrive in a Changing Economy*. New York: Free Press.

National Academy Foundation. 1995. *A General Statistical Overview of the National Academy Foundation and Its Member Programs*. New York: National Academy Foundation.

————. April 10, 1991. *Proposal to the National Diffusion Network Development Demonstration Projects, U.S. Department of Education, for Wider Dissemination of the Academy of Finance Program of the National Academy Foundation*. New York: National Academy Foundation.

————. January 1994. *The Academy of Travel & Tourism, Application Submitted to National Diffusion Network of the U.S. Education Department*. New York: National Academy Foundation.

National Academy of Sciences, Panel on Secondary School Education and the Changing Workplace. 1984. *High Schools and the Changing Workplace: The Employer's View*. Washington, D.C.: National Academy Press.

National Alliance of Business. 1992. *Real Jobs for Real People: An Employer's Guide to Youth Apprenticeship*. Washington, D.C.: National Alliance of Business.

National Alliance of Business and Scholastic Inc. April 1995. *Education in the U.S.* Washington, D.C.: National Alliance of Business and Scholastic Inc.

National Center on Education and the Economy. 1994. *The Certificate of Initial Mastery: A Primer*. Washington, D.C.: National Center on Education and the Economy.

National Center on the Educational Quality of the Workforce. 1995. *First Findings from the EQW National Employer Survey*. EQW catalog no. RE01. Philadelphia: National Center on the Educational Quality of the Workforce, University of Pennsylvania.

———. 1995. *The Other Shoe: Education's Contribution to the Productivity of Establishments. A Second Round of Findings from the EQW National Employer Survey*. EQW catalog no. RE02. Philadelphia: National Center on the Educational Quality of the Workforce, University of Pennsylvania.

National Center on the Educational Quality of the Workforce, Advisory Board. 1995. *On Connecting School and Work*. EQW policy statement, no. PS02. Philadelphia: Advisory Board of the National Center on the Educational Quality of the Workforce, University of Pennsylvania.

National Commission on Excellence in Education. 1983. *A Nation at Risk: The Imperative for Educational Reform*. Washington, D.C.: U.S. Department of Education.

National Commission on Secondary Vocational Education. 1985. *The Unfinished Agenda: The Role of Vocational Education in the High School*. Washington, D.C.: U.S. Department of Education, Office of Vocational and Adult Education.

National Education Association. 1893. *Report of the Committee of Ten on Secondary School Studies*. Publication no. 205. Washington, D.C.: U.S. Government Printing Office, U.S. Office of Education.

National Employer Leadership Council. August 1996. *Connecting Learning and Earning: The Employer Participation Model*. Washington, D.C.: National Employer Leadership Council.

Newmann, Fred M., and Gary G. Wehlage. 1995. *Successful School Restructuring: A Report to the Public and Educators by the Center on Organization and Restructuring of Schools*. Madison: Center on Organization and Restructuring of Schools, University of Wisconsin.

Oakes, Jeannie. 1985. *Keeping Track: How Schools Structure Inequality.* New Haven: Yale University Press.

Olson, Lynn. 1994. "Technically Speaking." *Education Week.* In special report, "Learning to Earn." Washington, D.C.: Editorial Projects in Education.

Oregon Education Association. 1992. *1992 Oregon Education Association Representative Assembly Report.* Salem, Ore.: Oregon Education Association.

Orfield, Gary, and Faith G. Paul. 1994. *High Hopes, Long Odds: A Major Report on Hoosier Teens and the American Dream.* Indianapolis: Indiana Youth Institute.

Orr, Margaret Terry. November 1994. *Wisconsin Youth Apprenticeship Program in Printing: Preliminary Evaluation Findings.* Boston: Jobs for the Future.

———. 1996. *Wisconsin Youth Apprenticeship Program in Printing: Evaluation 1993–1995.* Boston: Jobs for the Future.

Osterman, Paul. 1980. *Getting Started: The Youth Labor Market.* Cambridge, Mass.: M.I.T. Press.

———. January 1994. "How Common Is Workplace Transformation and Who Adopts It?" *Industrial and Labor Relations Review* 47 (no. 2), pp. 173–188.

———. 1995. "Involving Employers in School-to-Work Programs." In *Learning to Work: Employer Involvement in School-to-Work Transition Programs.* Ed. Thomas R. Bailey. Washington, D.C.: The Brookings Institution.

———. 1991. *Is There a Problem with the Youth Labor Market and If So, How Should We Fix It?* Cambridge, Mass.: Sloan School of Management, M.I.T.

Oxley, Diana. March 1994. "Organizing Schools into Small Units: Alternatives to Homogeneous Grouping." *Phi Delta Kappan,* pp. 521–526.

Packer, Arnold. 1994. *An Associate Degree in High-Performance Manufacturing.* Baltimore: Institute for Policy Studies, Johns Hopkins University.

Packer, Arnold, and Marion W. Pines, with M. Frank Stluka and Christine Surowiec. 1996. *School-to-Work.* Princeton, N.J.: Eye on Education.

Parnell, Dale. 1985. *The Neglected Majority.* Washington, D.C.: Community College Press.

Pauly, Edward, Hilary Kopp, and Joshua Haimson. 1995. *Home-Grown Lessons: Innovative Programs Linking Work and High School.* San Francisco: Jossey-Bass Publishers.

Pepin, Joshua, et al. December 1996. "State School-to-Work System Development—1996." Washington, D.C.: National Governors' Association.

Powell, Arthur G., Eleanor Farrar, and David K. Cohen. 1985. *The Shopping Mall High School: Winners and Losers in the Educational Marketplace*. Boston: Houghton Mifflin.

Powell, Bill. March 18, 1996. "Sick at Heart?" *Newsweek*, International Edition.

Raizen, Senta A. December 1989. *Reforming Education for Work: A Cognitive Science Perspective*. Berkeley, Calif.: National Center for Research in Vocational Education, University of California, Berkeley.

Ravitch, Diane. 1995. *National Standards in American Education: A Citizen's Guide*. Washington, D.C.: The Brookings Institution.

Reich, Robert. February 22, 1993. *Youth Apprenticeship and Lifelong Learning: Some Preliminary Notions*. Washington, D.C.: U.S. Department of Labor, Office of Information.

Resnick, Lauren B. 1987. *Education and Learning to Think*. Washington, D.C.: National Academy Press.

Richman, Louis S. August 22, 1994. "The New Worker Elite." *Fortune*, pp. 56–66.

Rimer, Sara. March 7, 1996. "A Hometown Feels Less Like Home." *New York Times*, p. A1.

Riordan, Rob. October 1994. "Hands On, Heads Up: Making Connections in School-to-Work Programs." *Kaleidoscope*.

Rosenfeld, Stuart. August 1993. *What Goes Around Comes Around: Studies of Federal Vocational Policy*. Chapel Hill, N.C.: Regional Technology Strategies.

Rosenstock, Larry. February 1991. "The Walls Come Down: The Overdue Reunification of Vocational and Academic Education." *Phi Delta Kappan*.

Rosenstock, Larry, and Adria Steinberg. 1995. "Beyond the Shop: Reinventing Vocational Education." In *Democratic Schools*. Ed. Michael W. Apple and James A. Beane. Alexandria, Va.: Association for Supervision and Curriculum Development.

Rothman, Robert. May 1995. "The Certificate of Initial Mastery." *Educational Leadership*, pp. 41–45.

Schaeffer, Esther F., et al. June 1994. *Education for Employment in the New Economy: A Joint Project of the Center for Learning and Competitiveness and the National Alliance of Business*. College Park, Md.: Center for Learning and Competitiveness, University of Maryland.

Schneider, Barbara, Mihaly Csikszentmihalyi, and Shaunti Knauth. 1995. "Academic Challenge, Motivation, and Self-Esteem, the Daily Experiences of Students in High School." In *Restructuring Schools: Promising Practices and Policies.* Ed. Maureen T. Hallinan. New York: Plenum Publishing Corporation.

Schorr, Lisbeth B., with Daniel Schorr. 1988. *Within Our Reach: Breaking the Cycle of Disadvantage.* New York: Doubleday.

Scottish Office Education Department. March 1994. *Higher Still.* Edinburgh, Scotland: Scottish Office Education Department.

Secretary's Commission on Achieving Necessary Skills. 1991. *What Work Requires of Schools.* Washington, D.C.: U.S. Department of Labor.

Silverberg, Marsha. 1997. *Experiences and Lessons of the School-to-Work/Youth Apprenticeship Demonstration.* Washington, D.C.: U.S. Department of Labor.

Silverberg, Marsha, and Alan M. Hershey. 1995. *The Emergence of Tech-Prep at the State and Local Levels.* Report submitted to the U.S. Department of Education. Princeton, N.J.: Mathematica Policy Research, Inc.

Sizer, Theodore R. 1984. *Horace's Compromise: The Dilemma of the American High School.* Boston: Houghton Mifflin.

———. 1992. *Horace's School: Redesigning the American High School.* New York: Houghton Mifflin.

———. May 1994. "School to Work: Some Questions for Marc Tucker." Prepared for the National Governors' Association. Washington, D.C.: National Governors' Association.

Smith, Hedrick. 1995. *Rethinking America: A New Game Plan from the American Innovators: Schools, Business, People, Work.* New York: Random House.

Sommerfeld, Meg. May 8, 1996. "Math, Science Test Scores Up, NSF Reports." *Education Week,* p. 6.

———. March 22, 1995. "Pioneering Reform Act Under Attack in Oregon." *Education Week,* pp. 13, 19.

———. October 11, 1995. "Upper-Level Math, Science Enrollment Is Up, Study Says." *Education Week,* p. 10.

Southern Regional Education Board. 1996. *High School Graduation Standards: What We Expect and What We Get.* Atlanta: Southern Regional Education Board.

————. 1995. *Integrating Vocational and Academic Studies: What Three High Schools in Delaware are Doing.* Atlanta: Southern Regional Education Board.

————. 1981. *The Need for Quality: A Report to the SREB by Its Task Force on Higher Education and the Schools.* Atlanta: Southern Regional Education Board.

Stasz, Cathleen, et al. 1996. *Workplace Skills in Practice.* Santa Monica, Calif.: RAND.

Stearrett, William H., Jr. 1994. "New Castle County Vocational-Technical School District—Customer Satisfaction Research: Parents, Students, Staff."

————. Fall 1995. "The New Castle County Vocational-Technical School District: Analysis of State Assessment Results" (memo).

————. August 1995. "New Castle County Vocational-Technical School District—Performance Indicators: Report Card for the School Year 1994–95." Performance reports on Delcastle, Hodgson, and Howard high schools.

Steinberg, Laurence, with B. Bradford Brown and Sanford M. Dornbusch. 1996. *Beyond the Classroom: Why School Reform Has Failed and What Parents Need to Do.* New York: Simon & Schuster.

Stern, David, Marilyn Raby, and Charles Dayton. 1992. *Career Academies: Partnerships for Reconstructing American High Schools.* San Francisco: Jossey-Bass Publishers.

Stern, David, and Daniel Wagner. To be published in 1997. "School-to-Work Policies in Industrialized Countries as Responses to Push and Pull." In *International Perspectives on the School-to-Work Transition.* New York: Hampton Press.

Stern, David, Thomas R. Bailey, and Donna Merritt. June 1996. "School-to-Work Policy Insights from Recent International Development." Berkeley, Calif.: National Center for Research in Vocational Education, University of California, Berkeley.

Stern, David, et al. 1995. *School to Work: Research on Programs in the United States.* Washington, D.C.: Taylor and Francis/Falmer Press.

Stevenson, David, et al. July 1, 1994. "Sequences of Opportunities for Learning." *Sociology of Education* 67 (no. 3), pp. 184–198.

Technical Development Corporation. 1993. *An Evaluation of the Fenway Middle College High School.* Boston: Technical Development Corporation.

Tifft, Susan E. October 1992. *Youth Apprenticeships: Can They Work in America?* EQW Issues no. 3. Philadelphia: National Center for the Educational Quality of the Workforce, University of Pennsylvania.

Tokarska, Barbara, Yiu-Pong Si, Robert Thaler, and Robert L. Crain. December 1992. *Academic-Career Integration in Magnet High Schools: Assessing the Level of Implementation.* Berkeley, Calif.: National Center for Research in Vocational Education, University of California, Berkeley.

Traub, James. 1994. *City on a Hill: Testing the American Dream at City College.* New York: Addison-Wesley.

U.S. Congress, Office of Technology Assessment. September 1995. *Learning to Work: Making the Transition from School to Work.* Publication no. OTA-EHR-637. Washington, D.C.: U.S. Government Printing Office.

U.S. Department of Commerce. 1995. *The American Almanac, 1995–96: Statistical Abstract of the United States.* Austin, Tex.: Reference Press, Inc.

U.S. Department of Education. 1996. *The Condition of Education 1996.* National Center for Education Statistics publication NCES 96-304. Washington, D.C.: U.S. Government Printing Office.

———. 1982. *Digest of Education Statistics.* Washington, D.C.: U.S. Government Printing Office.

———. 1994. *Digest of Education Statistics.* National Center for Education Statistics publication NCES 94-115. Washington, D.C.: U.S. Government Printing Office.

———. 1996. *Pursuing Excellence.* National Center for Education Statistics publication NCES 97-198. Washington, D.C.: U.S. Government Printing Office.

———. 1994. *School-to-Work: What Does Research Say About It?* Washington, D.C.: Office of Research, Office of Educational Research and Improvement, U.S. Department of Education.

———. November 1993. *Statistics in Brief.* Washington, D.C.: U.S. Department of Education, National Center for Education Statistics.

———. May 1995. *Vocational Course-Taking and Achievement: An Analysis of High School Transcripts and 1990 NAEP Assessment Scores.* Washington, D.C.: U.S. Department of Education, National Center for Education Statistics.

U.S. Department of Education and the National Center for Research in Vocational Education. 1996. "New American High School," conference held in Washington, D.C., May 1996.

U.S. Department of Education and U.S. Department of Labor. September 1996. "Implementation of the School-to-Work Opportunities Act of 1994, Report to Congress." Washington, D.C.: National School-to-Work Office.

U.S. General Accounting Office. 1991. *Transition from School to Work: Linking Education and Work Site Training.* Publication no. GAO/HRD-91-105. Washington, D.C.: U.S. Government Printing Office.

————. 1993. *Transition from School to Work: States Are Developing New Strategies to Prepare Students for Jobs.* Publication no. GAO/HRD-93-139. Washington, D.C.: U.S. Government Printing Office.

Viadero, Debra. June 12, 1996. "Environmental Studies." *Education Week*, p. 38.

Vickers, Margaret. 1991. *Building a National System for School-to-Work Transition: Lessons from Britain and Australia.* Boston: Jobs for the Future.

————. May 1994. *Skill Standards and Skill Formation: Cross-National Perspectives on Alternative Training Strategies.* Boston: Jobs for the Future.

Villeneuve, Jennifer, and W. Norton Grubb. April 1995. *Indigenous School-to-Work Programs: Lessons from Cincinnati's Co-op Education.* Berkeley, Calif.: National Center for Research in Vocational Education, University of California, Berkeley.

Vogl, A. J., ed. June 1995. "Schools: Should Business Set Their Agenda?" *Across the Board* 32 (no. 6) (journal of the Conference Board, New York), pp. 16–23.

Walter, Diana, and Anita Turlington. "Tech Prep: A Practitioner's Perspective." In *The Tech Prep Associate Degree Challenge.* The Tech Prep Roundtable. Washington, D.C.: American Association of Community Colleges.

Westbrook, Robert B. 1991. *John Dewey and American Democracy.* Ithaca, N.Y.: Cornell University Press.

Whitelaw, Kevin. September 16, 1996. "Weighing Security and Success." *U.S. News & World Report*, "America's Best Colleges: 1997 Annual Guide," pp. 115–116.

Whiting, Basil J., and Wade D. Sayer. October 1995. "School-to-Work or School-to-What? Exploring Prospects for Building Employer Capacity in School-to-Work Programming." An Interim Report Prepared for the Pew Charitable Trusts. Philadelphia: Public/Private Ventures.

William T. Grant Commission on Work, Family, and Citizenship. 1988. *The Forgotten Half: Non-College Youth in America.* Washington, D.C.: Youth and America's Future.

Wills, Joan L. (with the assistance of the Center for Policy Research of the National Governors' Association, the Meridian Corporation, and the National Vocational Technical Education Foundation). 1993. *Overview of Education and Industry Skill Standards Systems in the United States and Other Countries.* Washington, D.C.: Institute for Educational Leadership.

Zemsky, Robert. 1994. *What Employers Want: Employer Perspectives on Youth, the Youth Labor Market, and Prospects for a National System of Youth Apprenticeships.* EQW Issues no. 6. Philadelphia: National Center on the Educational Quality of the Workforce, University of Pennsylvania.

Zemsky, Robert, and Penney Oedel. 1992. *Look Before You Leap.* EQW Issues no. 4. Philadelphia: National Center on the Educational Quality of the Workforce, University of Pennsylvania.

Index

313